REFERENCE GUIDES TO RHETORIC AND COMPOSITION
Series Editor, Charles Bazerman

REFERENCE GUIDES TO RHETORIC AND COMPOSITION
Series Editors: Charles Bazerman, Mary Jo Reiff, and Anis Bawarshi

The Series provides compact, comprehensive and convenient surveys of what has been learned through research and practice as composition has emerged as an academic discipline over the last half century. Each volume is devoted to a single topic that has been of interest in rhetoric and composition in recent years, to synthesize and make available the sum and parts of what has been learned on that topic. These reference guides are designed to help deepen classroom practice by making available the collective wisdom of the field and will provide the basis for new research. The Series is intended o be of use to teachers at all levels of education, researchers and scholars of writing, graduate students learning about the field, and all, nationally and internationally, who have interest in or responsibility for writing programs and the teaching of writing.

Parlor Press and The WAC Clearinghouse are collaborating so that these books will be widely available through low cost print editions and free electronic distribution. The publishers and the series editors are all teachers and researchers of writing, committed to the principle that knowledge should freely circulate. We see the opportunities that new technologies have for further democratizing knowledge. And we see that to share the power of writing is to share the means for all to articulate their needs, interest, and learning into the great experiment of literacy.

EXISTING BOOKS IN THE SERIES
Invention in Rhetoric and Composition (2004, Lauer)
Reference Guide to Writing across the Curriculum (2005, Bazerman, et al.)
Revision: History, Theory, and Practice (2006, Horning and Becker)
Writing Program Administration (2007, McLeod)
Community Literacy and the Rhetoric of Local Publics (2008, Long)
Argument in Composition (2009, Ramage, et al.)
Basic Writing (2010, Otte and Mlynarczyk)
Genre: An Introduction to History, Theory, Research, and Pedagogy (2010, Bawarshi and Reiff)
Reconnecting Reading and Writing (2013, Horning and Kraemer)
Style: An Introduction to History, Theory, Research, and Pedagogy (2014, Ray)

STYLE

AN INTRODUCTION TO HISTORY, THEORY, RESEARCH, AND PEDAGOGY

BRIAN RAY

Parlor Press
Anderson, South Carolina
www.parlorpress.com

The WAC Clearinghouse
Fort Collins, Colorado
http://wac.colostate.edu/

Parlor Press LLC, Anderson, South Carolina, USA
The WAC Clearinghouse, Fort Collins, Colorado 80523-1052

© 2015 by Parlor Press and The WAC Clearinghouse
All rights reserved.
Printed in the United States of America

SAN: 254-8879

Library of Congress Cataloging-in-Publication Data

Ray, Brian, 1982-
 Style : an introduction to history, theory, research, and pedagogy / Brian Ray.
    pages cm. -- (Reference guides to rhetoric and composition)
 Includes bibliographical references and index.
  ISBN 978-1-60235-612-2 (pbk. : alk. paper) -- ISBN 978-1-60235-613-9 (hardcover : alk. paper)
 1. Style, Literary--History. 2. Narration (Rhetoric)--History. 3. Knowledge, Theory of--History. 4. Language and education--History. I. Title.
 PN3383.S79R39 2014
 808.3--dc23
                            2014045752

1 2 3 4 5

Series logo designed by Karl Stolley. Copyediting by Jeff Ludwig.
This book is printed on acid-free paper.

Parlor Press, LLC is an independent publisher of scholarly and trade titles in print and multimedia formats. This book is available in paper, cloth and eBook formats from Parlor Press on the World Wide Web at http://www.parlorpress.com or through online and brick-and-mortar bookstores. For submission information or to find out about Parlor Press publications, write to Parlor Press, 3015 Brackenberry Drive, Anderson, South Carolina, 29621, or email editor@parlorpress.com.

The WAC Clearinghouse supports teachers of writing across the disciplines. Hosted by Colorado State University's Composition Program, it brings together four journals, three book series, and resources for teachers who use writing in their courses. This book will also be available free on the Internet at The WAC Clearinghouse (http://wac.colostate.edu/).

Contents

Acknowledgments *vii*
Series Editors' Preface *ix*
    Anis Bawarshi, Charles Bazerman, and Mary Jo Reiff

1 What Is Style, and Why Does It Matter? *3*
    Definitions of Style *7*
        Style as Form and Meaning *8*
        Style as Eloquence *10*
        Style as Grammar *12*
        Style as Voice *13*
        Style as Possibility and Risk *14*
    Conclusion: A Cacophony of Definitions *16*

2 Historical Review I: From Ancient Greece through Rome *19*
    Style Before the Sophists *20*
    Sophists (Fifth and Fourth Centuries BCE) *22*
    Plato (Fourth Century BCE) *24*
    Isocrates (Fifth and Fourth Centuries BCE) *27*
    Aristotle (Fourth Century BCE) *28*
    Roman Style: Cicero and Quintilian *34*
    Greco-Roman Rhetorical Curriculum: Imitation
        and the *Progymnasmata* *42*
    Later Greeks: Demetrius, Hermogenes, and Longinus
        (First — Fourth Century, CE) *45*
    Feminist and Non-Western Styles in the
        Classical and Ancient World *48*
    Augustine of Hippo (Fourth and Fifth Centuries CE) *53*

3 Historical Review II: From the Middle Ages through Nineteenth Century US *56*
    Boethius (Fifth and Sixth Centuries CE) *60*
    Christine de Pizan *61*
    Renaissance Style *63*
    Renaissance Curriculum *66*
    Erasmus *68*
    The Ramist Watershed *69*
    Style in the Enlightenment and the Standardization of English *71*
    Gutting the Classical Canon: Harvard and the
        New Curriculum, 1875–1940 *76*

4 Contemporary Views on Style   85
Style in Publics and Counterpublics   86
Style, Voice, and Discourse   90
Bakhtin, Dialogism, and Style   94
Bakhtin, Classical Rhetoric, and Postmodern Imitation   97

5 The Relationship Between Style, Voice, and Grammar   102
Linguistics and Style in Rhetoric and Composition   108
   Christensen's Rhetoric   113
   Winston Weathers and Alternate Style   115
   Sentence-Combining Pedagogies   117
   Rhetorical Grammar   119

6 Frontiers of Style in Rhetoric and Composition   123
Language Difference, Linguistic Diversity, and Style   124
Style, Voice, and Feedback in Second Language Writing   131
Women's Writing and Breaking Rules   135
Style, Academic Genres, and Writing Across
   the Curriculum (WAC)   137
Style, Digital Genres, and Multimodality   141
Conclusion   149

7 Researching Style: Methods in Rhetoric, Composition, and Related Disciplines   151
Rhetoric and Composition   151
Stylistics   156
Discourse Analysis   161
Rhetorical Analysis   164
From Style to Styles: An Overview of Sociolinguistics   168
   Dialectology   170
Corpus Linguistics and Stylistics   173
Research(es) on World Englishes and Global English   176

8 Teaching Strategies and Best Practices   182
T. R. Johnson and *The Rhetoric of Pleasure*   188
Textbooks: Linguistic and Sociolinguistic Approaches   191
Approaches Informed by Classical Rhetoric   201
Mixed Approaches   212
Final Thoughts on Teaching Style   218

Glossary   221
Annotated Bibliography: Further Readings on Style   228
Works Cited   234
About the Author   255
Index   257

Acknowledgments

The author would like to thank colleagues, friends, and family who helped make this book possible. Special thanks goes to series editors Charles Bazerman, Anis Bawarshi, and Mary Jo Reiff—who offered extensive feedback on drafts and pushed this book to its best form. I appreciated support and encouragement from scholars including Paul Butler, who read the manuscript as it neared completion. Thanks also to David Blakesley, editor of Parlor Press, for timely responses and attention to detail—as well as the close scrutiny of copyeditor Jeff Ludwig. It should be noted that this book is available online through generous efforts by Mike Palmquist, editor of the WAC Clearinghouse. Finally, a debt of gratitude is owed to all of the authors cited here, whose insights into style have provided the foundation for this project.

Series Editors' Preface

Anis Bawarshi, Charles Bazerman, and Mary Jo Reiff

As one of the five rhetorical canons, style has always had a central place in writing, but what that place is has not always been clearly understood. From the point of view of readers, style is something we prize in texts as providing a pleasurable journey through a writer's thoughts and as a mark of the quality of the writer's mind and spirit. Writers seek to have a style that will engage the readers and will mark their own authorial distinctiveness. Yet what style consists of, where it comes from, and what its value is has undergone constant redefinitions and controversies.

At various stages in its historical treatment, style has been conflated with grammatical correctness and clarity (often associated with plain style) while at other times it has been positioned in opposition to grammatical correctness and conflated with voice and individual expression. Style has been associated, at times, with invention and at other times distinguished from invention. It has been defined both as one of the canons of rhetoric and as the *only* canon of rhetoric. At times style has been used to promote the value of rhetoric, and at other times it has been used to degrade rhetoric as mere ornamentation. It has been synonymous, at times, with norms and standardization and at other times synonymous with innovation, risk, and difference. At the epicenter of this confusion is style's complex, co-dependent relationship with rhetoric and grammar: We cannot study and teach style without grammar, and yet its association with grammar (as grammatical correctness) has rendered style marginal. Likewise, we cannot recognize style as strategic performance without associating it with rhetoric, and yet this very association has also at times relegated style as ornament, at best, and dangerously manipulative at worst.

Because of the way style embodies core, long-standing tensions in rhetoric and composition studies, its study can provide important insights into our attitudes, at various times in the history of the field, about language, discourse, and representation. At the same time, because style is not a fixed concept but is fluid and multidimensional, an examination of its multiple, interlocking definitions can reveal interdependencies in what may seem to be stark contrasts. For instance, recognizing style as a continuum of choices rather than a set of dichotomies (academic or not-academic, high or low, correct or incorrect, standard or non-standard) enables us to understand how style is a condition of all language use and how it participates in a set of relations (grammatical, generic, interpersonal, social, affective) that shape meaning-making.

Style, then, can be fruitfully understood as performative, in keeping with contemporary interests in writing as situated, materially inflected, embodied, evocative performance. To consider style as performative suggests that style is a decision-making, epistemological practice, not only a product to be assessed but a set of relations and interactions readers and writers perform with texts in particular situations. Increasingly, these stylistic relations and interactions are recognized as spanning across media and modalities, involving the negotiation of language differences and cross-cultural relations, and marked by articulations as much as by silences, pauses, and ellipses.

This volume traces the historical roots of how style came to be separated from rhetoric and conflated with grammatical correctness in ways that have limited our understanding of the role of style in meaning making. Rather than fixing or promoting style as any one thing, Ray instead uses its myriad definitions to trace the genealogy of its uses, to examine its current standing and possibilities, and to explore future directions. Along the way, Ray reviews the linguistic turn in composition studies; the debates between linguistic and literary views of style; the relationship between writing process approaches and style; changing perspectives on style in the rhetorical tradition, from the ancient Greeks and Romans to the Middle Ages, the Renaissance, Enlightenment, and the new rhetoric of the twentieth century. He traces the relationship between style and contemporary scholarship in language difference, translingualism, feminism, genre studies, writing across the curriculum, multimodality, new media, and visual rhetorics. The last two chapters offer detailed coverage of research methodologies related to style as well as pedagogical implications, including a review of textbooks focused on style. The glossary targets key concepts in style, and the annotated bibliography provides useful references for further reading. Covering an impressive range of scholarship from antiquity to the present, interweaving major figures alongside lesser known but significant figures, drawing connections across time (as in the ways that Demetrius anticipates Bakhtin in equating style and genre, or how the Roman obsession with language purity reflects current debates about language standardization), and looking beyond western rhetorical traditions and their contributions to style, this volume reveals style as ubiquitous and crucial to contemporary work in rhetoric and composition studies.

Style

1 What Is Style, and Why Does It Matter?

Mention the word "style," and most writing teachers begin singing the praises of Strunk and White's well-known handbook, *Elements of Style*. Regarded as the most authoritative treatment of style in English, the manual presents numerous rules for usage and grammar as well as exhortations to avoid "all devices that are popularly believed to indicate style—all mannerisms, tricks, adornments" and focus instead on "plainness, simplicity, orderliness, [and] sincerity" (55). The manual goes on to elaborate on this plainness of style as the preferred absence of "fancy" or foreign words, figurative language, and any non-standard usage or phrases. In short, writers should always take as few risks as possible and write only in the safest, most objective kind of Standard English. They should blend in. Above all, writers should strive for definite, specific, concrete language.

This view of style has its place in certain communicative situations; however, it excludes a range of other possibilities while also maintaining a binary between plain and adorned styles. Today, many writing teachers have difficulty thinking outside of the Strunk and White box. They see style only as conformity to standards, as the domain of manuals and handbooks, and they avoid discussing style as a means of expression, experimentation, and risk. In the recent edited collection, *The Centrality of Style*, Nora Bacon (author of the textbook *The Well-Crafted Sentence*) addresses this dilemma head on, stating that writing and rhetoric teachers largely believe that "You can teach academic writing or you can teach style, but you can't teach both" (176). Bacon critiques the dominant notion of academic writing as plain and literal, and redefines the genre as open to stylistic play. Bacon's argument builds on Kate Ronald's 1999 essay, "Style: The Hidden Agenda in Composition Classrooms," in which Ronald describes academic prose as "objective, impersonal, formal, explicit, and organized around assertions, claims, and reasons that illustrate or defend those claims" (175). For Ronald, academic discourse demands an almost vacant or plain style that carries as little of the writer's personality as possible, meaning no excess or playfulness via literary style or the idioms and spontaneity that characterize oral discourse.

Ironically, most teachers do not necessarily believe what they teach when it comes to style. As Bacon indicates her essay, teachers may promote a stale version of academic discourse, but secretly hope to see some sense of voice or aesthetic in student papers. Teachers may often give students worse grades for slavishly adhering to the letter of academic style rather than gracefully bending the rules. Both Bacon and Ronald agree that the contradiction between style-as-taught and style-as-graded is damaging to students, leading to lower performance.

Many teachers today may also rely largely on handbooks as crutches, added to whatever they learned about style when they were once students. They may correct what they see as mistakes on student papers, as well as overuse of conversational or subjective language and idioms, humor, personal stories, or the dreaded "I," "you," and "we." They may present a "proper" style for academic writing that precludes certain syntactical choices, such as beginning sentences with conjunctions or using sentence fragments and run-ons. They may also call for "appropriate" lexical conformity to registers defined as "academic" or "slang." Most teachers agree these are sometimes necessary, but are not sufficient or universal; yet, we still cling to them.

This situation is exacerbated by the textbook publishing industry, an industry that churns out dozens of handbooks and textbooks annually and that contain short chapters consisting of "rules" for effective style from our own professional organizations.[1] In his 2008 book *Out of Style*, Paul Butler refers to these guides as "so-called style manuals," where "style tends to be conflated with grammar or [is] used reductively" (20). Butler cites the 2003 *Longman Writer's Companion* as an example, but one need only browse the composition sections of catalogs to find similar titles. For example, Part 3 of William Kelly's *Simple, Clear, and Correct* contains seven chapters on grammar and mechan-

---

1. Consider the seventh and most recent edition of the *MLA Handbook for Writers of Research Papers*. The *Handbook* boasts a blurb from *Newsweek* as "the style bible for most college students." The guide spends a great deal of time on the uniform and mechanical aspects of writing, not to mention formatting and documentation.

ics without any indication that they might be used for stylistic effect. Kelly uses the word "style" only once, to tell writers to place "a period between independent clauses to eliminate a comma splice or run-on sentence" in order to avoid long sentences (253). As with dozens of other textbooks, style is mainly about staying inconspicuous.

Style: An Introduction to History, Theory, Research, and Pedagogy charts a more diverse understanding of style than is seen in such guides, one based on a resurgence of interest in style as an area of research and pedagogy. The last several years of work in rhetoric and composition have seen a number of scholarly and pedagogical projects that promote style as a continuum of choices from plain to lively, rather than as a set of dichotomies. For instance, the authors collected in Christopher Schroeder, Helen Fox, and Patricia Bizzell's book *Alt Dis* each argue for an alternative conception of academic writing style, one that embraces a both/and approach. These scholars assert that academic writing can be clear and concise without requiring adherence to prescriptions; it can adhere to conventions while also producing a sense of satisfaction (even pleasure). Michael Spooner's contribution to *Alt Dis* effectively represents this purpose. Speaking about teachers as well as editors, Spooner defines their goal as "not to correct a text toward what the handbooks or readability indices allow, but to understand the writer's ideas and processes . . . to imagine small ways to help the writer deliver those ideas effectively" (160). Ultimately, Spooner envisions an "'alt' style" that permits a wider degree of experimentation with stylistic conventions (163).

A major premise of *Style* is that an in-depth, historical, and theoretical understanding of style helps teachers make writing more satisfying and relevant to students.[2] Consequently, students will more likely produce writing that is rhetorically effective. In particular, Jeanne Fahnestock promotes reclaiming classical style for college academic writing in a special issue of *Language and Literature* about rhetorical stylis-

---

2. T.R. Johnson makes a similar point in his essay 1999 *JAC* essay, "Discipline and Pleasure: 'Magic' and Sound." For Johnson, teachers and academics too often present writing as a highly disciplined and rigorous activity, in which anything approaching "fun" or "pleasure" raises immediate suspicion. As explored in the second chapter of this book, Johnson's solution to this problem lies in a return to sophistic and classical rhetorics, which placed a high priority on the sonic qualities of language, in order to invest our writing and teaching with more enjoyment.

tics, arguing for recovery of the lost "interconnectedness of argument and style" in the Western rhetorical tradition (224). As one example, Fahnestock presents the rhetorical device *sorites*, an argument made "through interlocking propositions which in effect produce the figure *gradatio*," sometimes described as "a series of compressed or overlapping syllogisms" (225). For example, I might use *sorites* to argue the following:

> Teachers care about their students. Teachers care about writing. Scholarship shows that teaching style to students improves their writing. Therefore, teachers should care about style.

Phrasing my argument through this device could have several effects on readers. First, it sounds direct and forceful. It is simple and clear. Therefore, it may serve as a memorable way of conveying this book's central purpose. Conversely, it also serves as a reminder and catalyst to me, as I develop and revise this book, to be aware of my audience and my own goals. *Sorites* is one of many such devices rediscovered by Fahnestock, all of them once seen as part and parcel of education in grammar, rhetoric, and dialectic. An entire tradition of correspondence exists between argumentative and stylistic strategies in treatises by Aristotle, Cicero, Agricola, and Melanchton.

The new momentum in our field calls for a thorough historical investigation into this long undervalued canon. My intention is to describe key shifts in studies of style from sophistic Greece through the contemporary era. By providing an orientation to where style has been during the last three thousand years, I aim to carefully assess the current state of stylistic studies and project possible futures regarding its impact on theories and pedagogies in the field. This assessment identifies the core principles, debates, and methods of teaching style as they evolved from one historical era to the next, explaining the relevance of these moments in the study and teaching of style to contemporary college teachers and students. Regarding the future of the study and teaching of style, this book articulates connections between approaches to style in rhetoric and composition and other disciplines to encourage further research and pedagogical innovation.

DEFINITIONS OF STYLE

Style has been defined in a variety of ways by scholars working in areas within and related to rhetoric and composition. Style has been discussed in terms of classical rhetorical devices and amplification of discourse, as the manipulation of punctuation and syntax for rhetorical effect, as risk and deviation from norms, and as voice and authenticity. Some definitions are precise, such as Louise Phelps's definition, given during a personal interview with Paul Butler, as "the deployment of linguistic resources in written discourse to express and create meaning" ("Diaspora" 7). Other definitions are vague, such as Jonathon Swift's motto, "proper words in proper places."[3] This book endeavors to arrange a series of lenses on style without becoming mired in the particulars of a single, totalizing definition.

Since classical Greece, one central debate on style has centered on the view of form versus meaning, or both. Seeing style as form means that it can only decorate discourse; it does not play a primary role in invention—the generation of ideas and arguments. In this view, style comes after the fact. Style as meaning, on the other hand, implies that the use of devices, as well as the manipulation of sentence length and choice of words based on sound (and so on), has an undeniable impact on the development of ideas and their interpretation by audiences. Style as meaning entails that the decisions writers make regarding imagery, metaphors, sounds, length, syntax, and punctuation all contribute to an idea rather than to its mere expression. Style as inventive entails that these decisions become part of the process of discovering and shaping arguments, and therefore part of the entire composing process—not simply the editing and proofing stages.

In a 1980 *College English* article, John T. Gage grapples with the knotted concept of style as "at once a linguistic, a rhetorical, and a

---

3. Barry Brummett's *A Rhetoric of Style* analyzes the canon in terms of language, image, fashion, gender, and a commodity that encompasses all of popular culture in late capitalist societies—style as excess. For Brummett, style is an entire system of signification that enables judgment and identification between different socioeconomic classes. Although this definition is ambitious and helpful in understanding the relevance of style in a broad sense, this book takes more narrow approach, and limits its scope to prose style, albeit with nods to ways in which other modes of signification have been influential.

philosophical concept," and explains that it is a contentious term because "It is possible to be satisfied with a definition of style on one of these levels . . . only to discover that it raises problems in another" (615).[4] Gage's piece is of particular interest to contemporary stylistic studies because he ultimately adopts a flexible position that writing teachers must draw on multiple theories, rather than cling to one. We often see definitions of style in contest with one another, rather than in cooperation. Consider the central debate mentioned earlier about whether "Style is either separate from invention or . . . one of the aspects of invention" (Gage 618). New Critics often argue that "every change in style is a change in meaning," in opposition to an idea among linguists that the same propositional content can be expressed in many similar ways (618). What Gage struggles to explain in 1980 as the need "to have it both ways" has been taken up in the projects of stylistic revivalists (616). Seeing style through these central questions helps students and teachers as they encounter different orientations to style. The rest of this chapter presents a set of distinctive definitions.

Style as Form and Meaning

Many writing teachers view style as a way of altering the form of an idea, but not the idea itself. They might see the most appropriate style for academic writing as plain and transparent. Stylisticians tend to argue the contrary: that these differences *do* alter meaning—sometimes slightly, other times drastically—and that thinking about these differences helps writers shape their ideas. In *A Matter of Style*, Matthew Clark warns us to resist the notion "that meaning simply exists, prior to language, and that the job of language is merely to represent that pre-existing meaning" (45). Clark insists that "expression often helps to form meaning, and . . . the possibilities of expression influence the possibilities of meaning" (45). Consider the following short sentences that express the same basic idea:

---

4 Gage shows as much through Varro's treatment, in *De Lingua Latina*, of analogist theories (i.e., that language is representative of an ordered universe) and of anomalists ones (i.e., that language is disordered, irregular, and inadequate). Such disagreements carried over into debates about generative grammar, a theory that Gage sees as conveying the analogists' faith in mapping a coherent and logical structure onto language.

1. Professor Chapman gave me a lot of feedback on my dissertation chapter last week.

2. Chapman ripped apart my dissertation chapter a few days ago.

3. The second chapter of my dissertation had a lot of problems, but Dr. Chapman helped point them out and gave me suggestions on how to revise.

Here, it is easy to see how different choices in diction, tone, and sentence position convey different notions of the speaker and his or her relationship to the professor. The first sentence might seem straightforward and objective. The second sentence implies an antagonistic relationship with the professor. By contrast, the third sentence suggests a sense of gratitude, framing the conflict around the writer's own problems with the dissertation. It would be hard to imagine these three sentences as spoken by the same person.

Part of the reason why teachers and scholars might resist such a nuanced view of language and meaning is that we think of meaning itself as a monolithic concept, but, in fact, several types of meaning exist. Leonora Woodman's 1982 *JAC* article, "Teaching Style: A Process-Centered View," defines these different types of meaning. First there is "sense," or the essential information conveyed in different grammatical forms. Take the sentence "Man bites dog" and the passive form, "Dog is bitten by man." These two sentences emphasize different aspects of an event, but fundamentally convey the same sense. The difference between active and passive voice is not unlike switching camera angles to emphasize one actor or another in the same scene.

Style *does* have a significant impact if we think of meaning in other terms. Woodman describes other types of meaning as she revisits I. A. Richards's point that meaning exists in layers, including "mere sense, sense and implications, feeling, the speaker's attitudes to whatever it is, to his audience, the speaker's confidence, and other things" (qtd. in Woodman 117). Using a different verb or a longer sentence, or introducing harsher sounding words to generate cacophonous sounds adds implications not explicitly stated; it also generates emotions that do not rest on semantic content. Regardless of whether they see style as a matter of meaning or form, all rhetoricians note the impact that style has on audiences. The actual ability to produce emotional or rhetorical effects by manipulating language is often referred to as eloquence, explored in the next section. Rhetoricians who take a view of style as form and meaning tend to place a great deal of importance on eloquence. As Chapter 2 shows, the Roman rhetoricians Cicero and Quintilian established a vital link between eloquence and good character.

Style as Eloquence

The term eloquence often appears synonymously with style, especially in the classical period through to the Renaissance. When rhetoricians speak of eloquence, they usually describe the writer as having mastered a range of styles. As such, style as eloquence has particular connotations with emotional value and sensation. Cicero and Quintilian saw eloquence as the chief end of all discourse, and they defined three main styles for different rhetorical situations—the low or plain, the middle, and the grand.[5] Eloquence often refers to the grand style, reserved only for serious topics or sections of speeches where a rhetor wants to drive home the major points of a case, making them vivid.

Scholars in stylistics are currently trying to recover and repurpose such terms as eloquence by tracing their histories and making a case for their reintroduction into college writing instruction. T. R. Johnson's work on style emphasizes the magical, transportive qualities of language in the sophistic era. Johnson promotes Gorgias as an exemplar of classical eloquence that conflicts with contemporary understandings of style as a matter of mechanical correctness. An eloquent style is not usually a plain style, and Gorgias's eloquence, like Cicero's, appeared, even to some of his contemporaries, as bloated and Asiatic (as alien or strange). Gorgias was a crowd-pleaser, but his style grated on the more conservative tastes of Aristotle. As Johnson observes, today, the Aristotelian or Attic model persists in college writing instruction as well as the public discourse on style that emphasizes clarity, efficiency, and overall plainness.

We must also remain aware of the ethnic and classist associations of eloquence at points in history. Feminist and postcolonial writers view eloquence with some suspicion given its often privileged advocates that define eloquence via expectations or "tastes" that are endorsed by a ruling establishment that perpetuates itself through educational and cultural norms. What qualifies as "eloquent" often depends on a subject

---

5. A number of classical rhetoricians in William Dominik's 1997 edited collection, *Roman Eloquence*, treat this subject within the contexts of antiquity.

position with power and influence over others. The Greeks and the Romans defined their language in contrast to the supposedly barbaric ineloquence of other cultures—that same attitude formed the foundation of linguistic discrimination from Renaissance England through to contemporary debates on college education. Thus, the term "eloquence" carries heavy undertones of judgment about ethnicity, gender, nationality, and social class.

In the 2009 book, *Race and Rhetoric in the Renaissance: Barbarian Errors*, Ian Smith highlights the linguistic xenophobia of classical Greece and Imperial Rome that set a costly precedent for early modern Africans during Renaissance England, as the rising intellectual culture of Anglo-Saxons sought to displace its own barbarous reputation by projecting it onto linguistic others that were far less "eloquent" in their "failed language" (Smith 8). For Smith, "eloquence became the marketable norm [in Athens and elsewhere] . . . the *de rigueur* commodity in the fifth century" (24). In the 2006 book *Vulgar Eloquence*, Sean Keilen takes a similar stance on the need felt by Renaissance poets to reinvent themselves and their history in order to become inheritors of Greek and Roman traditions. Seen this way, eloquence has been to style what prestigious varieties of English is to other languages around the world today—a risky investment in a dominant code, to borrow a metaphor from Catharine Prendergast's *Buying into English*.

Eloquence has become an infrequent term in college writing classes, given its associations with ornament and literary texts. As Chapter 3 explores, part of the reason lies in the origins of college composition at Harvard in the late 1800s, when Adams Sherman Hill emphasized the rules of correctness and clarity over and above other qualities of writing, including aspects of style concerned with effective deviation from such rules. Style as eloquence carries the stigma of simply ornamenting discourse in the latter stages of drafting rather than throughout the composing process. When we praise the eloquence of a writer or speaker, it may seem as though we are suggesting that a speech sounds nice despite its lack substance. If teachers embrace a redefinition of eloquence, one flexible enough to accommodate non-standard Englishes and other languages, it might assist in destabilizing the stereotype of academic writing as rigidly formal, impersonal, and authoritarian. An eloquent academic essay will never read or sound like an eloquent play or poem, but it can still draw on aspects of style to achieve a balance between the goals of analysis and knowledge production on the one hand, and emotional engagement on the other.

Style as Grammar

Style and grammar have almost always been discussed in relation to one another, though classical rhetoricians tended to elevate style. Classical rhetoricians such as Cicero and Quintilian maintained that eloquence was the crowning achievement of rhetoric, and that grammatically accurate writing and speaking were necessary preconditions for eloquence.[6] While grammar was technically a part of style, it was not the whole of style. This basic view of grammar as a subordinate component of style, held through the nineteenth century until the formation of college composition courses in the US, saw correctness and clarity as the chief purpose of writing—eloquence or distinction was ancillary. Toward the end of the twentieth century, scholars such as Martha Kolln and Joseph Williams advocated the use of grammar in the service of style. Patrick Hartwell defines these approaches as "stylistic grammars" because they rely on the terminology of descriptive grammar, or linguistics, to help students develop an awareness of language as a rhetorical tool. Such approaches differ from school grammars because they focus on choice and effect, not merely on correctness.

Grammar and style cover much of the same territory, albeit through different terminologies. In the linguistic sense, grammar is a technical language that helps explain how sentences and passages function and how they achieve meaning. In the opening to her 1971 book *Grammar as Style*, Virginia Tufte states that "grammar and style can be thought of in some way as a single subject" (1). Although different definitions of grammar exist, Tufte defines them fundamentally as syntax, or the arrangement of words, where the rhetorical effects described as style become the most apparent.

Style as grammar, or grammar as style, drives arguments by Joseph Williams, Martha Kolln, and Laura Michicche, all of whom use terminology from linguistics as fundamental principles in teaching awareness of style. In particular, Kolln and Michicche use the term

---

6. George Campbell sums up the traditionalist view nicely that "the grammatical art hath its completion in syntax; the oratorical, as far as the body of expression is concerned, in style" (*Philosophy of Rhetoric* 35).

"rhetorical grammar," meaning instruction in the rhetorical effects of grammar, to help students realize the many choices they have when organizing information at the sentence-level. A rhetorical view of grammar and style is summed up nicely by Mikkel Bakhtin's assertion, in "The Problem of Speech Genres," that "the speaker's very selection of a particular grammatical form is a stylistic act" (66). In many ways, style is the exercise of choice among grammatical options.

Style as Voice

Teachers can and should teach style partly through grammar, since the styles of the writers we admire can be broken down, analyzed, explained, and imitated using the specific vocabulary of grammar. However, stylistically effective writing is not merely the sum of its parts. However precise and technical our terms, every writer develops a unique style or voice in ways that teachers and theorists cannot ever completely compartmentalize and dissect. The term "voice" is often used interchangeably with "style," though it is helpful to distinguish them. Voice refers to the impressions readers develop of a writer or speaker that exceed the explanatory power of grammatical and stylistic vocabularies. Paul Matsuda defines style as a component of voice, specifically as "the use of particular sets of discursive features. . .that contribute to—as well as constrain—the construction of voice" ("Voice in Japanese" 41). To get at the distinctiveness of someone's use of stylistic resources, it may help to think in terms of voice.

Peter Elbow explains voice and its relationship to style in a 2007 *College English* essay titled "Voice in Writing Again: Embracing Contraries." A long-time advocate of voice in student writing, Elbow defines the term as "language as sounded, heard, and existing in time" (175). Voice refers to any aspect of writing or speech that lends a sense of distinction or uniqueness—a presence or a way of marking someone's use of language as different from others. Students should learn to write with a sense of voice because, as Elbow argues, "Readers usually experience 'audible' voiced writing as clearer than writing they don't hear" (177), and so it enhances their rhetorical effectiveness. Moreover, helping students balance academic writing with their own voices—the way they speak in their everyday conversations—can help make writing a less intimidating task.

Traditionally, style is a formal branch of classical rhetoric with its own vocabulary; today, scholars of style in our field sometimes draw additional terms from grammar and linguistics. This large catalogue of terms can make style seem complex and overwhelming to college students. The loose terminology of voice is more flexible, emphasizing the relationship between readers and writers, not the text in isolation. As such, it can prompt students to reflect more deeply about the social and emotional impact of their writing, and resists giving them a set of ready-made labels. As Elbow acknowledges,

> Many of the textual features that people describe in terms of voice can also be described as matters of *style*. And there's a huge and sophisticated scholarly literature about style in writing. But the voice metaphor often works better for students and others who are not sophisticated about language. (177)

A disadvantage of treating style as voice lies in subjectivity and, to some extent, lack of specificity. Elbow admits that "The voice formulation is a personal subjective projection—and it implies a subjective guess about how others will react and even about the mind and feelings of the writer" (178). Teaching style as voice does not exclude other approaches, such as grammatical or rhetorical. Voice is merely another avenue of approach. Comments on student papers and class discussions can use the lens of style as grammar as well as voice, for example.

Style as Possibility and Risk

Since Mina Shaughnessy's opening to *Errors and Expectations*, it has been well-documented that attention to grammar alone can have disastrous consequences for the confidence students have in their abilities as writers (see also Braddock; Hillocks). If students are constantly penalized and punished for their errors, they become so reluctant to take chances with their writing that they become paralyzed, or they only stay within the safety zone established by their teachers. Meanwhile, as Nora Bacon and Kate Ronald argue, teachers then unknowingly penalize students for staying within that zone. Thus, students face style as a double-edged sword. If they take risks with their writing and fail, they are penalized. If they don't take risks at all, they are still penalized for lack of voice or confidence. To take risks in their writing, students must be able to fail without fear of reprisal.

A 1985 *College English* article on feminist styles, Pamela Annas attests to the benefits of breaking this trend, of treating writing as a series of possibilities rather than constraints:

> One semester two women in the course blocked when I asked them to write about their backgrounds in relation to writing and language. One said in class, "Thinking about my background. Well, you can't do anything about it, but . . . my attitude was, I'm mad, I'm angry, I'm bitter, so I'm not finishing this paper." She was upset at the anger she had found in herself, but she also thought that what she really had to say wouldn't be acceptable. So she turned in something that was bland, numb, and lifeless. During this discussion I suggested that she rewrite the paper, beginning with "I'm mad, I'm angry, I'm bitter," and go on from there. When she did that, her writing unblocked, and though much of what she wrote in the rest of the semester had a bitter edge, her writing was pro-lific and vivid. (367)

Such writers block often stems from a limited definition of style as adherence not only to grammatical rules, but also to exhortations about distance, objectivity, precision, clarity, and linearity in academic writing. The revival of style in rhetoric and composition seeks a balanced approach similar to the one seen in Annas's essay: style as a set of principles designed to open rather than close possibilities in prose.

An earlier 1981 *College Composition and Communication* (*CCC*) essay, Jane Walpole also problematizes the idea of norms and neutrality, showing them as always inherently subjective. Accepting the idea of synonymous meaning, or sense (see Hirsch, "Stylistics and Synonymity"), Walpole proposes the definition of style as what "encompasses all the alternate choices that make *this* discussion of X different from *that* discussion of X" (206). She cites a similar definition from Richard Young and Alton Becker, that "a particular style is a characteristic series of choices throughout the entire process of writing, including both discovery (invention) and linguistic selection and grouping (arrangement)" (qtd. in Walpole 206). Style as option is intimately related to every stage in the writing process.

This view of style drives from the theories of Quintilian, who saw the end of style in *facilitas*, and also from Erasmus, who saw it as *copia* (abundance in a writer's language options). It also appears in language difference, especially Suresh Canagarajah's work on metalinguistic awareness and shuttling between different varieties of English. It also converges with a dialogic view of style in that the stylistic options available to writers include multiple voices that they can shift between as they rotate through various socio-discursive situations (see Halasek; Farmer). Finally, style as option calls to mind work in sociolinguistics on style-shifting, code-switching, and code-mixing, as well as the more recent term "code-meshing" used by rhetoric and composition scholars.

Conclusion: A Cacophony of Definitions

This introduction outlined some of the major modes of thought on style, but many other definitions exist. In fact, every theorist and author appears to define style in a slightly different manner with emphasis on one or more constituent elements. Paul Butler evokes the definition of style as deviation that is classically-attuned, but that also describes the practices of linguistically diverse students who employ non-standard codes (e.g., dialects, vernaculars) in their speech and writing. Holcomb discusses style as a performance of identity in his *Rhetoric Review* essay, "Performative Stylistics and the Question of Academic Prose," as well as in his book *Performing Prose*, co-authored with Jimmie Killingsworth. Sociolinguists use the term "style-shifting" when describing the linguistic choices users make in different situations with different audiences. Someone may shift between multiple social languages, including registers such as casual and formal, in order to accommodate or resist the perceived norms of their audiences. In a sociolinguistic sense, style thus also becomes an identity performance and a statement about one's position within a discursive community. Fahnestock's 2011 book *Rhetorical Style: The Uses of Language in Persuasion* contains a multitude of definitions from these areas.

This book encourages teachers and scholars to see the value in multiple, interlocking definitions of style, rather than siding with a particular theory or discipline. Style can describe readers' relationships with texts, the grammatical choices writers make, the importance of adhering to norms in certain contexts and deviating from them in others, the expression of social identity, and the emotional effects of particular devices on audiences. Each use of style has applications for particular contexts and projects, often reflecting unique theories about language, discourse, and representation. These theoretical frameworks operate in the background and, at times, come to the forefront of scholarly and pedagogical conversations about style. I try to deal with them concisely when they need articulation. Only when one theory begins to exclude others does it become overly rigid or unhelpful.

This book is organized to chart such uses of style historically while projecting current and future directions in stylistic studies. Chapter 1 maps some essential ways of understanding style. Chapters 2 and Chapter 3 narrate a history of style from the classical period through the nineteenth century. Beginning with origins of style in epic poetry, these chapters consider disputing positions on style by the sophists, Plato, and Aristotle as Greece moved from a largely oral to a literate culture. A central disagreement arises in this moment between style as epistemological or as representational. The sophists saw style as foundational to or as conveying meaning, whereas Plato and then Aristotle reduced style's significance to the transmission of meaning. For several subsequent centuries, theories of style cycled through variations on this theme—style evolved in treatises during the Roman era, the Middle Ages, the Renaissance, and the Enlightenment. These chapters trace the continued cycle of evolution into the early twentieth century, and focus particularly on the rise of the New Curriculum at Harvard and its preoccupation with grammar and correctness.

Chapters 4, 5, and 6 give an overview of contemporary work on style in rhetoric and composition, including sections on language difference, basic writing, multimodality, feminist and alternative rhetorics, and creative writing. In these chapters I describe stylistic studies as an interdisciplinary project focused on reviving its role in invention in order to resolve tensions and disagreements from the past hundred years that, in many ways, illustrate a microcosm of the larger history of style. I also consider the role of style in publics and counterpublics, including the tendency to frame style as a commodity. Educators, academics, and linguistic minorities tend to form counterpublics against a dominant public that is insistent on Standard English and correct, efficient prose as the primary means toward self-improvement and socio-economic mobility.

Chapter 7 identifies specific areas within and related to composition that can help advance the study of style. For each area, I state its primary interest in style and describe its main research methodologies, including foundational texts, modes of inquiry, what qualifies as evidence, what major questions, and what major issues the area negotiates related to style. These areas include specializations within composition, such as historical and archival research, as well as qualitative and quantitative research methods. Areas outside the traditional scope of composition include sociolinguistics and the related fields of corpus linguistics and World Englishes.

Chapter 7 also explores stylistics and pragmatics. Scholars such as Paul Butler, Jeanne Fahnestock, and T. R. Johnson draw heavily on these two areas. I consider the history and methods of stylistics to help readers more fully appreciate their influence on rhetoric and composition. Namely, I describe how stylistics began as a literary enterprise, but has evolved into the study of style in a variety of everyday rhetorical situations. Finally, Chapter 8 offers practical strategies for teaching style in college writing classes, and revisits pedagogies introduced in earlier chapters and sections. Chapter 8 describes several key textbooks, organized by theoretical influences, that devote specific attention to style. For each book, I account for its strengths and weaknesses and its suitability for introductory and advanced writing courses.

2 Historical Review I: From Ancient Greece through Rome

This chapter traces the evolution of thought on style from Ancient Greece through the end of antiquity, emphasizing primary texts and interpretations by contemporary historians. Teachers may want to consult the classical treatises described here to develop a sense of what style has meant to different rhetoricians over time. Most of the authors of these treatises were themselves educators and, even if they do not provide particular instructions about how to teach style, their discussions of this canon directly impact promoting the value of style in contemporary college classrooms. These treatises take a range of positions regarding the importance of style to the overall theorizing and teaching of rhetoric and writing. Some treatises address style as a small part of a larger rhetorical system, some discuss style as a substantial means of developing arguments, and others are devoted entirely to style, and see it as the most central aspect of effective discourse.

Aristotle treated style as one small component of rhetoric, and emphasized clarity and plainness. By contrast, later rhetoricians such as Demetrius, Longinus, and (much later) Erasmus elevated style as a significant rhetorical tool, encouraging students to develop a wide repertoire of rhetorical devices to enhance their persuasiveness with different audiences. The Roman rhetorician Quintilian's *Education of the Orator* remains the most thorough and comprehensive catalog of stylistic devices and their appropriate use in different rhetorical situations.

A discussion of St. Augustine's adaptation of the classical tradition for preaching concludes this chapter. Augustine redefined rhetoric as preaching, and appropriated most of Cicero and Quintilian's thoughts on style for spreading the gospels. In many ways, Augustine was the last classical rhetorician. After the classical era, rhetoric shifted from a subject devoted primarily to oratory, falling from its place as the culminating part of a student's education. In the Middle Ages, Boethius split rhetoric and philosophy, relegating the whole of rhetoric to the adornment of thought, and thus aligned with a mimetic (representational) view of language. As such, rhetoric became mainly a matter of style, and altogether less important than invention—now the domain of dialectic. Chapter 3 shows how the late Middle Ages in particular saw style as used mainly to polish sermons and poetry, and to compose letters. Rhetoric occupied a lower place as stylistic embellishment until the Renaissance.

Style Before the Sophists

Before the classical era (fourth century BCE), style extended beyond *logos* (speech) to a range of behaviors, including body language, dress, tone of voice, and facial gestures, as well as to "certain types of arguments, structural devices, and techniques of characterization such as slander, or, conversely, self-praise" (Worman 11). In Homeric Greece, no measurable separation existed between thought and language, and even the "word to 'say' and the word to 'mean' were the same (*legein*), different verbs only appearing later" (Cole 42). Therefore, differences in stylistic expression were not merely adaptations of the same idea; they *were* different ideas. We can infer from this equation of thought and language that stylistic decisions were a matter of meaning and of invention. For example, we might recognize a difference in a phrase like "Please come with me to Troy" versus "You must come with me to Troy." The second is not simply a more emphatic instance of the first sentence; it has a different meaning altogether.

The Greeks did not distinguish style from invention or form from content until Aristotle. What we call style today surfaces as early as *The Illiad*, where different styles are observable throughout the speeches and actions of characters. In the reference book, *Classical Rhetorics and Rhetoricians*, Patrick O'Sullivan states that rhetoricians "linked figures such as Nestor, Menelaus, and Odysseus with the major stylistic categories of their day," comparing and contrasting the plain style of Menelaus with the grand styles of Odysseus and Priam (217). The idea of plain, middle, and grand styles did not fully take shape until Quintilian's work, but the seeds of the tripartite division seem to lie in epic verse. Thomas Cole observes that strategies used in epic poems by Odysseus to deceive others eventually became codified as rhetorical devices such as *evidentia*, in which vivid detail of a past event proves it happened (Cole 39).

Aspects of style—including meter, rhyme, and alliteration—originally developed as pneumonic devices used by Homeric *aoidos* (bards), and later *rhapsodes*, who were precursors to the sophists. The role of the *aoidos* was initially to chant epic tales. In the seventh and sixth centuries BCE, they came to embody more of what modern readers would call a *rhapsode*—those who "claimed expertise as Homeric scholars but also as Homeric philologists and phoneticians," serving as "linguistic 'guardians' of Homeric pronunciation" (Cole 17). Thus, an *aodios* was a performer, whereas *rhapsodes* were also interpreters and critics. Both would have recited their tales to music, keeping time with a lyre or staff.

Stylistic conventions for prose evolved from these early poetic, rhapsodic devices. According to Richard Enos, prose style developed during the fifth and sixth centuries BCE, first in Ionia, and then spreading throughout the rest of Attica. Early Ioninan prose writers (logographers) still prized poetic devices and figurative language when writing philosophical, scientific, political, or historical works—so much that they sometimes elevated sound above accuracy (Enos 25). The most well-known logographer is Heroditus, whom Enos analyzes for his narrative style. While it may not be beneficial to encourage students to lie for the sake of style, the fact that early prose historians cared as much or more about their style as the content of their work may surprise students trained to see style as less important, as a matter of rules rather than a major aspect of composition.

Recognizing the origins of contemporary prose style in this period of Western history can liberate teachers from reductive or narrow definitions of style that concentrate only on the surface-level conventions of academic discourse. If style was once an inseparable component of discourse and persuasion, then it is possible to recuperate this definition of style for contemporary writing instruction. This recuperation entails helping students develop an appreciation of how words and sentences sound and how their choice of diction, phrasing, and rhetorical structure can go far beyond the simple adherenceto guides and manuals. In essence, claiming this period for style means granting agency to students in their linguistic choices.

Sophists (Fifth and Fourth Centuries BCE)

The sophists conceived of style as generative rather than ornamental. In other words, style assists in the invention of ideas, not merely their expression to an audience after the fact. For the sophists, Gorgias in particular, language always carried the particular worldview of a rhetor with it, and thus could never be objective or transparent, as Plato and Aristotle later asserted. In "On Being," Gorgias maintains that nothing is knowable or true in itself, and language always mediates the development of ideas. If language determines our perceptions of reality, it follows that stylistic choices are inventive in that they give us a means of altering those perceptions, not merely decorating them for different audiences. Sophists such as Gorgias were the first rhetorical theorists in the Western tradition to recognize and harness the inventive potentials of style.

In the *Encomium of Helen*, Gorgias speaks of stylistic eloquence as a hypnotic drug, stating that "Sacred incantations sung with words are bearers of pleasure and banishers of pain, for, merging with opinion in the soul, the power of the incantation is wont to beguile it and persuade it and alter it by witchcraft" (45). Patricia Bizzell and Bruce Herzberg describe the prose of the sophists, Gorgias in particular, as "musical," deploying "the devices of the poets" (23). The sophists inherited the poetic tradition of the Homeric rhapsodes, and applied poetic techniques to rhetorical discourse.

Michelle Ballif interprets Gorgias's work as making important, early articulations regarding the inherent instability of language, a view that complicates the promotion of the plain style (i.e., simple, literal language) as best suited to the expression of ideas. In *Seduction, Sophistry, and the Woman with the Rhetorical Figure*, Ballif reads Gorgias as rejecting the Athenian emphasis on "the so-called plain style on the grounds that (1) truth is not . . . pure and clear; (2) truth cannot be known . . . and (3) truth cannot be communicated—that it certainly is not transparent" (76). Ballif concludes that the "speakable is not plain—it is (always already) deception" (76). As the next sections show, Plato and Aristotle denied the inherent instability and deception of language, and posited the plain style as the ideal form for conveying truth.

The fundamental difference between sophistic and Platonic or Aristotelian views of language affected opinions about the role of style in rhetoric. Because language was inherently unstable and always lied, the use of style was seen not as a wild thing to be tamed, but a set of tools. Aristotelian rhetoric saw language as stable, but corrupted when used improperly or unethically to advance personal interests; therefore, style had to be sterilized and reduced to the simplest possible medium so as to not interfere in philosophical pursuits of truth, ethics, and justice. The Aristotelian view led to vilifying the sophists as deceptive, superficial, and immoral until the last century. A more positive view of the sophists evolved during a reassessment of sophistic rhetorics during the 1990s, where such attention helps explain and contextualize the reanimation of stylistic studies. This recuperation of the sophists includes work by scholars such as Susan Jarratt, John Poulakos, Victor Vitanza, and Edward Schiappa.

Other well-known sophistic works include fragments by Protagoras and Antiphon, as well as the anonymous *Dissoi Logoi*, a text that uses the sophistic view of language as inherently subjective to advance the value of arguing on multiple sides of any issue. Unfortunately, few extant treatises exist by the sophists. Many of their writings appear in textual fragments, gathered in a collection by Rosamond Kent Sprague. Sean Patrick O'Rourke lists Anaximenes's *Rhetorica ad Alexandrium* as one of the only surviving handbooks of the sophists "imparting skills to the practitioner" (20) rather than in-depth theories or prescriptions.

Scott Consigny was among the first rhetoric historians in the 1990s to challenge the once-dominant view that sophistic rhetorics elevated style above content. Distinguishing his view from other historical accounts, Consigny identifies Gorgias's style as neither mimetic (representational) nor epistemological (knowledge-producing) but as hermeneutic, meaning that Gorgias "would presumably reject the notion that any one discourse and hence any one 'style,' whether it be that of the funeral orator, literary critic, attorney or philosopher, has a privileged access to the truth" (50). Edward Schiappa's The *Beginnings of Rhetorical Theory in Classical Greece* reconsiders Gorgias's use of stylistic devices to redeem him from the traditional view that his style was inappropriate for rhetoric (85–113). While scholars disagree over the extent to which the sophists subscribed to mimetic, epistemic, or hermeneutic theories of language, they tend to agree in their view of sophistic style as more than ornamental.

A wealth of other works rehabilitates the sophists. John Poulakos describes the sophistic stance similarly to Consigney and Schiappa by acknowledging the inherent contingency of knowledge expressed through language. Susan Jarratt re-interprets sophistic theories of language through the lenses of social-epistemic, feminist, Freirean, and poststructural theories of language and literacy. Like Ballif, Jarratt recognizes Plato and Aristotle's association of sophistic style with deception:

> The devaluation of both the sophists and women operates as their reduction to a "style" devoid of substance. Both rhetoric and women are trivialized by identification with sensuality, costume, and color—all of which supposed to be manipulated in attempts to persuade through deception. The Greek goddess of persuasion, Peitho, is linked with marriage goddesses—not for her domestic skill but because of her seductive powers and trickery. (65)

For Jarratt, the prose styles of French feminist writers such as Helena Cixous share stylistic traits with the sophists, including antithesis and a "propensity for poetry's loosely connected narrative syntax in prose" that challenges "the philosophers Plato and Aristotle with a threatening disorder" and help to construct an alternative epistemic that values "physical pleasure in language" rather than seeing it merely as a transparent vehicle for truths (72).[7]

Plato (Fourth Century BCE)

Plato's dialogues rarely discuss style explicitly, but we can infer an implicit theory from his criticisms of sophistic eloquence. When taken together with chapters of the *Republic*, Plato's dialogues suggest that rhetors should use a plain, unadorned style rather than an ornate one. While many sophists such as Gorgias and Protagoras saw the stylistic play of language as a source of pleasure and an end of itself, Plato defined language as a medium best used for discovering and expressing

---

7. Victor Vitanza's *Negation, Subjectivity, and the History of Rhetoric* declares postmodern and poststructural turns in rhetorical and literary scholarship as a dawn of a third sophistic because of their view of style as generative and language as formative.

truth, making language necessarily plain and literal. In many cases, Plato regarded the sophistic orientation to language as dangerous, since it could persuade people toward ideas that were harmful to them and to the state.

Plato articulated his ideas through a series of conversations between fictionalized versions of historical characters. (The *Republic* is composed entirely of such dialogues.) Plato's protagonist in these dialogues is his teacher, Socrates, and most of what historians know about him is based on these works. Throughout several of his dialogues, as well as sections of *The Republic*, Plato distinguishes knowledge from expression while privileging one over the other. Socrates often voices an unfair, subjective suspicion of style, including metaphor, and criticizes poets and sophists for misrepresenting reality. In the dialogue "Ion," when Ion attempts to explain the importance of verse, he is cut off from explaining how a rhapsode may not know more than a general, but can certainly teach a general how to explain military strategy more persuasively.

In a 2009 *JAC* essay, T. R. Johnson pinpoints pleasure as a breaking point between Plato and the sophists, namely Gorgias. Johnson characterizes the sophistic goal of rhetoric as "*terpsis* or aesthetic pleasure, because pleasure makes persuasion possible," something that provides "the ground on which author and audience merge, a sign that persuasion is succeeding and the crowd is changing" (444). Plato and Aristotle disparaged this notion of style, and define it in opposition to a more Attic, restrained version meant to assist in dialectic. Johnson describes fourth century Greece as an era when rhetoric, eloquence, and magic itself "came to be used unfavorably and to be applied to anything that was deceptive" (444).

In the dialogue "Gorgias," Plato presents eloquence as harmful in that it only helps rhetors achieve selfish goals by persuading others. When debating Polus, one of Gorgias's pupils, Socrates vilifies eloquence as flattery, as it "pretends to be that into which she has crept, and cares nothing for what is the best, but dangles what is most pleasant for the moment as a bait for folly, and deceives it into thinking that she is of the highest value" (98). Therefore, eloquence is not an art or medicine in Plato's view, but mere "cookery" that seeks to make anything pleasant for the moment, but lacks any "account . . . of the real nature of things" (98). Socrates promotes a view of rhetoric as self-regulation for the sake of justice, one of the chief virtues. Rhetoric for any purpose other than the unadorned expression of truth is immoral. According to Johnson, "Whereas Gorgias had equated rhetoric with both pleasure and medicine, Plato insisted that since what is pleasurable is not necessarily beneficial, not the same as Truth and Goodness, Rhetoric is therefore a spurious art, quite unlike medicine" (445). For Plato, rhetoric served only as a means of pursuing universal truths about how to live a just and ethical life. As such, rhetoric had no place for style, except in the most limited sense of conveying ideas clearly.

In the "Phaedrus," Plato discusses aspects of style more directly. Here, Plato dismisses the idea of eloquence altogether, having Socrates declare attempts to study rhetorical devices as useless. In the place of eloquence, Plato posits rhetoric as an ethical discourse in which one attains knowledge through analysis and synthesis that persuades other souls. Again, Plato sees rhetoric as ethical only when it expresses a truth arrived at independently of public deliberation, and deliberation about uncertain political matters is labeled "sophistry" because it never attains a definite universal knowledge. Once again, Plato makes the case for a plain, direct style of discourse in which reason is used to persuade someone toward truths, rather than style as the manipulation of emotions through skillful use of language.

It may help to compare Plato's view of language in these dialogues to that of Gorgias's in "Encomium of Helen," in which Gorgias promotes the hypnotic powers of eloquent language, but does not dismiss them as inherently immoral. Gorgias defends Helen, who is seduced by Paris in *The Illiad* to flee with him to Troy, abandoning her marriage and igniting a long, bloody war with Greece. His argument is that Helen was carried away by Paris's eloquence, a fact that acquits her of any wrongdoing. Whereas Gorgias's point is respect and awe for such power, it was exactly this power that alarmed Plato—such instances are what provoke his adamant stance on rhetoric as a tool toward advancing truth and justice, not the manipulation of language to persuade others toward any opinion or action.

In Book X of *The Republic*, Plato expels poets from the ideal city because "this whole genre of poetry deforms its audience's minds, unless they have the antidote, which is recognition of what this kind of poetry is actually like" (344). For Plato, poetry only imitates representations of true forms, and therefore it is extremely deceptive. To rationalize the rejection of poetic discourse altogether, Plato sets up a complicated chain of argument. First, Socrates asks his interlocutor,

Glaucon, to imagine painters as twice removed from reality by creating representations of beds and tables that are made by craftsmen who, in turn, are representing the ideal form of beds and tables ("made by God"). In turn, poets imitate images and thus are "thrice removed from truth." Therefore, works of epic verse by Homer deceive audiences into believing that they reveal knowledge about their subjects, such as military tactics, virtue, or politics.

Plato's theories of poetry as imitation and deception laid a foundation for future debates about its role in rhetoric. For Plato, a plain style ensured the clear transmission of ideas; therefore, the use of imagery, metaphor, and other devices could only lead people astray from greater truths about how to live and behave ethically. Plato, of course, was not the only classical theorist to disparage the sophists. Isocrates, for one, privileged invention over eloquence partly to avoid the label of sophist; he also dismissed sophists as preoccupied with style, as it was unhelpful in debates about civic matters. Aristotle privileged invention, and relegated style to the mere transmission of arguments. As I illustrate in later sections, in Aristotle's view, the best that style could do was not get in the way of communication.

Isocrates (Fifth and Fourth Centuries BCE)

Although Isocrates was a rival of Plato and a student of Gorgias, the two shared a derision of the sophists as overly concerned with eloquence for its own sake. Isocrates situated rhetoric as a tool for democracy, and defined language as a foundation of civic society. As he argues in *Antidosis*, "there is no institution devised by man which the power of speech has not helped us to establish" (in Bizzell and Herzberg 75). Similar to Plato, Isocrates blames the sophists for the decay of Athenian society, saying they have "plunged [it] into such a state of topsy-turvy and confusion that some of our people no longer use words in their proper meaning but wrest them from the most honorable associations and apply them to the basest pursuits" (78). Isocrates refers here to sophistic practices such as *dissoi logoi* (the use of eloquence to make weaker arguments appear stronger), thus disrupting the supposedly rightful representational relationship between words and objects.

Isocrates did not completely share Plato's aversion to style. He was, in fact, instrumental in the transition of style from oral to written discourse. Style often deals with the sounds of words and the rhythm of sentences, and the manipulation of these sounds for rhetorical effect. Isocrates was not skilled at speaking; he used writing as the central medium to express his thoughts on rhetorical education. What the sophists did with oral discourse, Isocrates did with prose. In David Christopher Ryan's estimation, Isocrates's emphasis on the stylistics of written prose rather than oratory played a significant role in Greece's transition from an oral to literary culture, and his "literary paideia" had a profound influence on the Attic Orators Demosthenes, Aeschines, and Lysias, who all worked at "governing written language . . . to evoke an intellectual and aesthetic response by controlling the sound of written words" through "carefully crafted prose rhythm . . . meant to satisfy solitary readers who read prose works aloud" (71).

Until Isocrates, style was the domain of oral discourse. Written discourse primarily served as an aid to speech writers. Writing for any other purpose did not merit attention to style. Isocrates changed this by writing works intended for reading aloud, thus forming the beginnings of a literate reading public. As such, Isocrates devoted his attention to how his works sounded to the individual's ear in private settings, rather than in public forums, where speeches were delivered. During later classical Greece, we see the spread of literacy and the composition of works that were not necessarily intended as speeches.

Today, when teachers encourage students to "read your work aloud," they usually mean so to assist in finding typos and grammatical errors. However, this advice applies equally to prompting students to actually witness how their words and sentences fit together into larger pieces of discourse that have a similar effect on readers as a speech, even if they are reading silently. Therefore, it is important to note this period in history as a point in which prose style emerged as an adaptation of the criteria originally developed for elegant speeches and poetry. Many of the tropes and figures recovered by contemporary stylisticians for composition pedagogy were, in fact, designed to enhance speeches, and they were first used by poets.

Aristotle (Fourth Century BCE)

The term style as we know it today may owe largely to the work of Aristotle. According to Thomas Cole, the "sharp isolation of style and arrangement as a subject for independent treatment is probably an Aristotelian innovation," given that neither the sophists nor Plato discussed them separately from other aspects of rhetoric (11). It is still hard to make a conclusive statement that Aristotle was the absolute first to explicitly address style, given that handbooks on oratorical technique may have existed in the fifth century BCE, but did not survive (Worman; Cole; Schiappa; Kennedy). These included works by Polus and Antisthenes, both believed to be students of Gorgias. Nevertheless, as Nancy Worman notes, Aristotle played a crucial part in the transition of style from *kosmos*, a holistic trait that linked verbal, visual, and embodied eloquence with character (21), to the decoration or embellishment of words (*lexis*).

In *On Rhetoric*, Aristotle may have reluctantly added treatment of style because it "has some small necessary place in all teaching" of rhetoric, and "does make some difference in regard to clarity, though not a great difference" (3.1.6.1404a). Richard Graff situates Aristotle's views on style within Greece's evolution from orality to literacy, describing how "the Greek language did not come ready-fitted with a proper equivalent for the modern term 'prose,'" and so were obliged to "understand their object in negative terms, as not-poetry or non-verse, and to discriminate between prose and poetry primarily at the level of expression or style" (305). As the earlier discussion of the sophists illustrates, Plato and Aristotle found the use of poetic devices for rhetorical discourse inappropriate because it concealed or distracted from the truths of dialectic and logical reasoning. Poetry necessarily dealt with representations and falsehoods, and so their use of figurative language was a given; but, rhetorical discourse should only use plain language and employ figurative language sparingly, and only to clearly explain ideas.

Aristotle's *On Rhetoric* does not provide an extensive list of rhetorical devices (as later treatises would), nor does it directly mention figures of thought and speech. Aristotle concentrates his treatment of style on metaphor—defined as "an apt transference of words" (3.2.1405b), and maintains that metaphors "should not be far-fetched but taken from things that are related and of similar species, so that it is clear the term is related" (3.2.1405b). He also introduces the techniques of "bringing before the eyes," understood as vivid imagery and *energeia*, the portrayal of things in motion—making them seem lively (3.11.1412a). Metaphor serves as the primary means of these techniques, when applied specifically to the representation of ideas or events. For instance,

Aristotle writes that a line such as "now then the Greeks darting forward on their feet" uses the metaphor of a dart to bring running "before the eyes" (3.11.1412a). Aristotle barely mentions other devices, though he classifies similes, proverbs, and well-done hyperbole as kinds of metaphor.

It is important to realize that while Aristotle often pulls examples from drama and poetry, he is trying to lay down principles for a prose style, governed by the restrained use of metaphor, for the purpose of imparting information or truths achieved through philosophical inquiry. Thus, for Aristotle, the four virtues of style consist of clarity (*saphe*), ordinary speech, correctness, and propriety (*prepon*). As he says, "the subject matter is less remarkable" in prose, as well as in formal speeches; therefore, style is a matter of plain speaking rather than ornament (3.2.1404b). In all such rhetorical situations, the rhetor "should compose without being noticed and should seem to speak not artificially but naturally" (3.2.1404b). In chapter 7 of Book III, Aristotle goes into even more detail regarding the appropriate rhetorical styles for different states of genus (e.g., man or woman, young or old, Spartan or Thessalian) and emotion (e.g., anger, passion, fear). For instance, excessive use of figurative language is appropriate to a state of anger or passion, even in rhetorical discourse.

Aristotle identifies the opposites of virtues as frigidities. The first mentioned is "doubling words"; we would understand this today as hyphenation. For example, Aristotle finds phrases like "beggar-mused flatterers" stylistically awkward because they disrupt rhythm. The second frigidity is gloss—when rhetoricians refer to common people and things through obscure descriptions. For instance, Lycophron refers to Xerxes as "a monster man." The third frigidity is the use of "long or untimely" epithets, and Aristotle describes these as especially vexing when they substitute for substance. The fourth and final frigidity occurs in inappropriate metaphors, either because they are "laughable" when the subject is serious or "too lofty and tragic" when the subject is ordinary (3.3.1406b).

Regarding rhythm, Aristotle is very specific about the appropriate pace for rhetorical discourse or prose. George Kennedy's commentary refers to Aristotle's treatment as "unsatisfactory" because his distinctions between prose and poetry collapse, not only because lyric poetry often used the same rhythms reserved for prose, but also because the examples of rhythmic prose themselves are lines from poems (Kennedy 213). Although the specifics of this section are not all that helpful for contemporary writing teachers, it is worth noting Aristotle's emphasis on artifice. Like many writing textbooks and style manuals today, Aristotle held that the best style was the least noticeable—the plainest—and this manifests throughout his treatment of style, even regarding rhythm. Aristotle argues that prose "should be neither metrical nor unrhythmical" because, first, rhythmic prose "seems to have been consciously shaped" and, second, because it "diverts attention . . . for it causes [the listener] to pay attention to when the same foot will come again" (3.8.1409a.). Specifically, Aristotle warns against what he calls the heroic meter (dactyls), and ordinary meter (iambs). Instead, he recommends a third meter, referred to as the paean—three short syllables and one long.

Aristotle's principles of style are often perfunctory, and are sometimes subjective. For instance, he shows disdain for hyperbole, and refers to it as "adolescent," as evidence of how young men are apt to exaggerate (3.2.1413b). In *Classical Rhetoric and Rhetoricians*, Neil O'Sullivan defines Aristotle's prescriptions for style as "at best idiosyncratic" and "an essentially subjective aesthetic judgment that has its roots in the polemic's of Alcidamas's [a student of Gorgias] generation about the nature of poetry and prose" (16). In a 2001 *RSQ* article, Richard Graff attributes Aristotle's disdain for excessive poetic devices, those common in sophistic oratory, to his preference for written literary texts (19). As Graff argues, Aristotle's "emphasis on the visual dimension of texts is especially prominent in the account of style . . . which at several points reveals Aristotle's sensitivity to the opportunities and challenges presented by the medium of writing and the practice of reading" (20).

While conventional readings see Aristotle's theory of style as mimetic and privileging transparency, not all scholars agree. In *Rereading Aristotle's Rhetoric*, Jeanne Fahnestock interprets Book III of *On Rhetoric* in light of pragmatics, outlining Aristotle's division of style into metaphor; antithesis, or "sentence patterning" that balances opposing ideas; and *energeia* (vividness). Fahnestock argues that Aristotle "groups them in chapter 10 on the basis of what they all can accomplish" (171) and finds parallels between figures of thought such as antithesis and lines of argument, as covered in Book II and *The Topics* (176). In general, a pragmatic perspective on style sees figures of thought and expression as "a stylistic prompt or syntactic frame for invention," despite modern epistemological "discomfort that any such notion of purely verbal invention produces" (178). The idea that poetic devices actively construct thought and meaning while being written or spoken disrupts the unidirectional flow of form and content and, when applied to Aristotle, it becomes a progressive reading of an ostensibly conservative treatise.

Aristotle's definition of metaphor and his discussion of "bringing before the eyes" receive particular focus in historical scholarship on rhetoric. Kennedy's translation references a large body of secondary sources on Aristotle's conception of metaphor, defined in *Poetics* as "a movement [*epiphora*] of an alien [*allotrios*] name either from genus to species or from species to genus or from species to species or by analogy" (21.1457b7–9.). In *Rhetoric*, Aristotle elaborates on this definition through examples, describing "begging" and "praying" as two different species in the larger genus of asking. Therefore, one can adorn begging or denigrate praying by referring to one as the other.

A counterpart to metaphor appears later in Book III that Aristotle calls *energeia* (actualization). *Energeia* contributes to a "bringing before the eyes," understood in contemporary terms as vividness or descriptive imagery. Sara Newman reads *Rhetoric* and *Poetics* in light of Aristotle's philosophical works to assert that "bringing before the eyes . . . functions neither in the traditional, ornamental sense that it is accessory to persuasion, nor in the contemporary sense that . . . [it] constructs meaning" (22–23), but as a blend of the two. As Newman interprets Aristotle, vivid imagery does more than simply beautify an argument; though, it should not become a rhetor's sole purpose, either. Similar to Fahnestock, Newman concludes that "style contributes substantively to argument" (23) in Aristotle's framework, despite the conventional view that it works best as invisible. It is possible that Aristotle saw style as inventive, and that portions of *Rhetoric* that discuss are strongly worded to correct what he saw as the stylistic excess of the sophists. In short, Aristotle may have seen the sophists as privileging style to such an extent that they neglected other parts of rhetoric.

In both *Rhetoric* and *Poetics*, Aristotle declares that skill with language is innate and not teachable. In *Rhetoric*, he states, "Metaphor especially has clarity and sweetness and strangeness, and its use cannot be learned from someone else" (3.2.1405a). In *Poetics*, he says that "an ability to use metaphor is a 'sign of natural ability'" (22.17). Yet, Aristotle's treatment of rhetoric in general—namely invention and arrangement—holds that rhetoric is a teachable *techne*, or art. As stated earlier, for Aristotle, poetic language stood apart from rhetorical language—meaning that while logical and persuasive discourse was teachable, poetry was a gift. One could learn to become a competent speaker by studying and practicing, but in the classical view, one had to be born a poet to benefit from any training.

As such, in *Poetics*, Aristotle lays no rules for the use of metaphor similar to those he states in *Rhetoric*. It could be said that poets were permitted more stylistic latitude than writers in other genres, and Aristotle distinguishes poetry from other genres not merely through use of rhythm or figurative language, but in its purpose. For Aristotle, while rhetorical discourse and prose convey particular truths, poetry deals with universal truths. Rather than reject poets as Plato does, Aristotle situates poetry as a necessary component of society, albeit one that can corrupt if enjoyed excessively. Hence, Aristotle sets up different stylistic fields for poetry and prose. Aristotle advises rhetors to use plain language; yet, for poets, he recommends a mix of plain language with rare words and metaphors. Whereas the point of rhetoric lies in the pursuit and use of persuasion toward truth, the point of poetry lies in a balance of distinction and clarity (1458b). He defends poetry against critics who "made fun of the tragedians because they employ phrases which no one would use in conversation," arguing that figurative language "gives distinction to the diction" (1458b).

As Kennedy and others acknowledge, Aristotle was the first Western rhetorician to approach grammatical correctness systematically. For Aristotle, proper grammar is part of *lexis* (appropriate words in the right places), and it facilitates clarity—his chief aim for style. For Aristotle, grammar entails effective use of connectives (conjunctions); specific nouns rather than vague ones and circumlocutions; gender agreement (participles were gendered); agreement in number for plural and singular nouns; and appropriate syntax (to avoid solecisms). Classical Greek definitions of grammatical units differ notably from modern grammar. For instance, no Greek treatise offers a definition of sentences, clauses, or phrases. Instead, they use the term "period" when referring to any unit that appears to have a vaguely defined sense of completeness. In an introduction to chapter five of Book III of the *Rhetoric*, Kennedy states: "Although Protagoras and other sophists had made a start at the study of grammar, it was in Aristotle's time still a relatively undeveloped field of study. . . . Systematic grammars of the Greek language did not appear until the second century B.C.E" (207).

Nonetheless, Aristotle's views on correctness are historically important. Greek identity hinged on language, and those who did not speak Greek were considered barbarians. Later, the Romans followed a similar paradigm, in which identity, status, and morality involved proper, pure Latin without interference from other languages. (Even Greek was seen as inappropriate and distasteful in public forums.) The idea of linguistic purity and its social-political implications extend from this period through much of Western history. Moreover, debates about the homogeneity versus heterogeneity of language lie at the heart of contemporary issues, including the relationship of Standard English to other varieties. It is helpful to see such dominant codes as a set of stylistic conventions from which writers can depart, drawing from other vernaculars, dialects, and languages to decide what words and expressions to use, as well as decide about the grammar and syntax that varies from one variety of language to the next.

Roman Style: Cicero and Quintilian

Classical Greek rhetoricians presented the first theories of style. Almost all of our terminology for tropes, figures, and schemes comes from the annals of Roman rhetoric—especially Quintilian's exhaustive catalogue of devices in *The Orator's Education*.[8] We also inherited the three levels of style (plain, middle, and grand) and four virtues of style from the Romans. These frameworks for rhetoric filtered down through nearly two thousand years, and still haunt contemporary style guides and handbooks. Although Theophrastus originated the four virtues of style, his works are lost; so, Quintilian's detailed discussion of these virtues (an expansion of Cicero's) had the greatest influence on subsequent generations of rhetors.

The virtues (*latinitas, dignitas, decorum, ornatus*) present a kind of rubric for classical eloquence that outlines the importance of correct speech, dignity, appropriateness to the occasion, and the ability to ornament discourse with tropes and figures. Romans used the term *amplificatio* (amplification) to describe the process of ornamenting or

---

8. Fortenbough also sees Roman treatises as important sources for the reconstruction of theories presented by rhetoricans such as Theophrastus (321).

stylizing discourse. (The Greeks referred to it as *auxesis*). In the anonymous *Rhetorica ad Herennium,* and later in Cicero, we also see the first discussion of the three-tiered system of style that has either been adopted wholesale, or adapted by almost every rhetorician since. Of course, the Roman systems of eloquence described here are not without problems. While thorough and detailed, they define style rigidly and preclude use of anything but pure Latin, without much room for deviation, innovation, or error. Only in Quintilian do we begin to see some allowance for breaking rules for stylistic effect.

Before proceeding, it may be helpful to briefly define a few terms used throughout the rest of this book: *trope, figure,* and *scheme.* Here we are concerned with broad definitions rather than particular ones, because rhetoricians often quibble over stylistic devices that might fit into more than one of these categories. Roman rhetoricians broadly define *trope* as the deviation from ordinary word use, including use of metaphor, defined by Aristotle as language that refers to one thing as another. Other tropes include *synecdoche* (substituting a part for the whole), *metonymy* (referring to a person or thing by one of its qualities), *irony* (saying the opposite of what we mean), and *oxymoron* (juxtaposing antithetical ideas).

Whereas tropes usually refer to individual words and phrases, a *figure* refers to sentences and slightly longer stretches of discourse. In Book VIII of *The Orator's Education*, Quintilian defines figures as the use of language for effect. We might say that while all tropes are figures, not all figures are tropes. For example, rhetorical questions and impersonation are considered figures because they do not necessarily use metaphorical language, but are instead meant for effect; i.e., not meant literally as questions. In *Rhetorical Figures in Science,* Jeanne Fahnestock provides an overview of how classical rhetoricians classified and re-classified certain patterns of language as tropes or figures. Ultimately, she proposes a functional definition of figures that is less concerned with categories, in order to account for the use of figurative language that may fall outside the use of formal terms from the classical tradition.[9] Finally, *schemes* refer to the alteration of word order. Examples of schemes include the use of sentence structures such as

---

9. Fahnestock also recognizes the difficulty of telling figurative language apart from literal, arguing that these distinctions often depend on rhetorical contexts. What seems literal or figurative can change between situations, genres, and disciplines.

parallelism (the use of parallel clauses) and *climax* (arranging clauses by order of importance). One especially effective example of a scheme is John F. Kennedy's motto, as it uses an inversion of word order, called *chiasmus:* "Ask not what your country can do for you, but what you can do for your country." People do not usually arrange sentences like this, but when they do, it is striking and memorable. Thus, an effective way to conclude a speech or even a paragraph is through a scheme.

Like Isocrates, Cicero regarded style and eloquence as inseparable from public affairs and ethics, in contrast to Aristotelian and sophistic stances on style as morally neutral. Cicero's best-known rhetorical treatise is *De Oratore*, written as a dialogue between two main characters named Crassus and Antonius.[10] As Thomas Conley observes in his reading of Cicero's *De Oratore* in *Rhetoric in the European Tradition*, "Crassus places his observations on the four basic requisites of a good style [discussed below] . . . in a broad context of right reason and virtuous action" (35). In the Roman sense, style is not just a kind of rhetoric, but is bound with ethics. A style is only "good" if it helps persuade others of virtuous ideas. Whereas Plato defined this as the job of philosophy and dialectic, Cicero is interested not in pursuing eternal truths, but in using eloquence to persuade citizens toward virtuous actions in everyday situations.

In *De Oratore*, Cicero makes style a central concern of rhetoric—not the mere decoration of words after the fact. In Book III, he even says that it is foolish to separate style from content, because one cannot exist without the other. Those who try are "half-educated people" who "find it easier to deal with things they cannot grasp in their entirety," and so "split them apart and almost tear them to pieces" (3.24). His vision of the ideal orator treats eloquence as the expression of wisdom in a way that is pleasing and interesting to an audience. In his view, orators are more qualified as political leaders than as philosophers, because they have the power to persuade through the eloquent use of words.

Toward this end, Cicero introduces the four virtues of style (*latinitas, dignitas, decorum,* and *ornatus*). For Cicero, correct grammatical use of Latin and pronunciation is a prerequisite for style. A secondary component of *latinitas* is clarity. Discourse can be correct but still obscure—often through the overuse of ornament, awkward sentences, or

---

10 *De Oratore* is the original Latin title for the English translation, *On the Ideal Orator*, cited here.

archaic words. Cicero regards distinction (*dignitas*) as not merely clear, but also apt word choice and even the effective use of rhythm—qualities that make one's discourse seem unique. *Decorum* is discourse appropriate to the occasion that is effectively ornamented (*ornatus*) with the use of tropes and figures. The occasion of a rhetor's speech determines their use of figurative language, leading Cicero to prefer a balance of plain and ornamented speech. Overuse of tropes and figures can undermine the purpose of a speech, much like too much sweetness can make someone sick (3.100).

Cicero is also the first rhetorician to propose a three-tiered system of style: the plain style, the middle style, and the grand style. He mentions these tiers briefly in *De Oratore* (3.177), and develops them more fully in a later treatise, *Orator*, where he explains how the level of style corresponds to different rhetorical purposes in a way meant to help orators determine the relationship between the virtues of ornament and appropriateness. Sometimes people want to be swept off their feet with flowery language; other times, they want only the facts explained clearly and quickly; still other times, they want language that renders a particular subject interesting or entertaining. The plain style is appropriate for teaching or imparting information, and consists only of clear, precise language in the way prescribed by Aristotle. The middle style permits some degree of ornamentation in order to emphasize points for an audience. It is also the most universally appealing style, appropriate for instruction, entertainment, and to some degree, persuasion. The third level of style could contain any and all rhetorical devices, at the rhetor's discretion, to ignite an the passions of an audience. The grand style is reserved for serious subjects, and if used for the wrong occasion, could make a speech appear overwrought or contrived.

These divisions also appear in Quintilian's treatise, and are adapted by St. Augustine for religious rhetoric. The system may seem simplistic given the enormous variety of genres today, but may still help students and teachers think about writing situations within these three broad categories. After all, some genres require clarity and plain language foremost, whereas others might tolerate—or even call for—use of stylistic devices such as vivid imagery, metaphor, alliteration, or different sentence schemes.

For Cicero, the best style is the most expedient in a given situation.[11] According to Elaine Fantham, Cicero's notion of style as purposeful rather than decorative sets him apart from classical Greek rhetoricians—even the older sophists. Fantham describes Cicero's stance on style in *De Oratore* as the notion that "discourse pleases because of its richness of content, the variety, not of applied ornament, but of serious topics well handled" (279). Fantham's reading of Book III, specifically lines 96–198, focuses on Cicero's distinction between *ornatus* as adornment versus ornament as purpose, as ornament is intrinsic to any speech because "what is necessary and useful is beautiful" (280). As Cicero originally states, "what possesses the greatest utility at the same time has the most dignity, and often even the most beauty" (3.178–80). Therefore, "Cicero is dealing with a type of *ornatus* not found in traditional stylistic theory—the charm, power and variety of speech" (Fantham 280) for the sake of fulfilling a purpose rather than decorating. The most equivalent Greek terms to Cicero's notion of style lie between *poikilian* (verbal ornament) and *metabole* (transformation). Similar to Fantham's reading, Cecil Wooten sees Cicero as privileging the functional value of variety (blends of plain, middle, and grand styles) and rhythm, praising them at length as the Attic orator Demosthenes in *Orator*.

Cicero's own style flew against convention, and he elevates Demosthenes above the other Attic orators in *Brutus* to defend himself against descriptions of his bombastic style as sophistic and Asiatic (179); he explains it as unbecoming of any orator. What Cicero says here conflicts with his statements about the superiority of a stern, Attic style in *De Oratore*. We might think of his statements in *Brutus* as a partial revision of his earlier comments on style, largely intended to make him seem less hypocritical. Richard Leo Enos confirms this understanding of Cicero in *Classical Rhetoric and Rhetoricians*, stating that *Brutus,* in particular, responds to criticism of *De Oratore* by the Atticists, "many of who[m] favored a terser, plain style of rhetoric than what they believed Cicero presented" (107). Throughout Greek

---

11. Cicero recommends the plain style whenever possible but, ironically, he does not always practice what he preaches. He was known as a firebrand who often gave wildly passionate speeches. Cicero's contemporaries (known as the Atticists) criticized him for an "exuberant, emotional oratory" style in his speeches to the Roman senate and in the law courts (Wooten 178).

Historical Review I: From Ancient Greece through Rome 39

and Roman rhetorical treatises, excessive eloquence becomes associated with foreignness or Asianism.

Cicero's work serves as a foundation for Quintilian's much longer, more ambitious treatment of style in *The Orator's Education*. In many ways, Quintilian was Cicero's intellectual heir. Joy Connolly describes Quintilian's perspectives on style in Books VIII and IX of *The Orator's Education* as "the bedrock for compositional theory and rhetorical speech analysis even today" (327). Granted, Quintilian follows Aristotle and Theophrastus's four virtues of style: "linguistic accuracy and purity, clarity, ornament, and propriety [appropriateness]," and he does not innovate as much as catalogue different devices (Connolly 327). However, the value for Connolly lies in this very cataloguing of figures of thought and speech—more than one hundred of them—and in their extensive illustration through examples in poetry and prose (including written speeches) that heavily influenced subsequent eras. Before Quintilian, no one had accomplished an exhaustive catalogue, not even in the *Rhetorica ad Herennium*. Discussions of devices and their effects were scattered across many different treatises and handbooks.

Quintilian maintained (following Cicero) the centrality of rhetoric to public affairs and ethics; therefore, stylistic eloquence had sociopolitical consequences. Because language persuaded others toward virtuous actions, eloquent speech was inherently virtuous. The ideal of the "good man speaking well," explained by Quintilian in Book XII, was the pinnacle of rhetoric, and it could not be achieved by someone who was corrupt. According to Connolly, Quintilian also "condemns rhetoricians whose devotion to fine-tuning grammar or logic blinds them to the true nature of eloquence" (322). Doing so missed the forest for the trees.

Quintilian provides a much more detailed account of the four virtues than does Cicero. Addressing the stylistic virtue of *latinitas* (purity and correctness), Quintilian advises orators and writers against barbarisms, mistakes that render their speech or writing completely ineloquent and ugly. These barbarisms fall into three kinds: when the author

1. "inserts an African or Spanish term in Latin composition" (1.4.8);

2. is "said to have spoken like a barbarian" by making threatening or cruel remarks (1.4.9); or

3. is guilty of "adding a letter or syllable to any word he pleases, or taking one away, or substituting one for another, or putting one in place where it is not right for it to be" (1.4.10).

Latinitas is a political as well as moral virtue, Quintilian argues, and the absence of such barbarisms "declare[s] us to be natives of this city [Rome]," and shows "that our speech may appear truly Roman, and not merely to have been admitted [us] into citizenship" (8.1.3). Himself a foreigner from Spain, Quintilian places importance on utilizing style to access the prestige and political security of sounding Roman and, therefore, being treated more like an equal.

Quintilian discusses the virtue of clarity more in terms of what to avoid than what to seek out. For instance, he advises rhetors against circumlocution, overly long sentences, and overuse of parentheses—all of which obscure meaning and drag out what could be stated more simply. As he says, "just because [some rhetors] do not want to make the simple statement," they "proceed to join this string of words up to another of the same kind, stir them together, and spin it all out beyond the limits of anyone's breath" (8.2.18). Quintilian sees ornament as the real purpose of rhetoric, without which a speaker is unlikely to persuade an audience. Yet, Quintilian also warns that use of figures, tropes, and schemes "must be manly, strong, and chaste. It must not favor effeminate smoothness or false coloring of cosmetics; it must shine with health and vigor" (8.3.7). Concluding in the vein of Cicero, Quintilian states that "True beauty is never separated from usefulness" (8.3.11). Quintilian goes on to state that unrestrained use of ornament is appropriate for ceremonies, but less ornament is required for deliberative or political speeches, and still less for forensic speeches during trials. The rest of Book VIII deals largely with tropes, defined by Quintilian as "a shift of a word or phrase from its proper meaning to another," and he dispenses with what he sees as relatively inane debates among grammarians over their classification by figures of thought or expression. Quintilian maintains that some figures "assist in meaning" (8.6.3), while others provide pure ornament. Quintilian also seems to include schemes as tropes, and briefly defines and illustrates tropes such as metaphor, metonymy, synecdoche, and hyperbole.

Appropriateness is the most important of the four virtues for Cicero because, unless one's style "is adapted both to circumstances and to persons, it will not only fail to lend distinction . . . [it] will ruin it" (11.1.2). An effective rhetor must adjust style to different themes and emotions that range from the serious to the trivial, joyful to sorrowful, and angry to despairing. Without directly mentioning Cicero's three levels of style, Quintilian often references a kind of low or colloquial language necessary for addressing uneducated audiences, in contrast to more ornate, and even florid, styles for ceremonious occasions when one's purpose is to display talent. Appropriateness is also determined by circumstance, as when orators defend court cases regarding minor versus grave offenses, as well as by time and place (11.1.45–48). There is no strict set of rules for what style to construct for different times and places, but a trained and eloquent speaker should know the differences between public and private settings, crowded and secluded ones—whether at home or abroad. Rhetors should be able to shape the styles of their speeches according to such variations in the rhetorical situation, using more or less ornament and varying rhythm and diction accordingly. For example, someone pleading innocence in a murder trial could alienate his or her audience by speaking in a style that is too eloquent and ornate. After all, Quintilian asks, what kind of innocent person would be in such a calm state of mind to construct such a fine speech? In this case, unadorned, even rough speech may do more to persuade judges.

Quintilian also offers a range of prescriptions about style that seem overly rigid, but he was the product of an extremely conservative time. Like the Greeks, Romans saw Latin as the difference between humans and all other forms of life—including slaves. For the Romans, language did not mean communicating on an equal footing with others. As Laura Pernot observes, "The two verbs meaning 'to speak' in Latin, *fari* and *dicere*, belong to two strong roots (*fatum*, fate) and (*deik, dike*, justice)" (85). To speak was not to engage in conversation or dialogue, but "to decree, foretell, or promulgate rules" and "[w]hen poorly used, it [was] dangerous, creating deadly innovations" (Pernot 85). Kirchner notes that Roman culture valued linguistic purity so strongly that it's "corruption was also thought to be part and parcel of moral vice" (291).

Many teachers and scholars would now contest Quintilian's view that stylistically effective writing requires conformity to a specific code, whether that code is Latin, Elizabethan English, or Standard English. What Quintilian dismissed as barbarisms, in particular the insertion of words from other languages into one's writing, today can be appreciated as helping to make writing livelier, more personal, more expressive, and more evocative—all traits that are associated with style. Progressive college writing teachers often celebrate the diversity of languages and dialects that students sometimes tap as resources. Contemporary work on language difference and voice encourages the use of multiple codes within a single essay in order to lend a distinctive quality to prose that we may understand as an individualized style. These views are explained in more detail in Chapter 5 and Chapter 6.

Greco-Roman Rhetorical Curriculum: Imitation and the *Progymnasmata*

A great deal of what is known about Roman schooling derives from Quintilian, who describes grammatical education as preceding rhetorical education in the vein of the Greek model. Quintilian did suggest an overlap between grammatical and rhetorical instruction, with younger students spending part of the day with a rhetorician, and the other part with a grammarian (2.1.13). Murphy's chapter in *A Short History of Writing Instruction* describes the sequence of exercises in memorizing model texts, paraphrasing the models, and translating them. Memorization was meant to inculcate students with proper language use, paraphrase to facilitate the beginnings of a unique voice, and translation to develop efficiency and dexterity.

These imitation exercises accompanied the *progymnasmata* that, together, extended from grammatical to rhetorical education. The only major changes involved the complexity and length of the texts that students memorized, analyzed, and imitated. The movement proceeded from narrative-based forms such as allegories to more argument-based ones such as declamations and laws. Murphy points readers to the *progymnasmata* handbook by Hermogenes of Tarsus, the most reliable source for exercises used by the Romans; while written in the second century CE, it is the most faithful to the Roman curriculum.

The fourteen exercises known as the *progymnasmata* (preliminary exercises) trained young grammar-school students in amplification before the progressed to rhetorical study. As Jeanne Fahnestock explains in *Rhetorical Style*, amplification referred not only to the use of rhetorical devices, but also a more general facility or copiousness with language. These exercises began with relatively simple retellings of fables and concluded with difficult assignments in making arguments and proposing laws. They became especially important in Roman education, and Quintilian discusses them at length in *Education of the Orator*. Many of these exercises performed a dual role in that they trained orators in stylistic dexterity as well as arrangement, since many of them closely modeled the different parts of forensic, deliberative, and epideictic speeches. Regarding style, even the earliest of the exercises required students' attention to word choice, as they composed dialogue for characters to expand fables, and developed a repertoire for rephrasing and paraphrasing poems and stories. For example, the exercises referred to as *ethopoeia* (speech in character) called on students to construct a speech in the voice of a famous character from history or poetry. Thus, the *progymnasmata* instilled an awareness of linguistic choices and their appropriateness for different rhetorical purposes.

Richard Leo Enos's chapter on Greek education in James J. Murphy's collection, *A Short History of Writing Instruction*, narrates the teaching practices in Hellenistic culture as it transitioned from oral to literate. As Enos explains, the *progymnasmata* became central to the curriculum that was formalized in the fifth and fourth centuries BCE. This curriculum began with instruction to young children in the alphabet, and then proceeded from age seven to fourteen with instruction in grammar and literary criticism. Males underwent military service after this stage, and then, at the age of twenty, were permitted to study rhetoric. (The Romans followed this same progression.) The *progymnasmata* occupied the pre-rhetorical education of students, although, as Quintilian points out, the latter exercises were useful in rhetorical as well as grammatical education. In the edited volume, *Education in Greek and Roman Antiquity*, Ruth Webb summarizes several collections of *progymnasmata* to state that "handbooks from Theon onwards present all the exercises together," attesting to the fact that "their authors and readers saw the exercises as parts of a unified system to be taught by one master, or at least within a single school" (297). According to Marrou, some rhetoric teachers may have followed Quintilian's advice and taught all of the *progymnasmata*; others may have taught only the more advanced exercises.

As J. David Fleming describes them, these exercises constituted the second (or middle) stage of rhetorical practice—the first being *imitatio* (imitation) of models, and the third being *declamation*, or "composition proper" (107). The *progymnasmata* and imitation exercises went hand-in-hand, and their value to stylistic training cannot be understated. Often, individual exercises in these handbooks of *progymnas-*

mata present sample texts for reading, analysis, and imitation even before instructing students to begin a particular exercise. Both Greeks and Romans viewed the development of a rhetor's style as incumbent upon the skilled interpretation and imitation of classic speeches and poems. It was through the imitation of many influences that students observed and practiced the use of style via word choice, rhythm, grammar, and rhetorical devices. In these exercises, the imitation of great orators and poets constituted the process by which young rhetors discovered and developed their own styles or voices.

Slight differences exist among the various handbooks, but they all contain the following exercises (for an elaborated definition of these exercises, see Kennedy's translations of the *progymnasmata* handbooks):

1. Fable (the expansion or abbreviation of one of Aesop's stories)
2. Narrative (the retelling of a story taken from epic poetry or history)
3. Saying (recounting and explaining an anecdote or pithy saying)
4. Proverb (a similar exercise explaining an anonymous saying)
5. Refutation (attacking the credibility of a myth or legend)
6. Confirmation (doing the opposite with a myth or legend)
7. Commonplace (elaborating on a virtue of vice)
8. Encomium (giving praise or blame to an historical figure)
9. Invective (the opposite of encomium)
10. Comparison (comparing two persons or things, a double encomium)
11. Impersonation (speech from the perspective of a character or historical figure)
12. Description (a vivid description of an object or person)
13. Thesis or Theme (analysis of a complex issue from two or more sides)
14. Law (proposal of a law and its merits, or sometimes the opposite)

The steps laid out for the exercises in these handbooks encouraged students to experiment by elaborating and expanding on the source material. Style might even be said to have served as the primary goal of exercises such as description and impersonation. Exercises in description encouraged students to construct compelling visual images from words, describing objects in nature or a character's body language and facial expressions. In impersonation, students were judged on their ability to capture the particular voice or speaking style of someone. Students needed to consider the differences in rhythm, diction, and syntax of different types of characters; for example, understanding how a servant would speak in contrast to someone like Odysseus, Priam, Achilles, or Helen.

One of the most challenging exercises that students encountered was transliteration, or re-writing texts from one genre to another. For instance, Quintilian recommends rewriting verse as prose, and vice versa (10.5.4). Like other exercises, transliteration intended to train students in the stylistic and structural aspects of language. Marrou's *A History of Education in Antiquity* describes these educational practices in even greater detail, with emphasis on grammar, imitation, recitation, and analysis. Edward P. J. Corbett endeavors to recover transliteration for contemporary composition teaching in a 1971 *CCC* article and in his textbook, *Classical Rhetoric for the Modern Student*.

Later Greeks: Demetrius, Hermogenes, and Longinus (First — Fourth Century, CE)

Demetrius was perhaps the first theorist to treat style in terms of syntax in his treatise, *On Style*.[12] Aristotle had made some comments about grammar and rhythm in Book III of *Rhetoric*, but they were undeveloped. In the case of grammar, Aristotle did little more than name parts of speech, and distinguish periodic from progressive sentences. (Periodic sentences place the main clause at the end to build anticipation, at the expense of clarity.) Scott G. Reed states that Demetrius was the first to "relate style to sentence structure" (127), outlining the appropriate length of clauses and periods (sentences) for each of his four tiers of style: (1) elevated or "eloquent," (2) graceful or elegant, (3) plain, and (4) forceful. Because of its "dynamic, fluid approach . . . teachers and theorists of writing may profit greatly from reclaiming Demetrius from the margins of history" (Reed 127).

---

12. Much more scholarship exists on the contributions of Longinus than Demetrius. Reed attributes the marginal status of Demetrius to conflicting opinions on the authorship and date of the treatise, maintaining that 275 BCE remains the best estimate. Reed says that because of its problematic authenticity, "it does not even merit mention in Robert Connors' chapter on the subject" in *Composition-Rhetoric*, which gives a history of style from the Roman era through the nineteenth century (127).

No surviving texts from earlier periods offer a very thorough or nuanced method for navigating the rhetorical situations where one might want a middle ground between the plain and the bombastic style (e.g., Gorgias). Demetrius gives us a third space, as it were, between Aristotelian and sophistic styles, one that teachers and writers can adapt to present-day circumstances. Each tier of style in Demetrius's system corresponds to different techniques of using figures of thought and expression, diction, syntax, and rhythm. In the eloquent style, for example, long syllables are appropriate because it lengthens important words and lends dignity and gravity to sentences. Any meter is appropriate for elevated discourse, except iambic because "many people speak iambic lines without knowing it" in "ordinary talk" (Demetrius 2.42-45); therefore, the use of iambic makes the subject matter seem ordinary. Sentences or "periods" should have many clauses or "members" for the same reason: "they give the impression of length" (2.45-48). Ironically, elevated discourse should not be smooth, but instead benefits from "words hard to pronounce in combination," because "their very excess brings out the greatness" of certain subjects. Demetrius goes on to prescribe appropriate syntax, sparing use of metaphor and simile, neologisms, effective vowel combinations, and "epiphonemes," or phrases added to a sentence for the sole sake of "adornment" (2.105-108).

We might go about reclaiming Demetrius for college writing instruction by considering the broader point that certain stylistic traits of texts are more appropriate for some genres than others. In some ways, Demetrius anticipates Bakhtin's case in "The Problem of Speech Genres," nearly sixteen hundred years later, that a given set of stylistic conventions always accompanies a given genre. Arguable, Demetrius is the first to note this relationship between genre, stylistic purpose, and types of sentence construction. We will see similar arguments in Chapter 4 and Chapter 5 from composition scholars who write about the rhetorical or stylistic effects of grammar—including Martha Kolln, Laura Micciche, Virginia Tufte, and Joseph Williams.

The core premise of Longinus's *On the Sublime* rests on five principles, including: "full-blooded ideas"; "emotion"; "proper construction of figures"; "nobility of phrase"; and "general effect" (7.4-8). In *Rhetoric and Poetics in Antiquity*, Jeffrey Walker describes Longinus within the sophistic tradition, a return to Gorgianic hypnosis and rapture. Ned O'Gorman elevates the status of *On the Sublime* (generally seen as a style manual) to that of a pivotal treatise, "where the art of rhetoric is presented as possessing its own end and essence, freeing it from subordination and . . . external judgment" (O'Gorman 72). Longinus's sublime uses stylistic devices not as "the available means of persuasion or the well-being of the public per se," as Isocrates and Cicero mandated, "but the road (*methodos*) to ecstasy (*ekstasis*) via 'height' or *hypsos*'" (73). By situating ecstasy and sublimity (height, *hypsos*) as the end goal of every trope and figure, creating an "irresistible power of mastery [in order to] get the upper hand with every member of the audience" (Longinus 1.2-11). Longinus defines an end cause of rhetoric (ecstasy) that goes beyond persuading or moving an audience.

Longinus indeed gives style a different role in rhetoric than does Aristotle or Plato, defining style as the use of figurative language to make an audience focus simply on the emotional presence conveyed by a speech. Aristotle positioned style as the clear transmission of ideas, and therefore pushed for a plain, literal style in most rhetorical situations. Longinus's treatise liberates orators from these constraints and opens rhetoric once again to poetry and play in language. Teachers might consider whether it is possible to explain ideas clearly, on the one hand, while also bringing readers to a state of excitement about a given subject through the use of figurative language and rhythm. Many contemporary approaches to style in rhetoric and composition suggest that it is possible.

Another later Greek treatise by Hermogenes revised and elaborated on Roman theories of style by expanding the three tiers of style. In his work, *On Types of Style*, Hermogenes offers seven ideas of style that could be blended for a range of different occasions: clarity (making sure audiences understand); grandeur (impressing them); beauty (eliciting pleasure); rapidity or speed (avoiding boredom); ethos (adapting style to one's reputation and personality); verity or sincerity (style that conveys trust); and gravity (style moving audiences to action). Each aspect of style could be achieved through different tropes and figures. Rhetors wanting to express anger would use grandeur, in particular the subtype he calls asperity, by composing in short abrupt clauses, harsh alliteration, and a range of figures. When rhetors wish to project confidence, they would practice verity and use figures such as apostrophe, parenthesis, and an overall plainer style that listeners would associate with honesty and frankness. The seventh style, gravity, involves the appropriate use of the other six types at one's discretion. As with

Quintilian, Hermogenes places responsibility for negotiating the types of style within particular situations on the rhetor.

Cecil Wooten's introduction to his translation of Hermogenes states the influence of the work in later antiquity, noting that it all but replaced the Roman, three-tiered style. It became a common textbook in Byzantine schools, and in the mid-1400s it was introduced to Western Europe by George of Trebizond. Once translated into Latin, Hermogenes's *On Types of Style* had a major influence on the study and teaching of style during the European Renaissance. Its influence is discussed in the forthcoming section on Renaissance style.

FEMINIST AND NON-WESTERN STYLES IN THE CLASSICAL AND ANCIENT WORLD

Conventional histories often have a blind spot regarding the presence of linguistic others. These linguistic others include genders, cultures, and ethnicities—as well as other regions of the world where other rhetorics form. In many cases, not enough extant texts remain to construct a comprehensive portrait of non-masculine, non-Attic styles. Nonetheless, a growing body of work includes Cheryl Glenn's *Rhetoric Retold*, Roberta Binkley and Carol S. Lipson's *Rhetoric Before and Beyond the Greeks*, another collection by the same editors titled *Ancient Non-Greek Rhetorics*, Damian Baca and Victor Villanueva's *Rhetorics of the Americas*, and Andrea Lunsford's *Reclaiming Rhetorica*. A number of primary texts are gathered in the 2001 anthology, *Available Means: An Anthology of Women's Rhetoric*. Although the volume is heavily slanted toward the nineteenth and twentieth centuries, it does contain works by Aspasia, Sappho, Diotima, Hortensia, and Heloise.

Feminist historiography guiding such recovery work is critical not only of the exalted status of men in the rhetorical tradition, but also the phallogocentric discourse that dictates the ways histories are structured. A special 1992 issue of *Rhetoric Society Quarterly* outlines other possibilities than merely adding women to the existing historical narratives. Many feminist historical methods also rethink concepts such as linearity, order, and hierarchy. Michelle Ballif articulates the project as a question of liberation:

> What "hitherto unrecognized possibilities" could we explore if our narratives had no syllogistic, metonymic, linear or trian-

gular structure? If we broke the sequence (and the sentence)? What if there were no conditions of a narrative, no universal criteria for judging the Truth or legitimacy of a narrative? (96)

As such, understanding feminist contributions to the study of classical rhetoric mandates the re-evaluation of the theories of classical rhetoricians.

The project that Ballif describes has become central to the recovery work of the sophists, and Susan Jarratt in particular has mobilized sophistic views of language and eloquence toward interpretations of Helena Cixous's *ecriture feminine* (women's writing) and Julia Kristeva's *jouissance*. These ways of writing and crafting sentences carry with them alternative modes of thinking and organizing experience. Regarding style, rethinking the classical canon involves "rethinking the sentence" and the idea of speech, poetry, or prose as ideally transparent or, by contrast, opaque. It means envisioning roles for rhetorical style other than informing, delighting, and persuading. Work by Cheryl Glenn on rhetorical silence in *Unspoken* offers such a rhetorical frame, working from the idea that "[a]ll silence has meaning" (11) because it encompasses language, rather than acting as its opposite or absence. Glenn draws on work in linguistics to show how speakers often intentionally use silence for a variety of purposes that include indicating agreement, doubt, caution, anger, and also to emphasize points or signal a change in direction. For Glenn, silence serves to explain and gesture toward enigmas, hidden insights, or ideas and experiences that language does not fully capture. Phrases such as "the joy was beyond words" or "I'll tell you about that later" allude to silence that exceeds the ideology of clear expression through language.

All of these uses of silence depend on context, and writing often portrays silence through statements about what an author will not discuss or plans to delay. The strategic, or stylistic, use of silence creates a range of tones or voices outside the Western, Aristotelian notion of conveying ideas clearly: defiant, resilient, playful, suspenseful, haunting, or woeful. Glenn's rhetorical silence is a third way between the sophistic style, meant to overwhelm, and the Aristotelian style, meant to inform. Such a framework might lead researchers in stylistic studies to ask what role such devices as ellipses, pauses, breaks, and other ruptures in speech play in writing and its effect on audiences.

Greco-Roman culture did not simply discriminate against women; their language and rhetorical practices were based on an idea of excluding anything that did not conform to Hellenistic ideals—a plain and masculine Attic style in speaking and writing. Ian Smith's *Race and Rhetoric in the Renaissance* contains an insightful chapter on these early forms of language hegemony and their representation in the rhetorical and literary culture of classical Greece. In conventional histories like those by Kennedy and Enos, Isocrates is portrayed as an important figure in the advancement of literacy and Hellenismos (Greek nationality). As a counterpoint, Smith highlights the incitement of anxiety and the fear of cultural others that drives Isocrates's *Pangericus*, in which he urges war on Persia. A similar xenophobia appears in *Antidosis*, where Isocrates describes "the race of the Hellenes above the barbarians, namely, in the fact that you have been educated as have no other people in wisdom and speech" (*Antidosis* 293–94). The term "barbarian," or *barbarous*, itself meant non-Greek, and referred specifically to those who did not speak Greek and were thus considered sub-human. Barbarian speech was even stylistically parodied in Greek drama. As Smith points out, "Playwrights used a variety of acoustic effects to simulate the cacophony and disorder of barbarian speech as in Aeschylus's long list of pseudo-Persian military and place names deliberately contrived to be jarring" (28). In particular, he directs readers to *Persians* 598–61, 966–72, 993–9. This is not an isolated case, either. Smith provides several examples, including Aristophanes's *Women at the Thesmophoria*, where he describes "a representative figure of barbarian vulgarity and gullibility, an object lesson in the disasters that await the barbarian appropriation of power" (27). The distinct quality of barbarian speech as parodied in Greek tragedy was so pronounced that even translators have made efforts to convey it by appropriating elements of African American Vernacular (AAVE). Smith quotes from Greg Delanty's translation of *Orestes*, when a Phrygian slave relays news of a disaster befalling Helen of Troy:

> When dey grabbed her around her knees we, her slaves, jumped up, mumbling to each udder dat someding dodgy was up. A few of us taut dat was all baloney, but udders would have no truck wit dat and had dose two buckoes taped. Dey twigged dat a strike was going to be pulled on Hele by dat snake who did away wit his own Ma. (qtd. in Smith 28)

These perspectives show that style has always had an exchange value. It can mark distinction among eloquent speakers and writers while also excluding other groups according to pre-determined conventions governing the use of language. Especially, Smith's work reveals the lengths to which certain groups will go to establish themselves as linguistically dominant. Style is therefore not merely an ornament or even a method of invention, but also a means of asserting value claims and either reinforcing or undermining hierarchies.

A growing range of scholarship has begun addressing style in the rhetorical traditions of non-Western cultures. Such scholarship is useful for teachers that face increasingly diverse and international student populations. Understanding historical work on the role of style in other rhetorical traditions assists in the negotiation of students' stylistic decisions by contextualizing them. For instance, in the ancient Chinese rhetorical tradition, views on style oscillated between the *pianwen* (ornate) and *guwen*, or Confucian (plain). In *Chinese Rhetoric and Writing*, Andy Kirkpatrick and Zhichang Xu describe *pianwen* as "florid and verbose" (37), much like the sophistic rhetorical style of fourth century Greece that Aristotle dismissed. It became prominent during the mid-fifth century CE as a turn away from the simpler Confucian style that favored indirect and inductive argumentative strategies. The term *pianwen* most closely translates as "parallel prose" in English, and part of its verboseness stems from its structure. This style relied on "the use of four and six word parallel phrases, with four words in the first phrase, six words in the second and so on" to create "contrasting tone patterns across the phrases" (Kirkpatrick and Xu 39). The earliest manual devoted to rhetoric, Chen Kui's *Wen Ze* (*The Rules of Writing*), insists on the *guwen* style. Like Aristotle, Kui believed that "form should serve meaning" and include "the use of words, syntax and sentence construction" (57). Thus, the most appropriate style was always the clearest and most concise.

The Chinese rhetorical tradition yields both a direct and an indirect style of argument, although the indirect style is more common, hailing from the Confucian period. As Kirkpatrick and Xu explain, it is more common to use a frame-main sentence construction, meaning that sentences begin with subordinate clauses rather than direct ones. For example, an American might say, "You can't enter the building because there has been a fire" (25). A Chinese writer is more likely to say, "Because there has been a fire, you can't enter the building." Whereas the direct, agonist style of argument in the Western tradition emanated from the courts, in China there were no such courts, and so no forensic rhetoric. Since rhetors were always persuading, they had to phrase arguments indirectly as to seem less threatening to political superiors.

Other rhetorical traditions in the Middle East may challenge our assumptions about histories of style in the West. In the edited collection, *Rhetoric Before and Beyond the Greeks*, William W. Hallo briefly describes rhetorical training in Sumerian scribal schools before discussing rhetorical devices used in the opening lines of the epic of Gilgamesh and other works in cuneiform dating back to the twenty-third century BCE. The use of eloquent language appears to reinforce the power of ritual and harmony in such cultures, not necessarily the forensic (legal) or deliberative (political) forms of persuasion, as in Greece and Rome. In this vein, Roberta Binkley recovers the ancient Sumerian figure Enheduanna, whose *Exaltation of Inanna* makes use of repetition and metonymy in a 150-line poem interweaving praise of the deity Inanna with the narrative of her own banishment and return to power as high priestess of Ur. Binkley's discussion of Enehduanna's poetry and historical context in the twenty-third century BCE questions our discipline's emphasis on Athens and Rome as the primary sites of the early development of rhetoric. This recovery work suggests that a history of prose style, understanding its debts to oral discourse and poetry, extends back much further than classical Greece, and that Aristotle was the "first" to discuss style only in the sense of the Western tradition, whose texts are more familiar and accessible to contemporary teachers in the US. Meanwhile, a great deal of historical material from ancient Mesopotamia and other regions remains untranslated.

Although prior scholars have tried to map Greco-Roman stylistic devices onto the literary works of these cultures, scholars in comparative rhetoric express skepticism of such projects, as non-Western texts do not "provide us with a neatly prepackaged corpus of theoretical prescriptions or practical illustrations of the art of persuasion in public speaking" or in writing (Hallo 25). In another essay in the same collection, Jan Swearingen advocates an "emic" approach to rhetorical history, meaning the "study of 'rhetoric' of the Other in its own terms rather than in ours" (213). In other words, in many non-Western rhetorical traditions, there is no equivalent to Book III of Aristotle's *Rhetoric* or the *Rhetorica ad Herennium* of which we know. The construction of theories and approaches to style requires induction from close study of their surviving texts, not from applying ready-made theories of style from the Western tradition.

Augustine of Hippo (Fourth and Fifth Centuries CE)

Augustine defined stylistic eloquence mainly as a means of lending potency and clarity to sermons, and his approach to rhetoric is often compared to Plato's in the "Phaedrus" (Conley 77). Augustine himself was trained in the classical tradition, and studied law before his conversion to Christianity in 387 CE. Bizzell and Herzberg contextualize Augustine as an early philosopher of Christianity in a period when it was a growing, but not quite yet the universal European faith it would become in the medieval era. His book, *De Doctrina Christina* (*On Christian Doctrine*) was the first to treat scripture as a literary text in need of interpretation; Book II and Book III of the treatise lay out a theory of signs to interpret the Bible allegorically, rather than always literally. For Augustine, it was a priest's responsibility to learn correct and responsible interpretation of scripture, including the ability to discern the difference between literal language and language that serves a metaphorical or allegorical purpose.[13]

Book 4 of *On Christian Doctrine* devotes attention to style, although it "contains little if anything that cannot be found in the *De Oratore*" (Conley 77). While it is true that Augustine did not compose an original theory of style per se, we should appreciate his application of style to the emerging genre of sermons. Augustine's discussion of style and eloquence is important for defending its use against early theologians such as Tertullian (160–224 CE) and Jerome, who denied the role of Ciceronian eloquence in clerical matters. These scholars found the classical tradition unsuitable for any discussion of religious discourse not only because it was designed by pagans, but also because faith and persuasion were irreconcilable. There should be no need to make one's discourse more persuasive if already speaking the truth of God; therefore, any rhetorical approach to religious discourse was suspect.

Augustine realized the need to convey religious truths to different audiences in different situations, and Part IV of *On Christian Doctrine*

---

13. Augustine actually classifies language, or "signs," into four categories: unknown, literal and figurative; and ambiguous, literal and figurative. Unknown signs require knowledge of Hebrew and Greek in order to compare translations. Ambiguous signs require careful reading and interpretation in light of the overall context and purpose of a passage.

explains this task for the preacher who faces a range of audiences, including skeptics. Preaching does not require invention in the classical sense, only the discovery and interpretation of God's truths through scripture. Roxanne Mountford discusses Augustine's negotiation of rhetorical dimensions of religious discourse, stating that his primary goal lies in clear expression that "should always be chosen above grace" (79). As Augustine asks, "who is moved if he does not understand what is said, or whose attention is held if he is not pleased?" (4.58). In other words, clarity is the foundation of a sermon, as it is a necessary component of style throughout the classical tradition.

That said, preachers still needed to persuade listeners of divine truths, and sermons that were merely clear would not necessarily succeed in converting followers or inspiring them to divine action. Augustine authorizes preachers to use the principles of classical style, namely tropes and figures along with Cicero's three tiers of style: plain, middle, and grand. Augustine often refers to the plain style as "subdued," and is concerned mainly with imparting facts as a teacher does to students. The middle style can use some tropes and figures, but "if it does not have them at hand, it does not seek them out" (4.42). Augustine means here that an orator should provide detail, but should not go out of his or her way to amplify the emotion of a claim, since it may call attention to itself rather than to the content of the sermon. Augustine describes the grand style as appropriate "when something ought to be done, and we are speaking to those who ought to do it, although they do not wish to" (4.38). Mountford paraphrases Augustine on the three tiers: "The plain style is suited for moving the understanding, the moderate style for moving the will, the grand style for inspiring obedience" (79).

Augustine elaborates on the three tiers of style by arguing that a given speech can alternate between them; in fact, it should do so. He states, "No one should suppose that it is against the rule to mingle these three styles" and, in fact, "when a speech is surfeited with one style, it does not keep the listener's attention" (4.51). Preaching manuals from Augustine onward follow a four-part or six-part division following classical models of speeches. Here, Augustine does not provide orators with detailed rules about which level of style to use in each part, but instead instructs them to vary levels of style according to their purposes throughout a sermon. The typical progression of a sermon, like most speeches, is to begin with an introduction and then to proceed through the narration and evaluation of events, concluding on a strong note to compel listeners to action. As such, we can see speeches beginning with a subdued style and gradually rising to the grand style. Augustine illustrates this theory by describing a sermon he himself gave to citizens at Maurtiania to persuade them to give up their violent celebration of Mars, held annually in the month of October, in which men carried on a kind of gladiator-style combat. At the end of his sermon, he says, "I pleaded indeed in the grand style to the best of my power, to root out and dispel by my words so cruel and inveterate an evil from their hearts and lives" (4.53). According to Augustine, eight years passed after his sermon without the violent celebrations.

This chapter has covered views on style from the ancient through the classical eras, ending with Augustine, who was, in many ways, the last writer in antiquity to explicitly theorize rhetoric. During the periods discussed here, rhetoric emerged as a discrete discipline under Aristotle, and evolved through iterations by Roman and later Greek rhetoricians ranging from Cicero to Hermogenes. During these periods, rhetorics evolved outside of the Western patriarchal arena in ways that have important implications for researching and teaching style. Classical rhetoricians had less influence during the Middle Ages, as discussed in the next chapter, but their views on style survived through Augustine and echoed through the genres of letter writing, sermons, and poetry. The next chapter describes the historical shifts that occurred during the fifth and sixth centuries CE, spurred by Boethius's elevation of logic, leading to the diffusion of rhetoric into these other genres. The next chapter also covers historical eras such as the Renaissance and the Enlightenment—when classical rhetoric was revived and once again to influence debates about the role of style in writing and discourse.

3 Historical Review II: From the Middle Ages through Nineteenth Century US

It may be easy to see the Middle Ages as an arid period for the study of rhetoric or any of its canons. Although covering several hundred years, from the fall of the Roman Empire through the Renaissance, the medieval era receives only about one hundred pages of treatment in *The Rhetorical Tradition*—about half to one third of the length of other sections. True, there were no public forums for rhetoric as we find in classical Greece or the Roman republic, but rhetoric still occurred in less visible ways. A 2012 article in *Rhetoric Society Quarterly* by Shawn Ramsey addresses this covert rhetoric, pointing out that despite appearances,

> civic decision making operated in contexts that were obscured to most people; it was often consular in nature and conveyed in writings sent over broad distances, or it was practiced interpersonally at the courts or synods of the elite . . . although descriptions of the rules and the nature of these latter practices are somewhat scant in standard histories and chronicles. (473)[14]

Style becomes an indirect issue in the new genres that emerged during this period: sermons, poetic prose, and letters. In *The Present State of Scholarship in the History of Rhetoric*, Denise Stodola describes three

---

14. Conley describes the Middle Ages as a period in which numerous trajectories emerged from Ciceronian rhetoric that continued to receive substantial commentary until the early twelfth century, when Boethius's framework rose to prominence (74). Conley describes the "continually shifting and changing circumstances" of this long period as too complex to reduce; therefore, he limits his discussion to the theories and contexts of single authors (74).

major genres of the period: *ars praedicandi* (sermons and preaching), *ars dictaminis* (letter writing), and *ars poetria* (poetry or poetic prose).[15] Preaching was the closest heir to public oratory, and Augustine's *On Christine Doctrine* became the most influential preaching manual during this period. Seminaries used it to train priests in interpreting scripture as well as navigating the three tiers of style (plain, middle, grand) while composing sermons modeled on classical, four- and six-part orations. As stated in the section about Augustine in the last chapter, medieval sermons were very similar to ceremonial speeches; the exception is that their goal was the inspiration of divine emotions and acts of religious devotion.

Prose style became more poetic during the medieval period, since "treatises on poetry writing focused on ornaments for written texts, whether verse or prose" (Bizzel and Herzberg 503). The main forms of prose during the medieval period were sermons and letters—both made common use of tropes and figures as well as a particular type of poetic prose called the *cursus*. Medieval grammarians taught poetry and letter writing according to the classical model, explicating figurative language in classical Latin texts for students who then constructed imitations for recitation (Bizzel and Herzberg 504). Carol Dana Lanham stresses the influence of poetry on written prose style. Although classical rhetoricians such as Quintilian drew some distinctions between poetry and prose composition based on "metrical necessity," such differences started "fading rapidly, and many prose texts acquired a poetic coloring" as embellished prose became the means of lending gravity to the topic of a composition (Lanham 102). Moreover, grammar school teachers of the sixth through the twelfth centuries CE became authorities on both rhetoric and poetry, relying on texts such as Latin grammar books, rhetorics, glossaries, and *differentia* (usage books).[16] As such, they taught prose as a highly stylistic endeavor, with attention to figurative language and rhythm.

---

15. General resources include Murphy's *Medieval Eloquence,* his *Rhetoric in the Middle Ages,* and George A. Kennedy's *Classical Rhetoric and Its Christian and Secular Traditions from Ancient to Modern Times.* According to Stodola, "Murphy and Kennedy still dominate the filed in this particular category, and their texts . . . have become the standard classics" (45).

16. Some of these books were references, while others were used regularly by grammarians to guide their classes through the analysis and imitation of Latin literary works. Lanham indicates *scholia,* or marginal notes, as evi-

The main outlet of such stylistic prose was the letter, used by dukes, barons, princes, and other powerful members of a court to conduct diplomacy and maintain relations with the church. The art of letter writing emerged during the eleventh century as a way of communicating information about laws and commerce; letter writing also became a central mode of education, since training scribes to copy texts and write letters became the primary purpose of literacy instruction. As Bizzell and Herzberg note, in an illiterate culture, "The person who could compose letters . . . had access to considerable political power" (444). The first treatises on the art were composed by the monk Alberic at Monte Cassino, titled *Dictaminum Radii* (or *Flores Rhetorici*) and *Brevarium de Dictamine*. They offer models and formulas for letters based on those of Cicero, and "encouraged the use of rhetorical figures and rhythmic Latin, which would later develop into a form of Latin prose used especially in letters" (Bizzell and Herzberg 444). These original treatises provided the foundation for several more handbooks and instructional materials on letter writing, and the art eventually became a major conduit for the transmission of the rhetorical tradition and the stylistic training of students who were taught to imitate the letters of Cicero. Letter writing served as a kind of *ethopoeia*, one of the *progymnasmata* described in handbooks by Theon (First century CE), Nikolaus the Sophist (Fifth century CE), and Priscian (Sixth century CE). Carol Dana Lanham's chapter in *A Short History of Writing Instruction* describes exercises in imitation and the *progymnasmata* as taking on an epistolary form, in which scribes learned style by writing letters in the voices of historical and heroic fictional characters.

One of the most important figures during this period is Geoffrey of Vinsauf. His treatises on poetry, prose (including letter writing), and tropes and figures appeared between 1200 and 1216, and remained influential until well into the Renaissance. *Poetria Nova* covers poetry, *Documentum de Modo et Arte Dictandi et Versificandi* covers prose and letter writing, and *Summa de Coloribus Rhetoricis* offers a manual of tropes and figures drawn largely from the *Rhetorica ad Herennium*. Writers, including Chaucer and Erasmus, praised Vinsauf's theories and used them as models for their own literary and pedagogical works. Vinsauf's treatises were meant as classroom texts, and they "were widely used as school texts to supplement the lessons

---

dence of which were used for what purpose. She references secondary sources devoted to their study.

of the grammarian, not only during the period when most were composed, but later on into the early Renaissance" (Bizzell and Herzberg 505). As such, they contain lessons and opinions on types of style. Here, Vinsauf echoes the classical distinction between high, middle, and low styles, though emphasizing social class. The "ornate *difficultas* or *gravitas*" (high style) relies on figurative language and reflects serious subject matter, such as tragedy, while aiming at a noble audience. The "ornate *facilitas* or *levitas*" (low style) concerns comedic matters of interest to lower classes.

Rhetoric did go underground, so to speak, during the Middle Ages. As the next section shows, Boethius understates its importance to philosophical inquiry. His treatises influenced subsequent thinkers that wrote explicitly about philosophy rather than rhetorical discourse. That said, rhetoric did not simply become extinct, and neither did style. Rhetoric survived in the everyday genres of preaching, poetic prose, and letter writing. These emerging genres not only provided a kind of refuge for style, but also opened spaces for its unconventional use by women rhetors that had been largely denied the right to engage in public rhetoric.[17] After describing Boethius's influence on the trajectory of style during this period, the following sections describe how rhetors such as Christine de Pizan took advantage of the shift away from classical rhetorical speeches as the medium of style, making innovations in the canon that are important for its contemporary study and teaching.

---

17 As Ramsey's 2012 *RSQ* essay explores, letter writing was also a domain of considerable rhetorical power for women, who often composed letters to powerful figures, including kings, advisors, and popes, persuading them on political matters. He analyses a number of letters by Ermengarde of Narbonne, Matilda of Bolougne, and Eleanor of Aquitaine that were digitized and made publically available in Joan Ferrante's database *Epistolae: Letters of Medieval Women*. Ramsey's analysis reveals women using the genre of letter writing to exercise a kind of political persuasion that they had previously been precluded from. Their discourse is persuasive not through the use of masculine rhetorical style, but rather through the use of implication, innuendo, humility, flattery, and indirectness that was often more appropriate to the message and situation.

Boethius (Fifth and Sixth Centuries CE)

Boethius focuses almost exclusively on invention and the topics, and his work is interpreted by the histories of George Kennedy and Conley as contributing to the subordination of rhetoric to philosophy. According to Conley, central differences exist between Boethius and Augustine on the role of stylistic eloquence in discourse. For Augustine, rhetoric commanded dialectic, because the "'argument of a speech is to be found not in any underlying scheme but precisely in the development of loci, their amplification, and the graceful connections made in it among the particulars of the case" (Conley 81). This same idea of rhetoric as the graceful expression of knowledge is why Cicero positioned it as the most important discipline, stating in *De Oratore* that it should conclude a student's education.

Boethius, whose commentary on Cicero became widely influential on medieval thinkers, emphasized the reverse (dialectic over rhetoric) and made rhetoric "an appendage of dialectic" so that stylistic effectiveness no longer determined "whether a given rhetorical argument [was] a good one or not" (Conley 80). In *Classical Rhetoric and Rhetoricians*, Beth S. Bennett confirms this view, stating that, inevitably, as Boethius overtook Cicero in influence during the eleventh and twelfth centuries, "Not only did rhetoric become reduced to a subcategory of logical argumentation, but also it was removed from its classical foundations as a public practice" (91). Bennett sees Boethius as elevating logic while ignoring the practical necessity of appealing to an audience.[18]

Boethius addresses the role of rhetoric in philosophy in Book IV of his treatise, *Topica Boetii*—which was the original Medieval title for *De Topicis Differentiis*. Bizzell and Herzberg describe the treatise as a common text in medieval schools. Here, Boethius describes rhetoric in the classical, Aristotelian tradition as the persuasion of an audience in civic matters, and a counterpart to dialectic. Unlike Aristotle, Boethius discusses invention strategies without much in-depth exploration of the other four canons—memory, style, arrangement, and delivery.

---

18 In a 1998 issue of *RSQ*, Richard McNabb challenges this standard view, reading Boethius's *Consolation of Philosophy* through Ernesto Grassi to highlight the use of metaphorical language and rhetorical devices, suggesting that Boethius saw rhetoric as epistemic, and thus "a mode of investigating truth even in medieval discourse" (84).

What Boethius does *not* say about style is perhaps more important than what he *does* say. The fact that he treats rhetoric as an obligatory but peripheral matter to philosophical inquiry indicates that style—and even rhetoric itself—was the ornamentation of thought and, therefore, not a central concern.

Christine de Pizan

Studies of style in the European tradition, much like histories of rhetoric in general, have overlooked the contributions of women. They were often precluded from political arenas, denied the right to vote, or even forbidden to speak publically in Athens and Greece. In Medieval Europe, women were also often denied access to many rhetorical venues, unable to own property, unable to preach; in most cases, women were only given control domestic spheres. Domains of Medieval rhetoric primarily involved sermons, legal letters, trade, and poetry—all of which excluded women as primary agents. (A woman could help run a business, such as a shop or a tavern, but she could not own it or make business decisions about it by herself.) Consequently, the feminist historians explored in the last chapter explained the need to look in less conspicuous places for information about women's use of rhetoric. Understanding style requires that we also examine recently recovered figures, such as Christine de Pizan.

Regarded as the first professional female writer in the Western tradition, Christine published in a range of genres, including poems, histories, and philosophical books on women's political education. Her works most studied by rhetoricians include two books, defined as conduct books, titled *The Book of the City of Ladies* and *The Treasure of the City of Ladies*, in which Christine advises noble women on courtly conduct and political strategy. Bizzell and Herzberg historicize her work as evidence of the importance placed on eloquence in the late medieval period. Christine's conduct books were written for women in political situations who "had to use language effectively to be queens and courtiers, heads of religious houses, partners in family businesses and trades, and guides for the young" (de Pizan 540). Because they did not usually have direct authority over these institutions, women had to be especially persuasive and resourceful in their use of language.

In *The Treasure of the City of Ladies*, Christine does not directly engage in theories of style articulated by Aristotle, Cicero, Hermogenes, or Quintilian. We have to read between the lines, as it were, to understand her in terms of style. Above all, she advocates a peaceful or non-provocative style. As she says, the princess serves a rhetorical role by acting as a "mediator between the prince her husband . . . and her people" (Bizzel and Herzberg 546). Christine often describes women of the court as mediators and negotiators, or "the means of peace" (547), advising them to act humbly or with humility when speaking to anyone. In her view, the ideal style of speaking and writing is "gentle speech" that "softens and breaks its [bone's] hardness just as the water by its moisture and coldness extinguishes the heat of the fire" (547). We might understand this style in terms of the difference between Attic and Asiatic styles discussed by Cicero and Quintilian. A more forceful, Attic style may provoke resistance rather than persuade, whereas the "gentle speech" Christine describes can be extremely effective. Such a view of style is not far from the tendency of academics to use qualifying adverbs like "perhaps" and "likely," in addition to hedging, to soften the impact of their arguments and dissolve resistance.

Christine also advocates silence as a stylistic resource. Although Glenn does not address Christine directly in her book *Unspoken*, she does situate her earlier historical work on such figures as part of the motivation to treat silence as a rhetorical move. As such, Christine recognizes that women in medieval courts have a limited number of options when they are the subject of gossip or slander. While it may seem trivial today, a woman relied almost completely on her own honor; being seen as promiscuous or immature could have devastating consequences, especially for women in positions of some power, as the wife of a baron, count, prince, or a member of the court.[19] Consistent with the need to display humility, wisdom, and charity at all times, Christine carefully explains how nothing can be done in response to slander. By countering slander, or spreading it herself, a lady only becomes implicated in her own dishonor. Likewise, a woman who witnesses improprieties by members of any court should "pretend that you did not see the least thing and that you notice nothing, since it is not within

---

19. Other secondary work on Christine de Pizan includes Scott D. Tryoyan's *Medieval Rhetoric: A Casebook*, Julia Simms Holderness's "Compilatio, Commentary, and Conversation in Christine de Pizan" (*Medieval Studies* 20 (2003): 47–55.) A wealth of resources on medieval women's rhetoric is compiled in Denise Stodola's contribution to *The Present State of Scholarship in the History of Rhetoric*.

your ability to remedy it" (550). In both instances, Christine makes silence a position of agency; indeed, silence is more strategic than any use of words.

From our reading of Christine, we see the seed of an alternative approach to style that is not explored by male rhetoricians of the period. Aristotle, Cicero, and Quintilian's version of rhetoric deals mainly with addressing large, public audiences. Although it is unfortunate that, historically, women were denied access to these outlets, women rhetors nonetheless provide valuable accounts of persuasion that are not articulated in conventional treatises. From these alternative rhetorics, we can build a more complete set of stylistic resources, perhaps adding to the limited idea of three styles the notion of a "benevolent style" that are characterized by a different set of figures, tropes, and schemes that are meant to defuse, rather than to inform, delight, or persuade. Imagine a silent style employing a range of tactics meant to circumvent or subvert power relations in certain rhetorical situations—such a framework for non-masculine styles arises at least partly from the study of Christine de Pizan.

Renaissance Style

Classical rhetoric had faded during the middle and medieval eras, partly due to the unavailability of manuscripts and the fragmentation of public outlets for oratory. As the last sections explained, the primary modes of discourse were letter writing, preaching, and poetry—not the deliberative and epideictic forms of rhetoric for which classical treatises were written. Classical rhetoric returned to prominence during the Renaissance, as intellectuals re-discovered their value for more contemporary forms of discourse. Trevor McNeely argues that rhetoric "is *the* integrating principle behind the Renaissance revolution in both Italy and England" (9). The study of rhetoric deeply influenced poets ranging from Shakespeare to Milton, letter writing, and on public discourse. Style was once again seen as an essential component of virtuous discourse. According to Sir Philip Sydney's 1583 treatise *In Defense of Poesy*, poets were more moral than philosophers, and stood a greater chance of moving audiences to virtue.

The revival of style began with George of Trebizond's *Rhetoricorum Libri Quinque* and Aldo Manuzio's translations of Aristotle's *Rhetoric* and Hermogenes's works, all of which re-introduce classical Greek rhetoric to Western Europe. (As Shane Borrowman points out, such works survived largely thanks to Arabic and Byzantine philosophers.) During the early sixteenth century, scholars also began traveling beyond Christendom and bringing back large numbers of treatises on style from the classical era; due to the advent of printing technologies, such treatises quickly spread throughout European centers of education (Conley 120). During this period, Ciceronian rhetoric reemerged, and eloquence became central to discourse and deliberation.

According to Annabel Patterson, in *Hermogenes and the Renaissance*, the sheer volume of editions, translations, and commentaries on Hermogenes's work shows that his approach to style was favored over those of Cicero and Quintilian (17). According to Patterson, the reason for Hermogenes's influence lay in the preference of seven types of style to the three-part division of classical rhetoricians into high, middle, and low. As a wealth of new literary genres emerged during the sixteenth century, the classical division offered little guidance about how to adapt styles to different contexts beyond forensic, deliberative, and epideictic oratory or epic, tragic, and comedic verse. The classical division also provided a limited account of how to blend styles and, at times, even discouraged rhetors from doing so (29). Hermogenes's seven ideas of style enabled a system where "Any genre may admit a mixture of styles, and the greater the genre, the more styles it will admit; while the rigid matching of style to genre . . . is no longer desirable or possible" (34).

Peter Mack's *A History of Renaissance Rhetoric 1380–1620* highlights the still-potent influence of Cicero and Quintilian on Renaissance treatises covering tropes and figures, letter writing, and preaching. Mack describes nine separate manuals of tropes and figures used by grammar school teachers, all of them based on the classical treatises by Cicero, Quintilian, and the *Rhetorica ad Herennium*. These manuals differed mainly in their divisions and classifications of stylistic devices,[20] but the substance of their definitions and illustra-

---

20. For a brief example, Antonio Mancinelli's 1489 manual *Carmen de Figuris*, written in the form of a poem to aid students' memorization, lists ninety-eight different figures divided into faults (vices), schemes, and tropes. Johannes Despauterius's 1512 manual *De Figuris*, also in the form of a poem, omits figures of thought and lists seventy-seven total stylistic devices divided into fourteen figures of expression, eighteen schemes, twenty-seven tropes, and eighteen other miscellaneous figures.

tions through classical literature is relatively consistent. Omer Talon's 1548 *Rhetorica* may be the most significant of the manuals described by Mack, given Talon's simplified catalog of figures and its popularity—going through at least a hundred editions by 1620 (Mack 221). Talon condenses a large list of tropes to the four most prominent and commonly used—metonymy, irony, metaphor, and synecdoche (Mack 221). Talon's reasoning lay in simplification to ease the burden of so many devices on teachers and students and, according to Mack, "Later writers . . . were happy to focus their attention on these four essential tropes" (221). Today, many writing teachers are more likely to be familiar with these four.

The art of letter writing, having emerged during the middle ages, continued to thrive as a domain of rhetoric during the Renaissance, a period that saw "about 900 editions of individual works" devoted exclusively or in part to letter writing—some works went through a hundred editions (Mack 228). During this period, letter writing transitioned from a rigidly defined genre with a set form to a more dynamic and fluid art, due mainly to the revival of classical rhetoric, the discovery of Cicero's letters, and their influence on Erasmus, who was a key figure in the evolution of the genre, Letter writing manuals constituted a major form of communication between nobles, clergy, and the commercial classes during the fifteenth and sixteenth centuries. Moreover, instruction in grammar and letter writing constituted the primary modes of education.

Style itself was a point of emphasis in letter writing manuals. According to Mack, "Most manuals include some advice on appropriate style or useful formula phrases" (228). The manuals typically contain separate chapters or sections on sentence composition and variety, grammar, prose rhythm, and gatherings of proverbs and eloquent phrases useful for different occasions (Mack 231). One of the earliest and most influential of these manuals was Niccolo Perotti's 1468 *Rudimenta Grammatices*, a comprehensive grammar that included a long treatise on letters that advised the low or plain style (in most cases), but also recommended variation according to the addressee. These manuals evolved from their medieval counterparts to list as many as twenty different types of letters, as in the case of Francesco Negro's 1487 manual, *Modus Epistolandi*, that provides instructions and examples of forms such as commendation letters, requests, love letters, lamentations, and consolations. Mack especially attributes Erasmus's 1521

Manual De Conscribendis Epistolis with an orientation toward "thinking about the addressee, and the writer's relationship to the addressee, as . . . the chief factors in determining the approach and style to be adopted in a letter" (246). Erasmus's organic, classical approach to letter writing would become the most influential.

A number of preaching manuals appeared during the Renaissance, almost all of them importing classical approaches to style wholesale. Peter Mack devotes a brief chapter to them. Erasmus's 1535 manual *Ecclesiastes* was a more popular manual—printed ten times—that defined figures and tropes as useful for interpreting scripture as well as inciting divine emotions—love of God, hatred of sin, fear of divine justice. St. Augustine's *De Doctrina Christina* remained influential as a preaching manual. Most manuals either list tropes and figures copied directly from treatises like the *Rhetorica ad Herennium*, or insist on plain and modest language as the most appropriate for sermons. As Mack concludes, the key difference between rhetorical treatises and preaching manuals is that the latter were designed specifically for ordained priests who had already received classical training in grammar school and university.

Renaissance Curriculum

Writing did not become a major focus in Renaissance grammar schools until the 1570s, when made possible by the spread of printing technology and the production of paper. William Harrison Woodward describes the rhetorical curriculum at several European schools, most based on the classical tradition in which students copied, imitated, and translated works from Latin and Greek. Renaissance humanist schools closely followed the classical curriculum, including instruction in criticism of classical poets and orators, declamations on historical and contemporary topics, and letter writing. Students submitted writings to their instructor, and received written feedback for rewriting. These schools also stressed mastery in classical languages as a foundation for cultivating vernacular style in European languages. Woodward states,

> There can be no doubt that the great majority of humanist teachers in France or England, hardly less than in Italy (excepting the purists, like Erasmus), were concerned with rhetoric not as training in Latin only, but as an essential instrument

for the acquisition of a sound and cultivated vernacular style. (75)

The Renaissance curriculum saw "Roman oratory as the needful preparation for civic eloquence" (Woodward 75), given their primary purpose in training future public servants and leaders in the spheres of religion, politics, and commerce.

For Woodward, medieval and Renaissance teachers saw style as "a province of grammar" (200), rather than the reverse. Grammar school teachers taught style for everyday purposes, and rhetoric teachers introduced pupils to figures of thought and speech, used for special rhetorical occasions. The aim of education was to give students the ability to adapt style for purpose, occasion, and audience. The curriculum saw value in grammar, but not for its own sake. Woodward observes that grammatical and rhetorical instruction during the Renaissance "takes from grammar the laws of syntax, and adds to them the principles of logical and tasteful exposition, so producing prose writing both accurate and persuasive" (173–174). Pupils only learned the principles of grammar in so far as they applied to a specific piece of writing they were analyzing or imitating.

Other works consider the Renaissance curriculum with attention to instruction in imitation, translation, and analysis as they pertained to eloquence. These include Don Paul Abbot's chapter in *A Short History of Writing Instruction*, Donald Lemen Clark's *Milton at St. Paul's School*, Paul Grendler's *Schooling in Renaissance Italy*, and the edited collection by Winifred Bryan Horner and Michael Leff, titled *Rhetoric and Pedagogy: Its History, Philosophy, and Practice*. These works describe a curriculum in which students learned Latin grammar and underwent a rigorous, ten-hour school day consisting of exercises in letter writing, verse composition, themes, and oral declamations. Roger Ascham's 1570 treatise *The Scholemaster* highly recommends exercises in imitation and translation between Latin and English, methods seen as vital to any Renaissance curriculum in the development of eloquence. The conventional curriculum excluded women, but special historical consideration of women's rhetorical education includes Barbara Whitehead's *Women's Education in Early Modern Europe*. This collection includes essays that recover ways in which young women learned eloquence, voice, and agency despite being excluded from grammar schools and colleges. Admittedly, women's education in the Renaissance is a frontier for future study.

Erasmus

The curriculum of English grammar schools in the sixteenth and seventeenth centuries rested largely on a proposal by Erasmus in *De Ratione Studii*, in which he advances a classical education based on grammar, literary criticism, and imitation of great works. In the Ciceronian tradition, Erasmus equates eloquence with civic virtue. His model became the standard for St. Paul's school (where Milton attended) and most others. Erasmus produced three major works of relevance to rhetoricians and grammarians, all of them directly relevant to stylistic studies: *On Letter-Writing*, *On the Best Kind of Style*, and *De Copia*.

Although Erasmus was deeply influenced by Cicero and Quintilian, he criticized Renaissance humanists for failing to fully appreciate the point of decorum (Conley 121), and thus only parrot the views of Cicero and Quintilian on style, rather than apply them to contemporary discourse practices. *De Copia* was "designed to inculcate linguistic sensitivity and fluency" (Conley 120) that would develop what Quintilian referred to as *facilitas*, but adapted for a new age. Erasmus made a pointed argument against misappropriation of Cicero in his 1527 treatise *On the best Kind of Style*, elevating decorum over simplistic imitation. According to Peter Mack, the treatise maintained that the "key to style is always appropriateness to the situation," and that "[i]mitation must be critical, not slavish" (97). Students in Erasmus's curriculum were encouraged to read widely and synthesize a range of classical and contemporary styles, as Cicero himself advised.

First printed in 1519, *De Copia* became widely used in grammar schools throughout Europe. Erasmus focuses on style in Book I, with Book II devoted largely to matters of invention and dialectic. For Erasmus, style derived mainly from abundance of phrase, or copiousness, that employed a large vocabulary as much or more than tropes, figures, and prose rhythm. For Don Paul Abbott in *A Short History of Writing Instruction*, "*Copia* . . . is the very foundation of style" (163). An often-paraphrased example is Erasmus's variation on the simple phrase "Your letter pleased me greatly":

> Your letter mightily pleased me.
> To a wonderful degree did your letter please me.
> I was exceedingly pleased by your letter.
> The greatest joy was brought to me by your letter.
> Your epistle afforded me no small delight.

The first fourteen of his methods for varying the style of sentences describe alterations of diction and substituting one phrase with another to achieve a different tone, one appropriate to different circumstances (Mack 83). Book I also devotes some attention to the tropes and figures, drawing largely on Quintilian. Erasmus outlines six methods of variation based on Quintilian's treatment of metaphor, amplification, and figures of expression that include asyntedon, polysyntedon, epanalepsis, interrogation, dubitation, exclamation, occupation, and subiectio (Mack 84).

Erasmus's *De Copia* may have been so popular in grammar schools because it stressed the practical aspects of style and eloquence, introducing figures and exercises without exhaustive meditations on history and theory. His importance to contemporary writing teachers lies in his definition of style via copia, stressing the knowledge not only of tropes and figures, but also of words themselves. Although classical treatises acknowledged diction as one component of style, Erasmus was the first to devote so much detail to its impact on prose. Toward this end, Erasmus offered a range of advice to students, recommending extensive practice in variation of expression, transcription of poetry to prose, development of lists of metaphors for aid in composition, and imitation exercises rooted in the *progymnasmata*. Book I also contains lists of synonymous expressions and advice for varying sentences through different grammatical constructions.

The Ramist Watershed

The revival of classical rhetoric during the Renaissance ultimately encountered resistance from philosophers who saw invention and dialectic as their domain. Most histories of rhetoric concur on the marginalization of rhetoric, as a consequence of Peter Ramus's 1547 treatise *Brutus's Problems*, and his 1549 follow-up, *Arguments in Rhetoric Against Quintilian* (see Murphy's translations.) In these works, Ramus rejects Ciceronian civic rhetoric as well as Quintilian's emphatic stance on the moral component of discourse. Ramus also argues that any classical treatise, including Aristotle's, only distracts from the innate capabilities of reasoning in all humans, who should develop their intellects through other pursuits. Cicero may be a model of style, when not too Asiatic, but the parts of the *Orator* and the *Orator's Education* that treat invention and arrangement are redundant to philosophical dialectic.

Ramus endeavors to correct Quintilian's classification of tropes and figures, as well as the division of style into four virtues. *Latinitas* (purity of language) belongs to grammar, not to rhetoric. Likewise, *decorum* (appropriateness) is better left to dialectic because it involves reasoning rather than the application of ornament to ready-made ideas. (Anticipation of audience does not appear as a major concern here.) Classifications in Ramus's rhetorical system hinge on length rather than on rhetorical purpose or effect, as in Cicero and Quintilian; therefore, Rasmus defines tropes as devices consisting of single words and figures as devices of multiple words. Ramus also pairs down the number of tropes to four—metonymy, irony, metaphor, and synecdoche. By contrast, Quintilian defined tropes and figures somewhat synonymously, and he used them interchangeably to describe figurative language in single words as well as phrases, figures of thought and expression, and in devices such as *onomatopoeia, catachresis, epitheton,* and *allegory.*

Ramus's supposed correction of Quintilian serves his purpose to further limit the capabilities of rhetoric, rather than lend any actual clarity to theories of style. If rhetorical style no longer helps determine correctness, appropriateness, or any but four types of tropes, then it indeed becomes a matter of ornament. Doing so, the Ramist split pours a foundation for Enlightenment thought and scientific writing during the seventeenth and eighteenth centuries that was contested by few, with the important exception of Giambattista Vico in the Italian Humanist tradition. Vico's treatise in 1725, titled *The New Science*, proposed four domains of knowledge production, with poetic knowledge as the first, and metaphor as a means of generating ideas through understanding and conveying them through one another. Vico's philosophical-rhetorical system elevates figurative language—a key element of style—from a minor role in ornamenting thought to a central stage of invention. From this position, Vico asserts the democratizing effect of eloquence, defined as "wisdom, ornately and copiously delivered in words appropriate to the common opinion of mankind" (qtd. in Bizzell and Herzberg 877). Because humans are rooted in language, learning by it and persuaded by it, skilled use of language (style) is possible for anyone to learn; style can persuade anyone, regardless of his or her status or power.

Despite such alternate epistemologies, the Ramist tradition remained dominant in models of scientific prose, as advanced by Bacon, Locke, and prominent members of the Royal Society during the seventeenth century. As the next section shows, although Enlightenment rhetorics reconstructed Ciceronian ideals, the prominence of scientific writing marginalized it altogether in favor of a plain, non-rhetorical style meant as a vehicle to transmit scientific discoveries.

Style in the Enlightenment and the Standardization of English

The Ramist relegation of rhetoric to style and delivery ultimately "became moot" during the seventeenth century, as science overshadowed logic in the production of knowledge (Bizzel and Herzberg 792). In other words, scientific methods and empiricism pushed logic and reasoning back into rhetoric, and repositioned both philosophy and rhetoric as more appropriate to ethical, social, and political issues, where decisions relied not only on knowledge, but also persuasion. As a result, "The Ciceronian conception of rhetoric, which included all five classical canons . . . became once again the foundation of rhetorical study and remained so through the seventeenth and well into the eighteenth century" (Bizzell and Herzberg 792). Of course, the revitalization of Ciceronian rhetoric did not necessarily mean the return of rhetoric itself to public status. The return was accompanied by debates about the appropriateness of Ciceronian style for different types of discourse. Francis Bacon saw a plainer style more suited to most types of discourse. Bizzell and Herzberg describe this plainer, Senecan style:

> The so-called Senecan style had arisen as an alternative to the Ciceronian and became popular during the seventeenth century. But the Senecan style is plain because it avoids stylistic display for its own sake, not because it rejects all verbal ornament and ingenuity. It favors long sentences, less symmetrical than the Ciceronian periods but still carefully structured; it resists Latin borrowings but does not avoid them altogether; and it certainly employs tropes, although it leans toward the less flamboyant of them. Bacon had reservations about this style, too, warning that it often strained after wit and weight that was not earned by the thought expressed. (794)

Debates about style recall earlier disagreements during Cicero's own time, between the proponents of Attic (plain), Asiatic (florid), and Rhodian (middle) styles. The evolution of the sciences also led to a strong desire for transparent language, a main goal of the British Royal Society, founded in 1660. Thomas Sprat, a prominent member of the society, associated stylistic language with confusion and obfuscation. In *The History of the Royal-Society of London* (1667), Sprat declares the society's intention to "reject all the amplifications, digressions, and swellings of style: to return back to the primitive purity, and shortness, when men deliver'd so many things, almost in an equal number of words" (113).

The emerging scientists were unhappy with language as a mediator between the mind and reality, but seeing no alternative, they sought to strip language down so that it interfered as little as possible. In his *Essay Concerning Human Understanding*, John Locke directly acknowledges the problem of language, that "sounds have no natural connection with our ideas, but have all their signification from the arbitrary imposition of men" (qtd. in Bizzell and Herzberg 817). This fundamental reality of language leads Locke and other advocates of scientific prose not in the direction of the sophists, who embraced contingencies between words and meanings, but toward a more Aristotelian ideal. Ultimately, Locke condemns "all the artificial and figurative application of words eloquence hath invented" because they "are for nothing else but to insinuate wrong ideas, move the passions, and thereby mislead the judgment; and so indeed are perfect cheats" (qtd. in Bizzell and Herzberg 827). Scientific writing needed to be as devoid of artifice as possible, while endeavoring to cement the relationship between words and ideas.

Following Locke, Francis Bacon hoped to reform English based on his understanding of Chinese as "Characters Real, which express neither letters nor words . . . but things or notions; in insomuch as countries and provinces, which understand not one another's language, can nevertheless read one another's writing" (742). One of the most extreme positions during this era appears in Bishop Wilkins's 1668 *Essay Towards a Real Character and a Philosophic Language*. Here, Wilkins outlines a symbolic language that directly represents reality completely and without metaphor, a project ultimately abandoned and later satirized in Jonathon Swift's *Gulliver's Travels*.

In the 1776 multi-volume treatise, *The Philosophy of Rhetoric*, George Campbell parts ways with classical rhetoric on many issues; he also formulates a three-part theory of usage that rejects the emerging prescriptivism and correctness.[21] The second volume, "The Foundations and Essential Properties of Elocution," turns to the emergent science of linguistics and descriptive grammar for this theory. He lays out three components of usage: reputability, nationality, and presentness. In other words, writers find a guide to crafting their style in what esteemed speakers and writers concur is appropriate (i.e., the speaking habits of the majority population of the nation) and what habits are actually present at a given time and place. Such a method as Campbell's has no place for strict rules:

> It is not the business of grammar, as some critics seem preposterously to imagine, to give law to the fashions which regulate our speech. On the contrary, from its conformity to these, and from that alone, it derives all its authority and value. For, what is the grammar of any language? It is no other than a collection of general observations methodically digested, and comprising all the modes previously and independently established, by which the significations, derivations, and combinations of words in that language are ascertained. (139–40)

Throughout Book II, Campbell urges against steadfast rules and judgments regarding all aspects of style, including issues of grammar, usage, and diction. Regarding figurative language, Campbell even anticipates twentieth century discussions of dead metaphors, advancing a line of thought that concludes in Book III, as he declares that

> critics ought to show more reserve and modesty . . . in pronouncing either on the fitness or on the beauty of such as occur in ancient authors . . . [since] many words which appear as tropical to a learner of a distance age . . . may, through the imperceptible influence of use, have totally lost that appear-

---

21. Campbell's theories on language fit into a larger reworking of rhetoric. Moving away from the five canons altogether, Campbell proposes a rhetorical method in two phases. In the first phase, a speaker should "excite some desire or passion in the hearers" and, in the second, "satisfy their judgment that there is a connexion between the action to which he would persuade them" and conclude with "the gratification of [that] desire" (927).

ance to the natives [everyday speakers], who consider them purely as proper terms. (299)

Hugh Blair valued style, but did not adopt a classical approach—even if his theories and pedagogies aim toward the same goal as Cicero and Quintilian—the moral rhetor. Although Bizzell and Herzberg refer to Blair as "the Quintilian of his time" (947), in terms of his stature and ethical approach to rhetoric, they acknowledge that Blair himself found *The Orator's Education* overly systematic and "too concerned with . . . topics, arrangement, and figures" (Bizzell and Herzberg 948). For Blair, moral excellence was a prerequisite for eloquence, and these were achieved through education and exposure to "polite literature" (948). The insistence on polite literature and taste received criticism from Gregory Clark and Michael Halloran, in their essay in *Oratorical Culture in Nineteenth-Century America*, for elevating poetry above the three domains of classical rhetoric: forensic, deliberative, and epideictic. Bizzell and Herzberg add to this perspective that Blair "may support excessively conservative aesthetic, moral, and political values" (948).[22] Blair gave numerous lectures on figures of speech and kinds of style, as well as a handful on the history of eloquence. These are all collected in *The Lectures on Rhetoric and Belles Lettres*, appearing in 1783, the year Blair retired from teaching at the University of Edinburgh.

Linda Ferreira-Buckley and S. Michael Halloran's introduction to the most recent edition of Blair's lectures describes the immense popularity and influence on higher education in Europe and the US of these lectures. As they state, the lectures were "a powerful vehicle for introducing many eighteenth-and-nineteenth-century teachers, students, readers, and textbook writers to classical rhetoric" (xvi). The lectures influenced almost every textbook on rhetoric and writing published in the English-speaking world for the next century, including the first and second generation of college composition textbooks in the 1810s, and then again in the 1860s. The editors cite Winifred Bryan Horner's assessment of Blair's lectures as the "missing link" between classical rhetoric and "contemporary language studies," including "North American composition" (qtd. in Buckley and Halloran

---

22. H. Lewis Ulman elaborates on this in his 1994 book *Things, Thoughts, Words, and Actions: The Problems of Language in Late Eighteenth-Century British Rhetorical Theory*.

xix). In essence, Blair applies precepts from the classical tradition to contemporary forms of English prose, such as letters and essays.

Blair may dismiss the classical tradition for its tendency to catalogue every single figure of thought and expression, but he borrows heavily from Cicero and Quintilian in his lectures. Teachers who have not read Blair will still recognize many of his prescriptions for style. His first lecture on style explains the importance of clarity, as it entails proper diction and usage, as well as purity. Much like Quintilian, Blair warns against borrowing words from other languages as well as coining new ones, maintaining that "such innovations are more hazardous, and have a worse effect" than their use in poetry, where he still advises sparing use (101). His lectures about sentence structure in style briefly touch on periodic and cut-off sentences, advising writers to alternate them for effect. The remaining chapters march through a list of rules about the appropriate use of pronouns, sentence cohesion and unity, superfluous and redundant language, parallel structure, and, of course, ending sentences with adverbs and prepositions. Blair's subsequent lectures on style closely follow Quintilian in their definitions and illustrations of metaphor, and about figures such as hyperbole, personification, and antithesis. He then uses these as tools to analyze the styles of contemporary British authors that largely appeared in *The Spectator*, and classifies authors according to styles he identifies as simple, timid, vehement, verbose, concise, plain, flowery, and affected. If readers cannot already guess based on Blair's principles described above, his preferences veer toward plain, elegant, and simple styles.[23]

Richard Whatley does not make an especially unique contribution to style, though he is an important historical figure who discusses style. Bizzell and Herzberg describe Part III of his 1828 book, *Elements of Rhetoric* as "providing standard textbook advice on perspicuity and

---

23. The editors of Blair's lecturers make a curious argument about Blair's position on pedagogical imitation, citing a nineteenth lecture in which he promotes the classical practice of imitation, and warns writers against the "servile imitation" of a single author (xliv-xlv). The editors distinguish Blair from Quintilian on the practice of imitation by citing a single line in *The Orator's Education*, in which Quintilian remarks that he would be happy if he could imitate Cicero (10.2.25). Their reading of this passage goes against most scholarship on imitation that reads Quintilian as advising writers away from servile imitation, just as Blair does. The editors even concede this reading and, perhaps in their zeal for Blair, insist on what I have to see as a willful misinterpretation.

correctness" (1002). Whatley's approach to style rejects Blair's model of rhetoric and education based on literary style and taste, but follows Campbell in developing moral reasoning and evidence as a major component of rhetoric, meanwhile splitting from Campbell by resuscitating Aristotelian rhetoric (as a counterpart to logic and dialectic).

For Whately, scientific inquiry discovered truth, and rhetoric sought the available means of persuasion while also deriving a different, but not antithetical, kind of truth from testimony (i.e., personal and religious experience). Thus, *Elements of Rhetoric* addresses working class students and those preparing for divinity school, situating religious texts as their own sources of truth that have little or no need for invention derived from the scientific inquiry that was becoming more integrated into school and college curricula in Europe, and eventually the US, during the nineteenth century.

Competing views on language as meaning itself or as merely a conveyer of meaning should be familiar by now, and this period represents a turn toward language as the transmission of ideas. Likewise, style became a matter of conformity for scientists as well as humanists such as Blair. These developments, especially Blair's position on rhetoric and style, would shape the emergence of college composition in the US. This section's discussion of Blair has already noted his influence on American college composition, and the next section explains exactly what happened to style and rhetoric in the late nineteenth and early twentieth centuries.

Gutting the Classical Canon: Harvard and the New Curriculum, 1875–1940

The current status of style in public discourse, as well as in rhetoric and composition, has roots in the late nineteenth and early twentieth centuries. The theories and pedagogies developed during these decades had a formative effect on writing instruction for the next one hundred years, especially on the relationship of style to invention and grammar. Developments at elite universities such as Harvard did more than simply reduce rhetoric to a matter of ornamentation, as Ramus had done. Rhetorical education itself was replaced with a new emphasis on writing clear, grammatical prose. Although mechanical correctness had always been a part of the canon of style, it became the only component of style (and rhetoric) to survive this gutting of the classical curriculum. Alongside this shift to grammar, equally prescriptive instructional models emerged during this period on appropriate paragraph construction.

This period witnessed a dramatic shift away from classical rhetoric and style, and toward an emphasis on grammar and correctness, the influences of which are still tangible. These historical views are described in Albert Kitzhaber's *Rhetoric in American Colleges, 1850–1900*, as well as work by James Berlin, Sharon Crowley, and Robert Connors. Primary documents from this period are collected in John Brereton's *The Origins of Composition Studies in the American College, 1875–1925*. The four key rhetoricians in the US during the late nineteenth century were John Genung, Adams Sherman Hill, Fred Newton Scott, and Barrett Wendell. Kitzhaber refers to these as the "Big Four." Their views on theory and pedagogy were still partly classical: Connors points out that Genung "refused" to discuss punctuation in his rhetoric handbooks (17). Ultimately, all of them came to argue for the importance of instruction in clear, correct English over a classical curriculum based on oral declamations and education in Greek and Latin. One of the Big Four, Adams Sherman Hill, made reforms at Harvard that paved the way for the later, hyper-mechanization of writing during the 1920s and 1930s.

Historical work by Robert J. Connors describes this period as a "transition from emphasis on style and communicative effectiveness to primary emphasis on rule-governed mechanical correctness" ("Rhetoric of Mechanical Correctness" 13). While the study and teaching of style before the twentieth century usually included grammar and correctness, it had almost never been *only* concerned with these two aspects. Under Hill, Harvard manufactured a "literacy crisis" based on the mechanical mistakes in admission essays, and then created a full-year writing course that became a standard first-year requirement in 1885. As David Fleming notes in his 2011 book, *From Form to Meaning*, almost every major university had implemented a version of the required course by the turn of the twentieth century. Even institutions in the Midwest, such as the University of Wisconsin, created a course devoted to instruction in written English (Fleming 31). This type of college writing course remains so dominant, stylisticians assert, that it preempts most attempts to discuss style as anything other than mechanical correctness.

Teaching materials reflect this larger preoccupation with correctness that came to comprise all that college writing courses did. By 1910, students wrote themes, and the themes were almost exclusively corrected for grammar, clarity, spelling, and punctuation. In the essay "Handbooks: History of a Genre," Connors traces the development of such materials as college composition handbooks—now a staple of contemporary writing classes—from the 1870s through the 1970s, and identifies the emergence of pedagogies that combine style and grammar in the early years of the twentieth century. According to Connors, precursors existed to the modern composition handbook, but handbooks did not begin appearing in a recognizable form, with their emphasis on rules and rote exercises, until Edwin C. Woolley's 1907 *Handbook of Composition: A Compendium of Rules*, a text that listed more than three hundred precepts on grammar and style. In 1918, a revised edition appeared with simplified rules (one hundred, not three hundred) and more exercises.

Wooley's book had a profound influence on writing instruction; not only was the book popular, but Wooley directed the first-year English course at the University of Wisconsin from 1909 to 1916 (Fleming 36), where he shaped the curriculum around weekly, 500-word themes, based largely on personal experiences, that underwent scrutiny for grammatical correctness and logical paragraph organization. Woolley's handbook gave rise to competitors, the most significant being Garland Greever and Easley S. Jones's 1918 *The Century Handbook of Writing*. Even after Wooley stepped down in 1916, the theme model "would appear at intervals over the next fifty years in UW's Freshman English" (Fleming 36). Emphasis on the most prescriptive elements of style only strengthened over subsequent decades.

During the 1920s and 1930s, handbooks included only an impoverished version of rhetoric to accompany lists of mechanical rules and writing exercises. This trend culminated in John C. Hodge's 1941 *Harbrace Handbook of English*, the handbook that served as "the model for all handbooks after it" (Connors 21). As Connors describes this period, "It was the point at which books that had essentially been tools for home reference became complete classroom texts, filled with lessons and exercises . . . a tradition that still continues today" (20). The first edition of the *Harbrace Handbook* contained thirty-four chapters, two thirds of which are devoted to mechanical issues such as sentence fragments, comma splices, proper use of semicolons, and proper use of apostrophes. Each chapter contained a series of exercises asking students to identify and correct errors. Consider the second chapter, on sentence fragments:

> Identify each fragment as a phrase, a subordinate clause, or a group of phrases and subordinate clauses. Correct the error (1) by including the fragment with the main clause, (2) by making the fragment into a sentence, or (3) by providing a main clause for the group of phrases and subordinate clauses. Use your judgment to determine the most suitable method of correction. Identify the two sentences that are complete and need no revision.
>
> 1. A fitting epitaph for John Brown, one of the most radical abolitionists before the Civil War, who was so obsessed by his one idea that he died fighting valiantly for it.
> 2. The success of an individual depends to a great extent upon mental capacity. The key to success being the brain.
> 3. Advertising serves two purposes. A means of displaying merchandise and an opportunity to add to the appearance of the building. (28–29)

This single exercise gives students thirty such fragments to correct. Other exercises in the chapter underscore the importance of verbs in complete sentences, directing students to fill in blanks in sentences with the appropriate verbs, identify and underline verbs in sentences, and do the same with nouns. These basic types of exercises span the entire book, underscoring Connors's point regarding what early composition textbooks taught as writing. More than fifty years later, it is not hard to find writing textbooks and manuals like the early *Harbrace Handbook* that use similar exercises, with a similar approach to writing as correctness.

Such historical considerations show at least one of the origin points of contemporary pedagogies that set up a somewhat exclusionary attitude toward style, dismissing or ignoring alternatives to the correctness model. Historical work may help teachers today understand that most of what is taught as style is rooted in early twentieth-century notions of what was important about writing instruction—not voice per se, but correctness and propriety. Therefore, contemporary college writing instructors may realize that they do not have to perpetuate ideas about style and writing now a hundred years old, nor must they rely on textbooks that look new on the outside and yet subscribe to antiquated views, rather than keep up with advances in research on writing.

Connors's 1986 essay, "The Rhetoric of Mechanical Correctness" elaborates on how handbooks and textbooks led to the skill-and-drill culture of freshmen English in the 1930s, what James Berlin describes in *Rhetoric and Reality* as current-traditional. Speaking to the larger contexts and material conditions of the freshmen composition course, Connors portrays the changes occurring in the late nineteenth century as ones that "transmogrified the noble discipline of Aristotle, Cicero, Campbell, into a stultifying error hunt" (72). As the last two chapters have shown, classical rhetoricians did discuss correctness and clarity as requisites for style; however, style was not defined solely by these concerns, as it would be at the turn of the twentieth century in the US. As Connors states,

> From the classical period up through 1860 or so, the teaching of rhetoric concentrated on theoretical concerns and contained no mechanical material at all. Usage and style were, of course, major areas of rhetorical consideration, but the traditional prescriptive advice in these areas assumed a student able to handle grammatical construction and to produce an acceptable manuscript with complete facility. . . . Such elementary skills as handwriting, punctuation, capitalization, and spelling might be critiqued by the professor of rhetoric, but officially they had no place in rhetoric throughout most of history. (79)

According to Connors, several things changed, resulting in the devaluing of the classical curriculum and the rise of correctness. One of the most important changes occurred on a cultural level: through the establishment of an American class system in the mid-1800s that led to renewed interest in grammar and pronunciation, one that contradicted earlier egalitarianism.

This preoccupation with correctness accompanied a larger "linguistic insecurity" (Connors 72) within US intellectual culture, an insight by Connors that is explored further by Bruce Horner, John Trimbur, and Paul Matsuda. This insecurity merged with movements in higher education to reform college writing instruction, an effort spear-headed by Adams Sherman Hill in the wake of unsettling student performances on Harvard's entrance exams. In the 1870s, Hill redesigned the freshmen composition course to focus on writing themes, rather on than studying rhetoric and reciting classical texts. Composition teachers were subsequently inundated with papers to grade, so they turned even further away from the fusion of style and invention in rhetoric, and graded for correctness. Connors explains the methods and practices of writing instructors that grew out of these material conditions, such as the "Correction Card" or "Theme Card," and the notation systems that relied on symbols and abbreviations—all meant to compensate for teachers' workloads.

Brereton's history in *The Origins of Composition in The American College* places the first modern composition course at Harvard, as Connors does, arising from students' poor performance on the university's entrance examination. Brereton points out that the exam itself "did not reveal some long hidden weakness so much as supply Harvard with new, objective evidence to use in the effort to improve the secondary schools" that had been established largely to supply elite colleges with students, helping them meet their enrollment quotas (27). Among the historic documents gathered, Brereton includes an address by Hill to secondary teachers, urging instruction in mechanical correctness, and citing it as a primary reason for entrance exam failures.

The "New Curriculum" by Hill became dominant, as other colleges adopted Harvard's composition model. However, the curriculum did not become the model at *all* schools. If style came to represent complete adherence to rules under Hill at Harvard, other perspectives emerged that defined style beyond the correct sentence, as Fred Newton Scott did in emphasizing paragraphs as units of composition in the 1893 book, *Paragraph Writing*, used at the University of Michigan. Even more radical, John Genung at Amherst College conceived of style as the *liberation* from conventions that constrained the discoveries of truth and self. Brereton describes Genung's *The Study of Rhetoric in the College Course* (1877) as "the most thorough contemporary description of the changes that had overtaken rhetoric in the late nineteenth century by one of the most prominent thinkers about composition" (134). Genung states,

> He [the college student] needs to know that writing is not juggling with words, not making ideas show off, but expressing the truth, plainly, directly, completely . . . . We cannot hope, indeed, to make finished authors: time fails for requisite prac-

tice.... A carefully written, conscientious college essay is stiff and self-conscious; the thought is meager and commonplace, the style is wooden... I believe there must be a more or less wooden period in all earnest authorship. (144–146)

To get through this wooden stage, Genung advises teachers to inspire literary spontaneity in students, to "deprecate anything that shows for intentional good writing, and, making a kind of 'rattlin' and roarin' Willie' of the student, to keep him slashing ahead, always fluent, if not always so cunning, until he happens to write something eminently racy and individual" (147). According to Gengung, this method has little use for the classical tradition—from Aristotle through Blair and Whately. While Hill's model ignores classical rhetoric to focus solely on mechanical correctness in English, here Genung dismisses the classical tradition because its taxonomical, technical descriptions of stylistic devices hampered the very spontaneity he wished to induce. In many ways, what Genung describes parallels what process theorists such as Elbow might say decades later, when touting the benefits of voice and freewriting. In short, both Genung and Elbow stress the importance of keeping students "slashing ahead" to avoid the stiff, wooden, and self-conscious style of student papers that try too hard to imitate academic prose.

The New Curriculum also treats style at other levels of discourse, namely the paragraph. Barrett Wendell, who became a professor at Harvard shortly after Adams Sherman Hill, delivered a lecture in 1890 on paragraphs, one of eight collected in a volume titled *English Composition*, in which he divides effective paragraphing into unity, mass, and coherence. Essentially, a paragraph should have a beginning, middle, and end in order to write with precision and force. The idea of coherence stems from Alexander Bain's popular 1866 book, *English Composition and Rhetoric*, a book that was used to drill students in constructing orderly, deductive paragraphs with clear topic sentences, and to then proceed according to patterns of narration, description, or exposition.

Mike Duncan's 2007 *College English* article, "Whatever Happened to the Paragraph?," describes and analyzes a number of nineteenth- and early twentieth-century handbooks for their promotion of clear, simple, orderly paragraphs that must possess an internal consistency. These textbooks and guides define paragraphs as self-contained units that, almost by themselves, pile up into essays. To write well, then, students had to write correct sentences that must be ordered into correct paragraphs. According to Duncan, even John Genung at Amherst College hands down a series of rules about topic sentences and proper ordering or sentences. As Duncan puts it, Wendell and Genung "were perhaps the greatest advocates of Bain's prescriptive approach" (475).

A number of secondary sources provide alternative accounts of this period, with an emphasis on other sites of education and other disciplinary perspectives. These sources consider the mid-to-late nineteenth century with more attention to writing instruction outside the sphere of universities like Harvard, Yale, Amherst College, and Princeton. Not all of these histories provide an exact account of how issues of style were taught in relation to the other canons, but they create a space for future research about the dynamic between style and invention at non-elite institutions. Jessica Enoch's 2008 *Refiguring Rhetorical Education* describes the civic roles women teachers claimed when educating freed slaves, Native Americans, and Mexican border-town citizens in the late nineteenth and early twentieth centuries. David Gold's 2008 book, *Rhetoric at the Margins*, describes rhetorical education at a normal school, a women's university, and a private black college, where the classical curriculum survived in spite of its displacement from large research universities. One professor described in Gold's book, Melvin Tolson, was a fiery orator in the vein of Cicero who instilled the same love of words in his students; yet, he also made his students diagram sentences. The educators described in Enoch's books often inhabit contact zones in which they negotiated multiple rhetorical conventions, languages, and grammars. If we are interested in an expansive understanding of style, these are important sources to consider, even if style is not an explicit topic in the historical work that currently exists.

A 2012 essay by David Gold on revisionist historiography describes many other projects, including: Thomas Miller's *The Formation of College English* (1997) and *The Evolution of College English* (2011), a history of schools outside the purview of the Big Four schools; Jacqueline Jones Royster's *Traces of a Stream* (2000), an account of African-American rhetorical education beyond higher education; Charles Paine's *The Resistant Writer* (1999), a redemptive look at Adams Sherman Hill; and Patricia Donahue and Flesher Moon's edited volume, *Local Histories* (2007), descriptions of other institutions that did not follow the Harvard model. Finally, Gold points readers to Jean Ferguson Carr, Stephen Carr, and Lucille M. Schultz's *Archives of Instruction* (2005), a study of composition handbooks from the nineteenth century that, as I see it, is a useful complement to Connors's work on these materials.

These developments during the late nineteenth century may have had the most direct impact on the current status of style in scholarship, textbooks, and instructional methods—not merely because it is the closest chronologically. This period in the history of style signals a shift to a climate of absolute rules contained in books that teachers still use, often unknowingly or even reluctantly, to regulate students rather than help them develop their own sense of style through experimentation with language.

This is not usually mean-spirited on the part of educators themselves, since writing in the "correct" style is viewed as a necessary step to a college degree and employment. In many colleges, writing instruction is a task taken on by graduate students, adjuncts, and other untenured faculty who often see the simple, straightforward guidelines and rules of style guides as a life-saver rather than as a straightjacket. No doubt, teaching style any other way requires a considerable deal of thought, planning, and individual time with students. It is even common for students to seek out easy-to-follow prescriptions on sentence and paragraph construction, and ignore the potential of images, sounds, and textures they can create through a wider toolbox of stylistic strategies.

The next three chapters give cause for optimism regarding the role of style in writing instruction by exploring a number of theories and pedagogies that are either gaining traction or renewed attention since the 1960s and 1970s—a period seen by contemporary scholars of style as a brief golden era in which rhetoric and composition shirked the burden of prescriptivism. By the mid-twentieth century, a number of pedagogies emerged as relevant to understanding style as decisions made at the local level that ultimately contribute to the overall tone or voice of a writer. These movements include generative rhetoric, alternate style, sentence-combining pedagogies, and rhetorical grammar. As the next chapter shows, contemporary scholars discuss the study and teaching of style as a series of choices made within sentences, paragraphs, and passages that culminate in distinctive prose.

4 Contemporary Views on Style

Previous chapters have shown tensions regarding the role of style in rhetoric and education from the ancient and classical eras in Greece and Rome, as well as non-western cultures, through to the early twentieth century in Europe and the US. This chapter and the next two chapters focus on the relevance of style to specializations within our discipline, including basic writing, language difference, and digital rhetorics. Even if rhetoric and composition scholars do not directly use the term "style," they discuss stylistic issues. Understanding style as ubiquitous in rhetoric and composition helps teachers and students become aware of the relationship between decisions at the level of the sentences or passage and their contributions to a writer's overall style or voice.

Advocates of style in rhetoric and composition today include Paul Butler, Tom Pace, T. R. Johnson, Susan Peck MacDonald, Tara Lockhart, Jeanne Fahnestock, Chris Holcomb, and Jimmie Killingsworth. These theorists discuss style explicitly, and they take an interdisciplinary approach that often combines classical rhetoric, linguistics, sociolinguistics, and stylistics. For instance, Holcomb's *Rhetoric Review* essay "Performative Stylistics and the Question of Academic Prose," draws on classical rhetoric, stylistics, and sociolinguistics to analyze debates between Judith Butler, Terry Eagleton, and Gayatri Spivak on the responsibilities of academics to write in a clear style for large, public readerships. Fahnestock explores style in these same areas as well as genre theory, writing in the sciences, and multimodality. These authors—Butler, Fahnestock, Holcomb, Johnson, Pace, Killingsworth—form a visible and largely coherent movement calling for a return to style in our field.

Paul Butler makes the case for renewed attention to style, while using it to synthesize theories of language in sociolinguistics, dialectology, hybrid academic writing, language difference, and rhetorical grammar. As Butler states, an underlying principle in all of these areas is a view that "form (style) and content (meaning) are inextricably linked" because meaning "is connotative . . . and comes from various rhetorical elements—humor, irony or sarcasm, emphasis, and even ethos . . . conveyed through form" ("Public Intellectual" 78). As Butler argues in his 2008 book *Out of Style*, we can make more precise arguments about language if we move style to the forefront of our research and teaching.

Too often, Butler maintains, style is associated with grammatical correctness, and is thus dismissed as another way to constrain student agency rather than nurture it through a comprehensive set of strategies and tools. By neglecting style, scholars and teachers cede the topic to public discourse—where traditional grammarians and prescriptivists dominate, and journalists and popular intellectuals routinely accuse college writing teachers of lowering standards. The next section, on style in publics and counterpublics, attends directly to such discussions. Ironically, Quintilian made a similar statement about rhetoricians, relinquishing the *progymnasmata* to grammar-school teachers, a decision through which rhetoric "has all but been driven out of its rightful possessions" (2.1.6). It would appear that history has a way of repeating itself, even with regard to writing and rhetoric.

STYLE IN PUBLICS AND COUNTERPUBLICS

Public derisions of composition for failing to teach students how to write clearly and correctly are not hard to find. For example, Stanley Fish has notoriously argued in a *New York Times* op-ed, titled "Devoid of Content," that college writing classes should only teach grammar and style, and by style he means clear sentences that reproduce the norms of academic discourse.[24] Similar pieces have been written by Heather MacDonald, Louise Menand, and George Will.[25] We see similar discourses in popular books, such as Lynn Truss's *Eats, Shoots, and*

---

24. Fish has elaborated the stance in his 2005 op-ed piece "Devoid of Content" into an entire book, titled *How to Write a Sentence*, a blend of his own approach to literary stylistics with a tutorial in Chomsky's Transformational Generative Grammar—the basis by which we understand language through phrases and clauses that can be combined in nearly infinite ways.

25. Another compelling example of such public discourse on style is a 2011 online opinion column in *Forbes*, in which Brown University graduate Michael Ellsberg accuses higher education of encouraging college students to

Leaves or Strunk and White's *Elements of Style*. It helps to see various methods of studying and teaching style in rhetoric and composition as forming "counterpublics" against these prevailing discourses, and these have implications for other areas of writing instruction—such as linguistic diversity and language rights. As Kathryn T. Flannery states in her 1995 book, *The Emperor's New Clothes*, "style is never innocent" (28). Style often serves as a site of socio-political struggle, where different values are contested across public and academic boundaries.

Scholars in rhetoric and composition have responded to public criticism by interrogating common assumptions about style. In a 2009 issue of *College English*, Catherine Prendergast historicizes public discourse on style, showing how "clarity, brevity, and correctness have defined the conventional wisdom of what counts as good style for the last fifty years" since the first edition of Strunk and White's *Elements of Style*, along with "many . . . progeny, including the far more interesting Lynn Truss's *Eats, Shoots, & Leaves: The Zero Tolerance Approach to Punctuation*" (13). In his recent book, *After the Public Turn*, Frank Farmer describes such discourse as "limit[ing] writing pedagogy strictly to considerations of form, that tend to conflate written style with prescriptive grammars, and that tends to dismiss as irrelevant any genuine motivation our students might have to write well" (134).

Paul Butler has also addressed this issue in his 2008 article, "Style and the Public Intellectual," proposing that rhetoric and composition should reclaim public discussions on writing, and to "go public with a renewed emphasis on style and to employ its disciplinary expertise" on the subject (62). As Butler observes in *Out of Style*, "The public conceptions controlling debates on style today—which often reduce style to the equivalent of grammar or prescriptive rules—have effectively usurped the topic from the discipline [of composition] itself" (19). Butler's fifth chapter provides a handful of evocative examples of this usurpation. In one, Heather Mac Donald's 1995 *Public Interest* article, "Why Johnny Can't Write," indicts rhetoric and composition for excusing teachers from the need to teach correctness. Mac Donald, a lawyer by profession, goes on to declare that "Every writing theory of the past thirty years has come up with reasons why it's not necessary to teach grammar and style . . . because grammatical errors

---

write like Talcott Parsons, an anthropologist whose prose Richard Lanham mocks in *Style: an Anti-Textbook*.

signify the author is politically engaged" (11). At best, we might say that MacDonald has an incomplete understanding of why research in composition turned away from an explicit focus on grammar. As Butler contends throughout his book, these views conflate style with correctness, missing the historical fact that correctness has always been only one component of the canon, not its essence.

Both Farmer and Butler embrace the idea of composition as a counterpublic, albeit with slight differences. Butler encourages rhetoric and composition scholars to take on the role of public intellectual, to bring the substantial body of knowledge about style of the field into public discussions, and position it actively against public intellectuals like Fish. Farmer admits that such a change would be an improvement over the current status of our discipline, but he offers a more complicated view of counterpublics based on the idea of bricoleurs, who "reject the honorific of *public intellectual* but would not reject any situational exigency to perform that function as needed" (149). Farmer reasons that if we write back to public deriders of our discipline, we can "use our expertise situationally, creatively, tactically," rather than being forced into a somewhat limited role as a talking head, simply summoned by editors of newspapers and magazines, and then rolled back into storage (149).

One of the most prevalent assumptions about style in public discourse is that academics write in a deliberately opaque style, and that this style discredits their opinions. For example, Terry Eagleton has criticized the prose of Judith Butler and Gayatri Spivak as "pretentiously opaque" (qtd. in Holcomb 204) in the *London Review of Books*. In response, Butler asserts the need for a voice that makes "readers pause and reflect on the power of language to shape the world" ("Bad Writer"). As Butler argues, if there is an affinity between radicalism and dense writing, it is their ability to frustrate norms. It is partly through difficult writing that radical intellectuals force readers to stop and pay attention to relationships between language and realities.[26] From this stance, a clear, plain style is not always the most appropriate

---

26. Chris Holcomb disagrees with Judith Butler in his 2005 *Rhetoric Review* essay, "Performative Stylistics and the Question of Academic Prose," stating that more often than not, radical prose serves an exclusionary, self-serving purpose rather than a democratic one.

end goal—a radical prose style challenges the Aristotelian ideals still pervasive in American attitudes about discourse and writing.

Michael Warner sees public critiques such as Eagleton's as "primitive" because they assume that "a clear style results in a popular audience and that political engagement requires having the most extensive audience possible" (137). Warner goes on to explain this misperception as a reason why "Anyone who dissents from it can only be heard as proposing inanities: that bad writing is necessary; that incomprehensibility should be cultivated; that speech in order to be politically radical must have no audience" (139). Writing in a difficult style may reduce the size of one's audience, but that does not make such writing bad, arrogant, or pretentious. We might deduce from Warner that it is important to teach students to appreciate difficult styles and to see that a plain or difficult style is each appropriate for different purposes. Doing so might invoke a future public more tolerant of linguistic and stylistic diversity. Min-Zhan Lu makes a similar point in her essays, including "Essay on the Work of Composition," in which she calls on teachers to help bring forth a more tolerant and receptive culture toward difference and deviation that extends beyond the academy.

This discussion of publics and counterpublics provides a foundation for the appreciation of academic orientations to style that privilege difference, deviation, and the negotiation of norms in student writing. When teachers merely teach style the way Strunk and White prescribe, or when they only correct students' mistakes in using style guides provided by MLA or textbook publishers, they are succumbing to a larger public narrative that circumscribes style as norming, confining, and regulatory. Incorporating other approaches does not exclude these norms, but it does not mandate their absolute authority. Even Quintilian advised students to break with traditions and rules, to take risks when they felt that a rhetorical situation called for doing so. The rest of this chapter teases out what this attitude entails in terms of teaching voice and grammar in college composition courses.

The next section defines voice, and situates scholarship on voice as a vital complement to pedagogies of style. Often, we use the terms "style" and "voice" interchangeably, without realizing their relationship. While the term "voice" may refer to many of the same traits as "style," the term brings our attention to the writer's presence. As Elbow argues, the term "style" can lead teachers and students down a path toward abstract analysis, while missing how a real person—or at least our perception of one—emerges from such analysis. Thinking about style in terms of voice helps make the purpose of deviation and resistance to publics more tangible. After all, it is the people and their voices—not merely texts and rhetorical effects—that struggle for recognition and freedom of expression.

Teachers may also conflate style, grammar, and correctness—just as many public intellectuals do. There are two consequences to this. On the one hand, teachers may perpetuate the dominant public and reproduce it in their classrooms, or they might resist teaching style and grammar altogether, seeing both as too authoritarian. During the 1980s in particular, composition scholarship seemed to mistakenly equate style with grammar, purging them both in favor of social-epistemic approaches (see Connors's "Erasure of the Sentence" and MacDonald's "Erasure of Language.") A complete and nuanced view of style must recognize its connection to grammar as a descriptive terminology, not grammar as a set of arbitrary rules. Chapter 1 mentioned Patrick Hartwell's category of "stylistic grammars" that includes work by Martha Kolln, Francis Christensen, and Joseph Williams. This chapter and the next contain sections that promote grammar as a source of stylistic creativity—affirming its connections with style and voice. In some ways, their work can help dissolve some of the troubled boundaries between public and counterpublic discourses on style. They show us that grammar is important, but also malleable—and especially important for students to learn as they craft their own voices.

STYLE, VOICE, AND DISCOURSE

The first chapter of this book includes a section defining style partly as a matter of voice, drawing on the work of process theorists such as Peter Elbow. The process movement emerged during the 1970s as part of a larger turn away from matters of form that had dominated college writing instruction since the New Curriculum. Many process theorists, such as Linda Flower and John Hayes, Janet Emig, and Mike Rose, concentrated on cognitive dimensions of the writing process, and developed scientific models to explain the writing process as a series of recursive stages that involved goal-setting and problem-solving (see Flower and Hayes's "A Cognitive Process Theory of Writing" as a prime example). As such, they devoted some passing attention to voice, tone, and grammar. Peter Elbow, often referred to as an expressivist for his focus on writing as self-expression, has always concentrated on voice (and style). As Elbow notes in his 2007 *College English* essay, "Voice in Writing Again," the two terms often mean the same thing, though he prefers the term "voice" over "style" because it circumvents the need to discuss grammar—a discussion he finds potentially confining, intimidating, and dehumanizing. In other words, describing prose with more evocative yet impressionistic terms such as "bossy" or "condescending" can help writers understand the rhetorical effects of their language choices more vividly than advising them about the overuse of subordinating clauses.

As Elbow states in *Writing with Power*, there is not only voice, but *real* voice. A writer's voice may be appropriate, fluid, and confident, but a writer's real voice is more than that; it is evocative. Writers can adopt many voices for different occasions, but only their *real* voice lends power to their prose. Admittedly, Elbow struggles to define the real voice he wants to help students achieve. As he tries to convey, real voice

> has the power to make you pay attention and understand—the words go deep. I don't know the objective characteristics that distinguish writing with real voice from writing with mere voice. For me it is a matter of hearing resonance rather than being able to point to things on the page. (299)

Elbow has an easier time defining what real voice is *not*, and describing how most conventional pedagogies that dwell on rules and conventions for college writing constrict voice rather than promote *real* voice. A term that Elbow and others use to describe voiceless writing is "Engfish," a term originally coined by Ken Macrorie in the book *Telling Writing*. Like Elbow, Macrorie was an early advocate of freewriting, a pedagogy prompting students to express their thoughts and feelings on any issue without pausing to organize or revise their writing for correctness. Process theorists like Elbow and Macrorie often attest to the power and clarity of unplanned freewriting when compared to the heavily revised, hyper-edited prose students produce when trying to complete assignments. Thinking of voice in terms of style, then, the idea is that students use freewriting to generate writing that is clearer, more honest, and more direct.

Many later social-epistemic schools of rhetoric and writing instruction characterized this approach as privileging some kind of inner truth or version of reality over social interaction. David Bartholomae, Joseph Harris, and James Berlin are especially pointed critics of Elbow's methods. These scholars stress the importance of discourse communities in the formation of a writer's voice, and see Elbow as over-privileging the individual writer and failing to fully account for how writers negotiate their need for self-expression with the expectations of academic writing. For instance, Harris points out the flaw in trying to find an allegedly authentic voice, comparing it to "saying blue jeans are more genuine than business suits" (33). Harris resists judgment claims about students' writing, such as "nam[ing] various passages as real or powerful without having to say why" (32). A section in chapter 6 explores similar complications of voice in scholarship on second-language writing. Elbow seems open to such criticism, and gestures toward qualities of voice that he cannot fully define or illustrate. In *Writing with Power*, he concedes that "Sometimes I fear I will never be clear about what I mean by voice. Certainly I have waxed incoherent on many occasions" (286).

Elbow has preferred this level of uncertainty rather than resorting to the language of grammar, at least until his recent book, *Vernacular Eloquence*. Here, Elbow seems to finally articulate a precise and thorough theory of what he means by voice in writing. He draws on research in linguistics regarding differences in spoken and written discourse—in particular, M. A. K. Halliday's 1987 book chapter, "Spoken and Written Modes of Meaning." Halliday describes spoken and written discourse as planned and unplanned. Both writing and speaking can, at times, seem planned or unplanned, and so they elude simple categorization. Elbow uses this framework to clarify his long-evolving definition of voice. When someone writes with voice, they draw on the everyday, unplanned patterns of conversation (even idioms) to disrupt the planned, hierarchical patterns of writing that can lead to unclear, wordy, impersonal, or disinterested prose. Thus, seeing style as voice highlights a broader goal of style, and gestures toward the ways style is not simply the use of grammar, or even stylistic devices or imagery or sound. Style is all of these, of course, but it is all aimed at creating a voice that is inviting to readers.

An interesting voice can take a variety of forms, a fact that Elbow has used to link his work with research in other areas of rhetoric and composition—namely, language difference. In *Vernacular Eloquence*, but also in an earlier contribution to the collection *Alt Dis*, Elbow addresses the use of vernacular languages such as Black English as a way of introducing more spontaneity, originality, and self into the early drafts of student papers, helping students negotiate their non-standard language varieties with the conventions of academic writing. In *Vernacular Eloquence*, he quotes from a freewrite by colleague Janet Bean, with whom he co-authored another essay on voice and language difference in *Composition Studies*, titled "Should We Invite Students to Write in Home Languages? Complicating the Yes/No Debate."[27] Bean writes that "we have to talk about the politics of standardization, about dialect and value, about the relativity of correctness . . . we have to stop believing in a pure standard English" (qtd. in Elbow 156). Endorsing this view, Elbow's latest work on voice suggests to researchers and teachers that we are never just teaching style or voice, but *styles* and *voices*. The patterns of everyday speech that can enliven writing may derive from many different forms of language, not merely from the ones currently authorized by higher education, dominant publics, and the textbook industry.

Such a view of voice and linguistic diversity becomes key in work on what Philip Marzluf describes as "diversity writing," the prose produced by marginalized students who perform authenticity through non-standard forms of English. For example, Southern students might deliberately use the word "y'all" in a paper, or students from Singapore might use "la," to prove certain aspects of their ethnic or geographic identifies. In his critique of voice in "Diversity Writing," Marzluf echoes Elbow's critics, with a special emphasis on linguistically diverse students. For Marzluf, while Elbow's pedagogy avoids the trap of equating voice with self, a misappropriation of voice may risk stereotyping and pigeon-holing students. He says, "To contend that students are closer to or more comfortable with certain types of language—or that vernaculars reveal students' selves more honestly—is rarely an innocent claim" (514). Such a view implies that all African-American students write better when they are encouraged to draw on AAVE, or that all white Southerners secretly yearn to write in the voices of their great-grandparents. If students come to see voice as the expression of a true self, rather than as a social construction, they may be pressured into seeing other voices, other styles of writing, as somehow inauthentic, fake, or depersonalizing.

---

27. This article also contains contributions by several language specialists, including Paul Kei Matsuda.

This section made three main points about style and voice. First, in many ways, style and voice are synonymous terms. Second, when pressing for a distinction, we see that voice can refer to the sense of presence a writer creates via style, and also specifically to the use of oral patterns to make prose more stylistically inviting. Third, it is helpful to think of "voice" not as uniform, but as varied. Writers may develop many voices, or their "voice" may draw from many different forms of a spoken language. Because writers can construct many voices, teachers should be cautious of endorsing one particular style or voice as superior—whether that means more in line with academic discourse or, conversely, more authentic. The idea of voice as voices will be taken further in the next section, on Bakhtin's approach to style and voice. Bakhtin's approach treats stylization as double-voicing, showing that that voice is already innately plural.

Bakhtin, Dialogism, and Style

If expressivists such as Elbow treat style in terms of voice, then Bakhtin's theories of heteroglossia, stylization, and dialogism encourage thought about style/voice as the negotiation of multiple voices. In fact, Harris hopes to redefine voice away from the expression of a unitary self, asserting that "we need to begin with the idea that our culture speaks to us through many competing voices" (34) and that writing is a process of responding to and appropriating them.[28] Bakhtin was one of the first theorists to argue for the inherent diversity within language (heteroglossia), explaining that a single speaker's social interactions within a given day may include a specialized language used at work, a different one at home with family, yet another with friends, and yet another in church. Moreover, these different tongues within a single language are always in dialogue with one another (dialogism). Each type of language evolves in relation to the other, as any speaker carries bits of language from one social sphere to another, always repeating and imitating what he or she has heard someone else say in one situation when it seems appropriate in another. To explain this process, Bakhtin posits the term *double-voicing*. Anytime we speak, we are not

---

28. Harris references Bakhtin directly, but consciously situates his discussion within the context of the Amherst School in the 1930s—where similar notions developed specific to college writing instruction.

simply voicing ourselves, but voicing the many others from whom we borrow language.

The idea of dialogized heteroglossia becomes realized in Bakhtin's illustration of the daily life of a Russian peasant, in the essay "Discourse in the Novel." Bakhtin describes the multiple social situations and their respective language genres, describing first how the peasant may see these as isolated from one another. However,

> As soon as a critical interanimation of languages began to occur in the consciousness of our peasant, as soon as it became clear that these were not only various different languages but even internally variegated languages . . . then the inviolability and predetermined quality of these languages came to an end, and the necessity of actively choosing one's orientation among them began. (296)

At this point, the peasant begins blending language conventions between "the language and world of prayer, the language and world of song, the language and world of labor and everyday life, and the specific language and world of local authorities," and so on (296). Each of these languages has its own norms in terms of diction and grammar, or sentence length and structure. While they might possess clear differences, they are not rigid; they are always in the process of changing each other. Teachers and students might think today of the ways they employ different choices at the local and global levels of discourse that signify a specific style.

Via Bakhtin, voice becomes *voices* and style becomes *styles*. It may be easy for teachers to simply tell students to write in a voice that "sounds natural" but, ultimately, writers never draw only on their own oral discourse patterns to develop a sense of voice. Rather, they are always appropriating phrases they have heard before and weaving them into their own texts. Far from plagiarism, this is the natural function of language according to Bakhtin—what he refers to as double-voiced discourse, as described in *Problems in Dostoevsky's Poetics*. Just as language is inherently diverse, it is also inherently populated with a range of intentions or purposes. Someone might make the same utterance in a semantic sense, but might do so in a context that completely changes the actual idea conveyed. (Just imagine someone saying "I love you" in an endearing tone, then hearing it uttered in return with a sarcastic undertone.) When someone appropriates a piece of discourse and deploys it in a different context, they are engaging in what Bakhtin calls double-voicing. All language is always double-voiced.

Seeing style and voice as inherently diverse means understanding one's voice as permeated and inflected by everyone they know and everything they have read. Different forms of double-voicing exist, including emulation, imitation, paraphrase, and quotation. In each case, one speaker borrows words from someone else and uses them for a different purpose. Bakhtin specifically refers to a kind of passive double-voicing as "stylization," in which writers adopt the style of someone they have read, either to conform to that style or to revive it for a contemporary time. By "passive," Bakhtin does not mean passive on the part of the writer, but on the part of the source. The writer who imitates or copies the style of another is being extremely active in the process of appropriation and redirection, but the source is passive in that it allows the adaptation to take place. According to Gary Saul Morson and Caryl Emerson, in *Creation of a Prosaics*, "The crucial point is that the stylizer constructs his [or her] utterance so that the voice of the other will be heard to sound within his [or her] own" (151).

Bakhtin's idea of style as heteroglossic double-voicing directly contradicts any idea that academic writing can be boiled down to one timeless, universal set of stylistic conventions or standards. Even within a single field, individual journals and editors have different conventions and preferences for how authors use language to construct their scholarly identities. Second, this notion of style presses teachers and scholars to recognize how different disciplines and their stylistic conventions ricochet off one another, as writers and editors carry habits and expectations back and forth between them. Moreover, we recognize that the wide variety of discourses students use will unavoidably seep into their academic writing—to deny that is to deny that language itself as porous.

Bakhtin went so far as to state that diversity described not only language, but also a kind of linguistic identity. Our very selves consist of multiple versions that are always shaping and evolving in relation to others. Chikako Kumamoto builds on this idea in a 2002 *College Composition and Communication* article on Bakhtin's conception of identity and its influence on language choices or, in Bakhtin's terms, "internal dialogization." She describes her own diverse set of selves as an eloquent "I," one that is "Japanese female . . . educated in an American parochial system, converted to Christianity in Japan . . .

completed graduate work in Milwaukee and Chicago, [and] trained in Renaissance studies" (74). Each identity constitutes a self that is connected to the others. If the self is selves, then how could anyone expect that a single, unchanging set of conventions could suffice to make this multiple "I" eloquent in every situation?

Bakhtin, Classical Rhetoric, and Postmodern Imitation

Postmodern pedagogies of imitation recognize a connection between Bakhtin's theories and the Greco-Roman tradition, a tradition that might otherwise be seen as authoritative, monolithic, and monolingual. In Chapter 2, I noted a kind of linguistic xenophobia in the classical tradition; however, contemporary scholarship has managed to separate classical approaches to style from such socio-cultural baggage. Writing in a 1995 issue of *JAC*, Mary Minock describes classroom practices based on her theoretical reading of Quintilian and Bakhtin, in which students re-read difficult texts as many as "seven times as homework over the course of a week and respond each time for at least a full single-spaced page" (503) in order to facilitate what she calls "unconscious imitation" (500). In unconscious, as opposed to intentional imitation, students still demonstrate "traces of syntactic imitation" (505) in their writing as they intuitively appropriate the voices of the authors they work with throughout the semester. Minock's pedagogy derives from Bakhtin's definition of "any gifted, creative exposition" as "always a free stylistic variation on another's discourse" (*Dialogic Imagination* 347).

Minock's use of Bakhtin highlights how imitation and mimicry occur in ordinary, everyday language use. She acknowledges that classical pedagogies of imitation were not meant to oppress students, but to direct what they already had an inclination to do—mimic one another. In fact, imitation is just as ordinary a linguistic act, according to Bakhtin, as stylistic figures of thought and expression. From a dialogic viewpoint, what rhetoricians developed as a learned activity already occurs spontaneously in language. Minock points out that Quintilian recognized this to some extent, saying that Books I and X of *The Orator's Education* raise "an extremely relevant point about the spontaneous unconscious imitation that comes from constant exposure" (500). The unconsciousness of mimicry and parody (ironic mimicry) becomes even clearer, as Minock attributes the inspiration for her pedagogy to discovering "quite accidently" that "all of my students . . . could spontaneously write spot commercials" despite the fact that "none of my students ever claimed they admired or had studied the spot commercial" (500). She goes on to say that "Their ability to generate the rhetoric and syntax of the genre was based on their unwritten dialogues with particular spot commercials that had been repeated with subtle shifts of context" (500).

The central import of Minock's pedagogy is that if students can instinctively learn the stylistic and generic features of any text through constant exposure and internalization in ways that Bakhtin theorized as the imitative nature of dialogue and interaction in speech genres, then this commonplace ability to produce through imitation can be harnessed according to more formal teaching methods, like those proposed by Quintilian. Carefully planned exercises in imitation can expedite this otherwise gradual process, through which students develop an original set of voices or styles of writing and speaking. Such methods, as described by scholars during the mid-twentieth century, are thus not confining, but freeing. They take what language does in ordinary circumstances according to Bakhtin—the imitation and appropriation of the words of others—and turns it into an object of study to give students more control over that process.

The co-ownership of utterances that makes languages dialogic—always multi-voiced—also makes all speech acts a form of imitation. Bakhtin defines originality (the product of invention) as always involving the processes of borrowing and imitating other discourses, whether they are works of literature or speech utterances. According to Bakhtin, only "extremely subtle and sometimes imperceptible transitions" exist between the development of what we might call an original style and the imitation of someone else's style (*Problems of Dostoyevsky's Poetics* 190). Bakhtin theorizes that language users are always directly or indirectly borrowing, adapting, and imitating one another—even in their daily conversational exchanges. This observation shows how what we perceive as an original or unique style is always rooted in prior discourses.

Bakhtin's concept of multi-voiced discourse holds that style is not developed by servile imitation, but by "listening to the other and trying to produce your own style in proportion to the other" ("On Rhetoric" 125). In this sense, imitation is not "mimetic behavior" in a strict sense, but rather a step in the process of crafting a "signature in relation to the signature of the other" (125). Drawing on Greco-Roman rhetorics to question the modern premises of authorship, John Muckelbauer lays out the implications of the imitation-novelty dynamic for teaching in the twentieth and twenty-first centuries. Muckelbauer argues that invention is a "necessary component of the repetitive translation from model to copy" (71), and treats imitation as a tool for the development of originality. This recognition leads Muckelbauer to endorse Edward P. J. Corbett's pedagogical use of imitation—an adaptation of Quintilian's advice to students and teachers to develop rhetorical skill by emulating model texts.

In 2005, a special issue of *Written Communication* focused on a recently translated essay by Bakhtin about grammar, style, and pedagogy, titled "Dialogic Origin and Dialogic Pedagogy of Grammar: Stylistics in Teaching Russian Language in Secondary School." A full annotated translation appears in a 2004 issue of the *Journal of Russian and East European Psychology*. In the essay, Bakhtin describes correlations between grammar and stylistic impression, comparing a paratactic sentence by Pushkin to a hypotactic variation of the sentence. The essay explores why hypotactic (complex) sentences are stylistically inferior, or "dry and pallid" when compared to simpler paratactic ones (21). Bakhtin's larger point is that Russian stylistics lacked a systematic method to account for grammatical forms and their "inherent representation and expressive potential"; moreover, "When we study certain areas of syntax . . . where the speaker or writer may choose between two or more equally grammatically correct syntactic forms," it is essential to have a way of determining the form that is more appropriate for a given purpose and situation (13). Bakhtin then describes a series of explicit teaching lessons devoted to the stylistic impact of the linguistic features of sentences.

In the issue, Bakhtin scholar Kay Halasek provides a detailed interpretation of the essay and its implications for contemporary writing instruction, namely that "No one style suits all rhetorical situations," and that there is a "rhetorical effect of grammar" (357–358). Although Bakhtin is sometimes seen as a critic of rhetoric, Halasek cites J. Zappen's position in the 2004 book, *The Rebirth of Dialogue*, that Bakhtin sought "not to reject but [to] dialogize" rhetoric; as such, the essay reads as an effort to do the same with grammar. She goes on to write, "Our very grammars are dialogic. Linguistics and grammar are not most productively described, Bakhtin argues, in terms of structural correctness but in terms of stylistic (and, I would argue, rhetorical) appeal and power" (360).

Frank Farmer interprets the essay as a meditation on style as existing not only in literary texts, but also originating from "dialogue, in living language, which in turn is mutually enriched by literary representations" (341). Thus, one major import of Bakhtin's essay on stylistic pedagogy is that teachers should "acknowledge (and thus honor) the everyday languages that our students bring to the classroom" not only as "sources for more refined literary works but the already present creativity that they possess" (345). It is worth noting, as Farmer references "Students' Right to their Own Language" (STROL), that contemporary arguments in favor of code-meshing and translingualism frequently describe the dialogic and heteroglossic dimensions of language as evidence.

In light of his own work on style, Joseph Williams treats Bakhtin's approach as a series of readers' reactions or responses to texts, rather than qualities of the writing itself. Although disagreeing with the larger theories of utterances behind Bakhtin's approach, he asserts agreement with

> Bakhtin's teaching methods: Contrast sentences with similar propositional content expressed in saliently different ways (e.g., parataxis vs. hypotaxis). This methodology is so clearly effective that we should wonder why it's so widely ignored. Most writing classes offer model sentences, paragraphs, and essays, but when what's good about them is not specifically contrasted with what might have been bad, students can't recognize what to avoid and what to emulate. (352)

Williams joins other Bakhtin scholars in endorsing imitation as a valuable pedagogical tool for helping students develop their own styles or voices.

This chapter has explained the significance of dialogic theories of language for the sake of understanding style and voice as inherently diverse. When we talk about style, voice, or their relationship, we should recognize that many styles exist. Every social situation we encounter has its own unique conventions governing language choices that we can interpret as styles of speaking or writing (e.g., diction, sentence length, level of formality, extent of figurative language). These styles are always evolving, and one style can influence another through the process of dialogism—where writers and speakers appropriate aspects of style when switching from one situation to another. Through dialogic approaches to style, we also come to understand that imitation is not the opposite of originality. In fact, it is through imitating the styles of many others that we develop our own voices. The more authors we see as models, the more we practice and experiment with their styles, and the more mature we become as writers. As the next chapter shows, style also overlaps with grammar—another issue that teachers sometimes see as antithetical or somehow subordinate to style. However, this book hopes to show how style, voice, and grammar ultimately inform one another—a complete understanding of style relies on seeing the connections between these three lenses on language.

5 The Relationship Between Style, Voice, and Grammar

Contemporary discussions of style often rely on the terminology of grammar, because it helps explain the rhetorical effects of language, both within sentences and at broader levels of discourse, such as paragraphs and passages. Earlier, we saw Elbow's difficulty in elaborating a theory of voice stemming partly from his resistance to grammar. While it is true that style is not a matter of grammatical correctness, style is a matter of using language in a way that grammar helps us to isolate and analyze. Work outlined here includes the stylistic grammars enumerated in Hartwell's article, "Grammar, Grammars, and the Teaching of Grammar." Unlike Harvard's New Curriculum, these pedagogies emphasize choice and innovation.

Many teachers may think of grammar as a monolithic concept. In fact, Hartwell identifies five different types of grammar. There is Grammar 1, innate grammar, or the unconscious syntactical rules that all native speakers "know" but struggle to explain. Grammar 2, linguistics or scientific grammar, tries to construct abstract models and principles that explain Grammar 1. Many teachers may recognize Grammar 3, linguistic etiquette, as the arbitrary set of rules that make up our idea of Standard English. In short, Grammar 3 can be defined more appropriately as usage—conventions that are currently accepted as dominant. Grammar 4 refers to grammar as it is presented in textbooks and handbooks; it is similar to Grammar 3, except that Grammar 4 also consists of yet more arbitrary rules about beginning sentences with conjunctions or using commas to breakup run-on sentences. Finally, Grammar 5 consists of the stylistic grammars that use the terms of Grammar 2 and and Grammar 4 to explain the rhetorical effects of prose.

This section focuses on what Hartwell refers to as Grammar 5, specifically a kind of metalinguistic ability, or "the active manipulation of language with conscious attention to surface form" and "stylistic effect" (579). Hartwell considers Grammar 5 a "vocabulary of style" to be actively engaged with, "to be molded and probed, shaped and reshaped, and, above all, enjoyed" (579). Works by Fahnestock, Kolln, Williams, Christensen, and Weathers employ grammatical terms without dragging in the baggage of prescriptive school grammars. Yet, rhetoric and composition scholars have developed an aversion to grammar since the 1980s—including these stylistic grammars. In her contribution to *Refiguring Prose Style*, Nicole Amare traces this aversion back to the Braddock Report published in 1963, a report she describes as having "told us that formal grammar instruction not only does not improve our students' writing but in fact may have an adverse effect on their compositions" (154). As Amare states, "We remain in the shadow of the Braddock study" (155).

In *Out of Style*, Paul Butler outlines a similar history beginning with Daniel Fogarty's 1959 *Roots for a New Rhetoric*, in which Butler represents then-current approaches as dominated by correctness and "style qualities" such as "clearness, force, coherence, interest, naturalness, and other devices" in opposition to a "new or improved teaching rhetoric" based on the theories of New Rhetoricians such as Kenneth Burke (118). Richard Young's "Paradigms and Problems" characterizes current-traditional rhetoric as preoccupied with "usage (syntax, spelling, punctuation) and with style (economy, clarity, emphasis)" (31). Sharon Crowley's *Methodical Memory* explores an over-emphasis on style rather than invention in current-traditional rhetoric. Finally, Maxine Hairston's Conference on College Composition and Communication (CCCC) chair's address, "The Winds of Change," argues that teachers who focus on "style, organization, and correctness" (7) often overlook the need for instruction in invention. According to Butler, all of these landmark events culminate in the diaspora or dissolution of style into several areas within composition. As such, teachers lack a coherent framework for discussing language choices at the micro, macro, and meso-discursive levels.

Susan Peck MacDonald addresses the field's turn to social-epistemic rhetoric during the 1980s and 1990s as a major reason for the marginalization of theories or pedagogies addressing sentence-level issues, including stylistic grammars. In the essay "The Erasure of Language," MacDonald argues that other disciplines that might enlighten our understanding of language issues—such as linguistics, as it offered much to composition during the 1950s and 1960s—now rarely surface in major journals. In her historical study of the CCCC, MacDonald writes,

> linguistic scholarship embedded in the early CCCC sessions was often significant. Workshop discussions were summarized and published in each October issue of *CCC* as a form of extended professional dialogue, the kind of dialogue crucial for the compact work of an "urbane" discipline . . . these linguists within English were speaking at CCCC with authority about what and how to teach language, and their understanding involved complex linguistic training . . . both Chomsky and Sheridan might be part of the same discussion involving language. (598)

According to MacDonald, as the field professionalized and turned away from sentence-level pedagogies during the 1980s, it exiled language in general and became unreceptive to subsequent work in other fields that could contribute to the study and teaching of college writing.

A definitive moment in debates on style and grammar came in 1984, when George Hillocks declared, after analyzing hundreds of case studies, that "The study of traditional school grammar (i.e., the definition of parts of speech, the parsing of sentences, etc.) has no effect on raising the quality of student writing. Every other focus of instruction examined in this review is stronger" (160). Moreover, he added: "Taught in certain ways, grammar and mechanics instruction has a deleterious effect on student writing," and that teachers and administrators who insisted on grammar drills for students "do them gross disservice which should not be tolerated" (248-249._ Hillocks's article all but silenced the debate about grammar instruction, regardless of its intent or methodology. In his contribution to *Concepts in Composition*, James D. Williams observes that the discipline's major journals—including *CCC*, *Research in the Teaching of English*, *Written Communication*, and *College English*—"did not produce a single article address[ing] the question of grammar's effect on writing performance" from 1986 onward" (317).

Without grammar, it is difficult to discuss style at any level, either within sentences or at a more discursive level. Coherence at the level of paragraphs and passages often relies on stylistic decisions at the sentence level. It is all tied together, and so failure to teach grammar leads to failures all the way along the chain—paragraphs, passages, and entire articles. There is no need to see grammar as antithetical to style. In fact, many of the stylistic devices in classical rhetoric can be explained using grammatical terminology. The classical sentence scheme known as *parison* refers to crafting coordinating or subordinating clauses of equal length and structure to achieve balance or parallelism in one sentence, or across many sentences. For example, someone might write, "Although Obama lost a state, he won a nation." There is also the famous saying by Neil Armstrong, "That's one small step for man, one giant leap for mankind." Both statements achieve balance by mirroring grammatical structures such as the two-verb phrases "lost a state" and "won a nation," or in the noun phrases, "small step for man" and "giant leap for mankind," both of which possess adjectives and prepositions in the same positions in each phrase.

The device *anaphora* can be explained as the repetition of words or phrases at the ends of clauses or sentences. So can the device *epistrophe*, the repetition of words at the beginning of clauses, or *symploce*—a combination of the previous two devices. Devices such as these affect sentences, but writers can repeat them across paragraphs or passages to achieve stylistic cohesion at the broader levels of discourse. This is especially true of anaphora; for example, Obama uses anaphora in his 2004 speech at the Democratic National Convention to promote his brand of hope as

> *the hope of* slaves sitting around a fire singing freedom songs; *the hope of* immigrants setting out for distant shores; *the hope of* a young naval lieutenant bravely patrolling the Mekong Delta; *the hope of* a millworker's son who dares to defy the odds; *the hope of* a skinny kid with a funny name who believes that America has a place for him, too. (emphasis added)

In this case, we need the language of grammar to explain the effects of this passage, as well as how the atoms of grammar enable its very construction. Obama effectively uses the repetition of a particular prepositional phrase, "the hope of," in a series of dependent clauses that are punctuated by semicolons rather than commas. Through the use of the prepositional structures, Obama links several key characters through himself, the "skinny kid with a funny name." One could only imagine how awkward the passage might sound if Obama had simply used possessive nouns, saying, for example, "slaves sitting around a fire singing freedom songs's hope" and so on.

Jeanne Fahnestock also treats syllogism and enthymeme as stylistic and grammatical units, because they are lines of argument that govern the organization of sentences (374–376). Rhetoricians from Aristotle to Quintilian regarded the syllogism as a method of generating arguments using major and minor premises, one famous example being, "Socrates is a man. All men are mortal. Therefore, Socrates is mortal." Here, the first sentence is the major premise, the second a minor premise, and the third a conclusion. The enthymeme is merely a rhetorical syllogism that is used to tie together opinions rather than facts. Seen through style, both become a way of creating links between sentences, similar to the ones described above based on similarity, difference, cause, or simultaneity. The syllogism and enthymeme organize information at the level of discourse, but they require stylistic skill in working with grammatical units. According to Fahnestock, "Students [of classical rhetoric] needed enough grammatical competence . . . to manipulate the three critical terms into the appropriate subject and predicate positions in comprehensible sentences" (375). Once again, style occurs at the level of sentences and discourse, and we understand it via grammatical terminology.

Grammar can help explain stylistic matters across sentences, at the level of paragraphs and passages. Fahnestock shows that to create cohesion, a writer can substitute a shorter word or phrase in one clause used in a prior one (347). For example, the phrase "done so" can refer back to a verbal construction in a previous clause or sentence. The stylistic device *ellipsis* can also create cohesion by omitting entire phrases without substitution, prompting readers to infer connections between clauses or sentences. The most prominent pattern for creating cohesion is the given/new or topic/comment pattern, in which writers use sentence position to arrange old and new information (Fahnestock 348). Writers normally make old, familiar, or assumed information part of their subjects or first clauses, and then introduce newer information later in the predicate. Linguists use the phrase "right branching" to refer to sentences that reveal new information or more detail about a topic as they progress. These patterns enable writers to organize information in paragraphs and stretches of prose, generating a sense of cohesion that readers associate with stylistic effectiveness. Clumsily organized passages, with ineffective grammatical structuring of old and new information, often come off as stylistically immature or undeveloped.

Writers also develop coherence through manipulation meaning relations between sentences, adding introductory clauses or individual words such as "likewise," "however," "furthermore," "consequently," or "meanwhile" to scaffold relationships of similarity, contrast, addition, cause, or temporal simultaneity (Fahnestock 356–57). Such words lend cohesion when relationships between sentences could be unclear. For example, imagine a writer evaluating a source: "The article contains some factual inaccuracies. It presents an interesting theory." The relationship becomes clearer with a word like "nonetheless" at the beginning of the second sentence, explaining that the writer still values the source despite the factual problems. Fahnestock also describes restatement as a stylistic move in which phrases like "in other words" or "to put it simply" lend coherence and clarity to paragraphs and passages (360). These are grammatical decisions that also create a sense of style or voice at the discursive level. Academic writers rely on these strategies to guide readers through complex sequences of information.

Parataxis and hypotaxis qualify as yet other grammatical patterns that work at a larger, discursive level. The difference between parataxis and hypotaxis lies in the loose coordination of ideas using conjunctions and the intentional refrain from subordinating clause structures. Hemingway's distinctive style of writing owes to his use of paratactic structures. In the last few sentences of *A Farewell to Arms*, for example, main character mourns his dead fiancé:

> But after I got them [the doctors] to leave and shut the door and turned off the light it wasn't any good. It was like saying good-by to a statue. After a while I went out and left the hospital and walked back to the hotel in the rain. (355)

The paratactic organization of these sentences emphasizes the seemingly random and relentless event of experiencing someone's sudden death. Readers might see the narrator's failure to link these sentences as well-suited to the psychological state of someone who has just lost a fiancé. By contrast, many nineteenth century writers often show a much higher degree of organization by relying on subordinating clauses, as such a pattern suited the hierarchical social structures in which their characters were embedded. Edgar Allen Poe often used hypotaxis in long, twisting sentences that conveyed the inner mazes of human emotion.

Now that we have a firmer appreciation for the relationship between style and grammar, we can look at specific stylistic grammars that have emerged over the past fifty years. The next section provides a brief account of the linguistic turn in composition during the 1950s. During this period, composition embraced linguistic theories of language and its explanatory power to help teachers and students define and practice style. Specifically, linguistics offered a technical vocabulary for talking about style that teachers found lacking in prior conversations. Several sections after that are devoted to theories and pedagogies of style by Francis Christensen, Winston Weathers, Martha Kolln, and Joseph Williams. These approaches all draw from linguistics and grammar to explain aspects of style.

Linguistics and Style in Rhetoric and Composition

Linguistics, Noam Chomsky's transformational grammar (TG) in particular, gave rhetoric and composition a useful set of terms for analyzing style and teaching it to students. Stylistic grammars that emerged starting in the 1970s rely on the language of TG. Before TG, articles on style in composition journals demonstrated a murky, fragmentary approach to its theory and pedagogy. They offered idiosyncratic ideas for assignments with little in the way of analysis, terminology, or method. Moreover, they accepted prescriptive grammar despite efforts by linguists as far back as the 1880s to demonstrate the ever-shifting values of usage (i.e., what counts as "acceptable" changes over time).[29] Charles Fries, also influential in the evolution of second-language writing at the University of Michigan, made concerted endeavors to inform college writing teachers about linguistics and descriptive grammar as an alternative to prescriptivism and mechanical correctness. The National Council of Teachers of English (NCTE)

---

29. Connors' essay in *The Territory of Language*, recollected in his *Selected Essays*, outlines several decades worth of linguistic research that never had much influence on writing instruction. These theorists include Thomas Lounsbury, Brander Matthews, and George P. Krapp, who went so far as to state that "in order to have a language become fixed, it is first necessary that those who speak it should become dead" (qtd. in Connors, *Selected Essays* 127).

published Fries's book, *English Grammar*, in 1940 with the intent of spreading linguistic knowledge; unfortunately, to little effect.

One *College English* article illustrates the approach to style before linguistics was accepted by the field. Written by plain-style proponent Rudolf Flesch, the article suggests assigning students sets of words to compose into sentences to illustrate "the great variety of expressions possible in stating even the simplest idea" (22). The notion echoes Cicero, Quintilian, and Erasmus without reference to the classical tradition. Flesch had already published books on readability in writing, such as *The Way to Write* (1946) and *The Art of Readable Writing* (1949), and he would publish *The Art of Plain Talk* in 1962, promoting what Francis Christensen later criticized as "The Flesch Doctrine," for its reductive insistence on plain style, simple words, and short sentences.[30] Another composition article from this decade describes classroom exercises in which students calculate the sentence length and types in their compositions to discover, as the author tells his students, that "You have a style of your own" (Rivenburgh 75).

Such microanalysis precedes workshops in which students read their in-class writings to each other, and then made suggestions for improvement in sentence variety that included combining shorter sentences and introducing clauses. Beneath these exercises lies a belief that "[a]s a student progresses toward adulthood he should write longer sentences and more of the complex type; he should vary his sentence patterns," although "[t]hrough carelessness and laziness . . . most college freshmen have got into a rut" (Rivenburgh 75). Although none of these authors cite classical treatises, they follow Roman prejudices in equating eloquence with virtue and flatness with moral vices such as "laziness." This trend changes after the publication of several books, including Fries's second attempt, titled *The Structure of English* (1952), Donald Lloyd and Harry Warfel's *American English in Its Cultural Setting* (1956), Harold Whitehall's *Structural Essentials of English* (1956), and Noam Chomsky's *Syntax and Structure* (1957), after which point composition scholars openly considered the merits of structural linguistics and TG for pedagogical purposes.

Briefly defined, a transformational grammar describes language through sentence positions that consist of different arrangements of

---

30. Interestingly, Flesch's 1949 book was re-published in 1996 by Collins, and was given a new title: *The Classic Guide to Better Writing: Step-by-Step Techniques and Exercises to Write Simply, Clearly, and Correctly*.

noun phrases, verb phrases, auxiliaries, and modals. For the first time, TG offered a unitary system of tree branches that parsed sentences into syntactically meaningful units. Sentence positionality is responsible for the infinite generative power of the English language, as speakers combine simple kernel sentences such as "The aardvark is eating" and "The aardvark is happy" in a seemingly infinite variety of ways. Sentence positionality and kernels later served as key ideas behind the sentence-combining movement of the 1970s, as well as rhetorical grammar (see Kolln and Micciche). It is essentially the same idea behind Erasmus's notion of *copia*, illustrated through hundreds of variations on the simple sentence, "Your letter pleased me greatly."

A number of books exist that distill Chomsky's theory for writing teachers while still doing justice to the complexity of TG. One of the earliest is Owen Thomas's *Transformational Grammar and the Teacher of English* (1965). Thomas notes the insufficiency of prevailing pedagogies addressing grammar and style, stating that they

> are based almost exclusively on the models of the eighteenth century English grammarians. They are largely prescriptive, and their "explanations" of such things as agreement and the passive voice are based upon an intuitive perception of the structure of English. (11)

While recognizing that writing teachers do not need to teach TG itself, Thomas maintains that teachers "have not made use of all the devices that modern scholarship offers us," and "have been content merely to preserve the traditional" (17).

Linguistic approaches to style and grammar appeared with increasing regularity in the 1960s. The linguistic approach was a refreshing alternative to those described earlier, not only because they offered a more precise terminology, but also because they did *not* fall into the trap of prescriptivism. Archibald Hill recognizes the socially-contingent dimension of style and "correctness" as shifting between discursive contexts. As an example, a school boy's language may be too casual for class, but passes as "correct enough" with "playmates." Hill even describes Standard English as inappropriate in some workplace environments, where one must communicate with speakers in different registers and dialects. From this view, phrases in student papers commonly perceived as incorrect actually involve the use of different linguistic registers. Telling students these phrases are "wrong" ignores other socio-linguistic spaces outside the classroom, and treats language in a vacuum.

The linguistic turn in rhetoric and composition also revealed the subjective nature of literary approaches to style. Linguist Eljenholm Nichols criticized writing instructors for their lack of rigorous terminology and specificity in analyzing written works, stating that "contemporary linguistic methodology . . . provide[s] important data for a definition of style, that subject on which English teachers are wont to wax eloquent" (261). Terms such as "limpid, flowing, sonorous, staccato, lyric, epic . . . may do well enough to label a reader's overall impression of a given style, but they do not really describe the stylistic features that produce the impression" (261). Nichols turns to syntax and constituent elements such as sentence position and the prevalence of conjunctions and appositives. Louis T. Milic echoes this critique when referring to the vague adjectives used by literary scholars to describe style. Milic labels the overuse of such terms a "Rhetoric of Metaphysics" (129) that contains "no method beyond the method of impressionistic description and a vague use of rhetoric" to analyze the various styles of authors (124). For Milic, the solution to this problem lies in "the study of style . . . by rigorous means derived from linguistics and the quantitative sciences," a source of knowledge that "seems to be the inevitable direction such work must take" (126). Here, Milic anticipates the emergence of stylistics, a sub-discipline of linguistics that became popular in the 1960s and 1970s, faded in 1980s, and then regained some prominence as a discipline, especially in Britain.

Arguments for more rigorous approaches to style continued with articles by Richard Ohmann, Martin Steinmann, and Seymour Chatman. In a 1967 *CCC* article, Chatman wrestles with definitions of style offered by prior scholars, and eventually settles on a linguistic one that takes into account the "personal idiosyncrasy of expression by which we recognize a writer" (72), a definition he elaborates on as a "pattern of choosable recurrents, the idiosyncratic selection of features he makes from the language's reservoir over and above the features it requires for its ordinary function" (75). Chatman supports this definition with a linguistic analysis of writers such as Samuel Johnson.

Some literary stylists responded with vehemence against linguists, as evidenced in an article by A. M. Tibbetts, who saw linguistics and stylistics as relying too much on "a manufactured, non-human language, which is rather like trying to explain the beauty of a woman's face by using calipers, a slide rule, and a book of logarithms" (634). Tibbetts's remarks directly implicate Richard Ohmann's "Literature as Sentences," published at the outset of his editorship of *College English* in 1966, in which Ohmann directly acknowledges the influence of Chomsky in his analysis of a sentence in James Joyce's story "Araby." Ohmann also published work that attempted to usher stylistics into rhetoric and composition, though it proved unsuccessful after a devastating (and amusing) critique of its methods by Stanley Fish in an essay titled "What is Stylistics and Why are People Saying Such Terrible Things About it?," and essay that was eventually collected in Fish's now-canonical *Is There a Text in This Class?* Debates on stylistics are explored in the next chapter, but for now. it is sufficient to understand stylistics as the application of linguistics to the analysis of prose, with influences from Chomskian grammar.

Tibbetts's remarks do not mention stylistics as a discipline, but they do contest this linguistic, empirical method of rhetorical research offered by Steinman and Ohmann, whom Tibbetts sees as ignoring the "great writers and rhetors" of prior ages and their pedagogical models based on "practice and imitation" (634). Steinmann and Ohmann responded to Tibbetts. Steinmann answers that reservations to linguistic study of language seem to

> belong to a depressingly large class of English teachers who believe their intuitions to be a leased wire to the World of Being enabling them to pronounce easily, authoritatively, and finally on all human questions, factual and moral; who, therefore, believe systematic pursuit of knowledge of any "fully human affair" to be either unnecessary, impossible, or immoral and fear that this "scientism" will . . . discredit their mystery . . . . Are Aristotle's "forensic," epideictic," and "enthymeme" folk terms? Quintilian's "metaplasm," "schematisim," and "trope?" Are they part of a manufactured, non-human language? (635)

Ohmann responds in a similar manner, observing that Tibbetts's view obviously "prefers appreciation to analysis," though one "does not explain without analysis," and therefore needs "the best analytic tools available" (635). This debate between classical, literary, and linguistic approaches to style continues through the 1960s, and ultimately shifts the discourse of teachers and scholars toward a view of style as depending on instruction in grammar, but not as a series of prescriptions and rules, as seen in the New Curriculum developed by Harvard. Linguistic frameworks for style promote knowledge of grammar to enhance a students' awareness of options when composing a text, as well as sensitivity to the effects that construction and organization of phrases and clauses could have on readers.

Over time, a linguistic conception of style that uses the explanatory and analytical power of grammar had considerable impact on rhetoric and composition regarding the ways that style was conceived and taught. The turn toward linguistics and its grammatical terminology laid the foundation for pedagogies such as Christenson rhetoric, sentence-combining, alternate style, and rhetorical grammar. These approaches, explored in the next three sections, all share a mission to educate students about the implications of grammatical decisions for their writing styles.

Christensen's Rhetoric

Francis Christensen's contributions to style include the essays "A Generative Rhetoric of the Sentence" in *CCC* in 1963, and "A Generative Rhetoric of the Paragraph" in *CCC* in 1965, both of which are collected in the six-essay volume, *Notes Toward a New Rhetoric* (1967). Despite similarities, Christensen distinguishes his approach from that of TG, declaring that "It is not derived from generative grammar; I used it before I ever heard of Chomsky" (2). Christensen resists the linguistic approach that relies on combining kernel sentences. Instead, the key to an effective style lies in the "cumulative sentence" in which modifiers advance the "main clause" through addition (5). For Christensen, sentences and paragraphs move from general levels to specific ones. Sentence cohesion can be achieved by ensuring smooth movement between these levels of generality and specificity.

Christensen's pedagogy is articulated most thoroughly in *A New Rhetoric*, where he contests the "Flesch doctrine" (xvi), referring to Rudolf Flesch's advocacy of plain writing, simple words, and short sentences.[31] Due to scholars such as Flesch, "we have no effective way to teach sentence improvement" (xv), he argues, based on his dissatisfac-

---

31. Rudolf Flesh recommends the plainest writing possible for college writers in works such as "Let's Face the Facts about Writing" (*College English*, 1950), and his books, *The Art of Readable Writing* (1949, *The Art of Plain Talk* (1946), *and The Way to Write* (1949).

tion with "chapters on the sentence in our handbooks and rhetorics [that] all adduce the rhetorical classification of sentences as loose, balanced, and periodic," and so constitute "some of our worst perversions of style" (xv). As an alternative, Christensen offers four principles of sentence and paragraph movement: addition, direction of movement, levels of generality, and texture (6–9). These are explained in the first chapter, and the rest of the book is dedicated to writing exercises and exemplary passages drawn from literary works. The principle of addition refers to the expansion of simple sentences by tacking on free-modifying clauses. This core principle leads to the second principle that sentences should be cumulative, moving rightward, as opposed to periodic sentences with clauses stacked in front of the main clause. Christensen's third principle holds that as sentences and paragraphs progress, they become more specific and concrete. Finally, the principle of texture refers to variation. By varying the length of phrases and sentences, writers keep readers from falling into a set pattern as they read, and thus pay less attention to content.

Christensen's rhetoric received as much criticism as praise. Some who adapted his ideas include Robert Beaugrande, who sought to mesh his rhetoric with Milic's theory of style to form a "generative stylistics" that would give students "the ability to go beyond the typical use of language toward the development of an individual style, to move . . . toward a set of registers to serve special goals, and to expand the options offered by the English language" (246). Despite a handful of adaptations, criticism almost immediately overshadowed Christensen's generative rhetoric. Whereas Christensen maintained that stylistic innovation could spur reflection and revision at a more global level, the discipline never fully accepted the idea. David Stevens epitomizes such reservations when he states that style is generative "only in a secondary (not to say unimportant) way—as, to use a crude analogy, a storeroom of wood-working tools might be generative by its affecting and serving a wood-craftsman in ways that would result in his making a knick-knack or a cabinet" (174). James Britton refers to Christensen's pedagogy as a series of rote exercises without context and a substantive theoretical foundation. Tom Pace interprets this criticism in *Refiguring Prose Style*: "What most of these critiques assume . . . is that learning to write eloquent and interesting sentences and paragraphs is somehow antithetical to learning to express ideas effectively" (22).

One problem with Christenson's approach may not lie in the above criticisms. Rather, Christenson's oversight may have been his dismissal of other syntactic structures, given his resistance to TG. It is true that the cumulative sentence is a powerful tool for writers, but it cannot be the only tool. Other stylistic grammars by Kolln and Williams treat grammar and its rhetorical effects more comprehensively, and they discuss a variety of sentence schemes inclusive of cumulative sentences, but not limited to them. While Christensen may have contributed to stylistic studies by showing the generative power of free-modifying phrases, teachers should be cautious of accepting his work at face value if it means the exclusion of other frameworks.

Winston Weathers and Alternate Style

Winston Weathers is another important, though largely forgotten, scholar who proposed a dynamic stylistic pedagogy. Weathers published three books: *Copy and Compose*, *A New Strategy of Style*, and *Alternative Style: Options in Composition*. These books build off of Weathers's central argument expressed in the 1980 *CCC* article, "Teaching Style: A Possible Anatomy," in which he calls on teachers to prove the relevance of style to students by showing them concrete strategies for negotiating rules in different rhetorical situations. As Tom Pace points out, "Weathers follows much of the same ideas about imitation that Corbett learned from the classical rhetoricians and that Erasmus encouraged students in the sixteenth century to practice" (17). Weathers offers a pedagogy of imitation that is dialogic in approach. Pace summarizes alternative style as follows: "The more styles students experiment with, Weathers argues, the more able they are to resist dominant structures of language and use language more democratically" (17).

In *Alternative Style*, Weathers grounds his pedagogy in a theory of Grammar A and Grammar B. Grammar A functions as the conventional rules students are expected to learn, and is akin to Patrick Hartwell's Grammar 4 (or school grammar), a series of exhortations about the proper use of mechanics and punctuation. When teachers correct students for beginning sentences with conjunctions or producing comma splices and run-on sentences, they promote Grammar A. By contrast, Grammar B is

> a mature and alternate . . . style used by competent writers and offering students of writing a well-tested set of options that, added to the traditional grammar of style, will give them a much more flexible voice, a much greater communication capacity, a much greater opportunity to put into effective language all the things they have to say. (8)

Grammar B is similar to Hartwell's category of stylistic grammars that use the descriptive language of linguistics (TG) to help writers understand their options. Writers may not be consciously thinking about Grammar B as they write, but it helps to practice and imitate patterns of language until they become natural—something they do not have to think about.

Like Christensen rhetoric, Weathers's work has also been marginalized. None of his books are currently in print, and they are difficult to find. In an interview with Wendy Bishop in 1996, Weathers recounts an anecdote illustrative of the contempt for his ideas and the larger turn away from style during the 1980s. Invited to give a keynote at the 1982 CCCC in San Francisco, Weathers ultimately spoke to a miniscule audience—a fraction of the average turnout at such an address:

> It was, in effect, boycotted . . . . Alas, though the conference attendance was large, I gave the address to about fifty people—in a vast, cavernous Hyatt Regency ballroom that would have held a thousand. It was obvious that that title of the address, or my reputation perhaps, had led vast numbers of people to stay away. (79)

Weathers's alternate style is a progressive one that echoes Bakhtin's work on dialogism, heteroglossia, and double-voicing. If Grammar A is the conception of language as rule-governed and static, it is one of the centripetal forces that seek to standardize language and make it coherent. If Grammar B is the alternative, having the tendency to disrupt standard practices in light of individual circumstances, then it is one of the centrifugal forces of language that work against conformity and standardization, maintaining diversity. Grammar A is authoritative, often shutting down a writer's confidence in writing him or herself into a discourse. Grammar B is more open, inviting writers to participate and appropriate conventions and principles for themselves.

Wendy Bishop's edited collection, *Elements of an Alternate Style*, includes a number of essays influenced by Weathers's pedagogy that advocate a more creative style in academic writing. One fairly representative essay of the collection is Elizabeth Rankin's "It's Not Just Mumbo Jumbo," an essay that discusses less conventional writing assignments modeled on a class she completed as an undergraduate on the eighteenth century novel. As Rankin says, "One assignment in that class was to write a new chapter for the novel *Tristram Shandy*, a chapter that would show, through imitation, an understanding of and appreciation for the innovative formal aspects of that work" (72). Rankin offers her own students a range of possibilities that include such experimental academic essays. In the book's appendix, "Responding to, Evaluating, and Grading Alternate Style," Bishop advises teachers to construct evaluation criteria for these types of assignments based on a student's ability to transition between styles, take risks, and reflect on stylistic decisions in cover letters to the instructor (176). Bishop's appendix includes samples of such guidelines as well as grading options. These materials may be helpful to teachers interested in addressing alternate style in the classroom.

Sentence-Combining Pedagogies

Sentence-combining pedagogies of the 1970s adapted TG grammar and Christensen rhetoric by devising assignment sequences in which students were given lists of short sentences and then asked to combine them into longer ones using subordinating and coordinating clauses. A 1983 *CCC* essay by Ross Winterowd traces the evolution of sentence-combining from Christensen to Donald Bateman and Frank Zidonis's *The Effect of Study of Transformational Grammar on the Writing of Ninth and Tenth Graders* (1966), through John Mellon's *Transformational Sentence-Combining* (1969), to Frank O'Hare's *Sentence-Combining: Improving Student Writing Without Formal Grammar Instruction* (1973). Winterowd then explains the often-overlooked theoretical foundation of sentence-combining within transformational grammar:

> early in life people acquire an almost total *competence* in their native language: a reservoir of potential that may or may not be realized in *performance* . . . sentence combining exercises give students access to the tacit knowledge in their reservoir of competence and thus allow them to develop *technique* [through which] they are able to switch registers and thus create chords that are, to them, unique. (83)

Winterowd points out a second major theoretical input from the distinction in transformational grammar between deep and surface structures that enables the understanding of roughly equivalent meaning from many variations. Someone can express roughly the same idea in one sentence, or in several. Winterowd attempts to inaugurate a new method for instruction in style that he calls "pedagogical stylistics," instruction based on research in linguistics, literature, and psychology. Although stylistics had been a discipline since Roman Jakobson's time, as discussed in Chapter 7, it had yet to fully catch on as a research method or pedagogy in the US.

Sentence-combining pedagogies were largely effective in helping students acquire technique, though they also fell out of favor due to the rise of post-process theories, specifically the social-epistemic approaches to rhetoric and writing advocated by James Berlin, David Bartholomae, and Patricia Bizzell during the 1980s that stressed writing as a social act, therefore teaching aspects of writing such as style less explicitly and more as matter of adapting to different discourse communities. For example, David Bartholomae's "Inventing the University" analyzes the language choices of first-year writing students, but without the explicit focus on rhetorical devices or syntax that seemed acontextual to social epistemics. Bartholomae emphasizes students' attempts to appropriate or "invent" for themselves the discourse conventions of academia, based on their perceptions of it. A social-epistemic pedagogy therefore attunes students to the socially-constructed nature of academic writing, rather than its formal features. However, contemporary stylisticians have argued that the discursive elements of academic writing manifest in these very formal traits, meriting attention.[32]

In a synthesis of more than four thousand articles on sentence-combining and writing instruction, Robert Connors acknowledges the empirical success of these pedagogies, as does James D. Williams in his contribution to *Concepts in Composition*. These studies include those notable to college writing teachers, such as Combs (1977); Daiker, Kerek, and Morenberg (1978); and Howie (1979). A cogent retrospective on sentence-combining pedagogies appears in A. Suresh

---

32. Ironically, among the scores of articles on sentence-combing, there exists a practical, how-to article in a 1981 issue of *CCC*, co-written by James Berlin, whose later book, *Rhetoric and Reality*, would usher in social-epistemic rhetorics and contribute to the marginalization of sentence-level scholarship.

Canagarajah's *Critical Academic Writing and Multilingual Students*, in which he indicates that "teachers who use sentence combining have to be mindful of its limitations" because it "sometimes encourages the misleading notion that the essay is generated by stringing one sentence with another to produce extended texts" (58). Like most contemporary theorists, Canagarajah maintains the importance of "larger discoursal and rhetorical processes that account for [an essay's] coherence," and cautions teachers that writers "who have syntactic fluency don't necessarily display complexity or effectiveness in their writing" (58). Thus, it is not necessarily that sentence-combining pedagogies themselves were preoccupied with form, but that they were (and are) easily misappropriated.

Sentence-combining and Christensen rhetoric were synthesized by at least one scholar, William Stull, whose textbook, *Combining and Creating*, shows the influence of TG as well as Christensen's generative rhetoric. *Combining and Creating* prompts students to combine sets of short sentences using different parts of speech, such as coordinating connectives (Chapter 2) and relative and subordinate clauses (Chapter 3 and Chapter 4). The rest of the book stresses the importance of the cumulative sentence, drawing directly on Christensen's four elements of effective style—addition, direction of movement, levels of structure, and texture (108–116). Following Christensen, Stull introduces students to a range of different types of free modifiers (e.g., prepositional, verbal, appositive, and absolute phrases), and provides exercises using them to combine short sentences.

Rhetorical Grammar

The past several sections have shown how different pedagogical approaches employed the descriptive grammar used by linguists for teaching writing. These sections also noted how social epistemic theories and pedagogies that arose during the 1980s faulted stylistic approaches for their preoccupation with formal, rather than contextual and discursive, aspects of writing. Rhetorical grammar serves as a response to this critique—a term coined by Martha Kolln in the 1980s, and revived by Laura Micciche in her 2004 article "Making The Case for Rhetorical Grammar." Micciche argues that "The grammatical choices we make—including pronoun use, active or passive constructions, and sentence patterns—represent relations between writers and the world" while expressing our attitude toward a given subject (719).

Rhetorical grammar is the study and practice of how language options have different effects for different audiences. For Micciche, "To shift the structure of a sentence alters the meaning of that sentence, as definitely and inflexibly as the position of a camera alters the meaning of the object photographed" (721). The ideas behind rhetorical grammar are now commonplace for stylisticians, and they appear to reconcile social-epistemic and stylistic frameworks.

Despite its unpopularity, rhetorical grammar rests on the ubiquity of grammar. As Micciche concedes, "In composition studies, grammar instruction is unquestionably unfashionable . . . frequently associated with 'low skills' courses that stigmatize and alienate poor writers while reproducing their status as disenfranchised" (716). It is precisely this negative perception that rhetorical grammar contests. Anticipating Micciche's stance, Martha Kolln challenges the growing suspicion about grammar and style in her 1981 *CCC* article, "Closing the Books on Alchemy," published in a special issue devoted to issues of language study that includes Joseph Williams's "The Phenomenology of Error." Acknowledging widespread attention to the Braddock Report of 1963 on the ineffectualness of grammar, Kolln critiques the methods and parameters of rhetorical grammar. She asks:

> What do [the authors] mean by "formal grammar"? Do they mean memorizing rules and definitions? Diagramming and parsing sentences? Or does "formal grammar" simply refer to an organized subject in the curriculum? And certainly they would have asked another, related question: If formal grammar has a negative effect, is there an alternative that might have a positive one? (139–140)[33]

For Kolln, grammar is always present in writing classrooms. Thus, the question is, "Do we acknowledge its presence and its importance?" (150). Sentence-combining pedagogies illustrate her point well, such as

---

33. Kolln turns to Henry C. Meckel's "Research on Teaching Composition," published in the *Handbook of Research on Teaching*. The study makes more reserved claims about grammar instruction, namely that "More research is needed on the kind of grammatical knowledge that may reasonably be expected to transfer to writing," and that "teachers cannot safely rely on textbooks used in schools but must depend on the expert opinion of linguists based on modern studies of the usage and structure of the language" (qtd. in Kolln 140–141).

Frank O'Hare's *Sentence-Combining: Improving Student Writing without Formal Grammar Instruction* and Daiker, Kerek, and Morenberg's *The Writer's Options* (2007), both of which work on the premise that students can improve their style without explicit attention to "the study of grammar, traditional or transformational" (O'Hare 30). As Kolln points out, sentence-combining pedagogues discuss the same structures of language as do linguists, but simply choose to label them "who statements" rather than "clause modifiers" (149). The argument laid out here informs the textbook that Kolln later produces, *Rhetorical Grammar*, now in its sixth edition (discussed in Chapter 8).

Rhetorical notions of grammar reposition commonplace attitudes about style, such as clarity, as situational and audience-based. In 1981, Rosemary L. Hake and Joseph M. Williams published the *College English* article, "Style and Its Consequences," finding that writing teachers do not always reward students for writing in a plainer, more active style. In fact, their study finds that high school and college teachers tended to rate student essays higher for using nominal sentences (sentences that focus on noun phrases) that are harder to read than verbal ones (sentences that focus on strong, active verbs). According to Hake and Williams's study, "graders overwhelmingly preferred the nominal version of each essay over its paired verbal version"; moreover, the preference was so strong that "it appears to have influenced their discursive judgments about other, more general components of the essay" (437). Their results challenged the dominant ideology that certain grammatical structures always led to a reader's perception of if the writing as well-written.[34] In 1981, Williams also published "The Phenomenology of Error," showing that even conservative writers often break their own stylistic rules—usually unconsciously, and without anyone noticing. Williams's own deliberate "errors" confront readers with the fact that many stylistic rules are the particular, eccentric preferences of writers, codified in handbooks and passively accepted. Williams's textbook, co-authored with Greg Colomb, titled *Style: Lessons in Clarity and Grace*, takes a rhetorical approach to clarity and

---

34. Two comments in the article raised questions about its assumptions and methods (Secor 1982; Yearwood 1983), with persuasive responses to each by Hake and Williams.

economy of style still evident in the current edition. It is explored in more detail in Chapter 8.[35]

Rhetorical grammar may never appeal to every teacher, but it is clearly different from acontextual approaches to grammar that value correctness. Approaching style through grammar requires the acquisition of a technical terminology, but one that is not so different from catalogues of tropes and schemes. In fact, many of the classical dimensions of style can be explained grammatically—especially schemes such as parallelism and antithesis, as these depend on knowledge of clauses. Writers may be able to develop a sophisticated style on their own, through arduous trial and effort, but rhetorical grammar endeavors to give writers a language in which to think about their styles critically at every point of their drafting process. As the next chapter shows, even scholars who contest the conforming pressure of Standard English, promoting linguistic diversity and heterogeneity in its place, use descriptive grammar to account for the choices writers make when deviating from language norms.

---

35. In a somewhat skeptical review of the textbook in a 1983 issue of *CCC*, Ian Pringle wonders whether any approach to style based on principles of clarity and efficiency, even linguistically-based and well-articulated, should be taught to freshmen, or whether they are best saved for upper-level writing classes or even education beyond college.

6 Frontiers of Style in Rhetoric and Composition

A number of specialized areas in the discipline have expanded our conceptions of what writing is and does. As such, they can also expand our knowledge of style and its relevance. Work in language difference challenges the dominance of written Standard English, and therefore destabilizes the idea of style as simply adhering to or departing from norms. Likewise, feminist accounts of writing and rhetoric recuperate alternative styles and argue for their place in traditional academic writing. Work in genre studies and Writing Across the Curriculum (WAC) shows the variations of style different disciplines and the importance of understanding how different discourse communities shape different stylistic conventions. Finally, work in digital rhetoric and multimodality broadens our understanding of writing as a textual, printed-based practice to engage its imbrications in a range of new genres and also in visual and aural forms of argument. Research in these digital and multimodal genres ushers forth new frameworks for style and stylistic possibilities for composing across genres and mediums.

This chapter synthesizes work over the past several decades, and states their implications for researching and teaching style as a wide range of options for engineering effective and engaging discourse—options that draw on the stylistic resources of multiple Englishes, languages, genres, mediums, and modes of communication. Discussion of these areas helps flesh out exactly what it means to think of style in relation to norms, and to promote style as making linguistic decisions not simply within one variety of English or set of conventions, but across many. The first section of this chapter shows that even students who we see as monolingual can benefit from a greater awareness of how the Standard English they speak is constantly under the influence of other languages, dialects, and registers—and therefore express an openness to non-standard codes as resources for stylistic experimentation.

Language Difference, Linguistic Diversity, and Style

Scholarship on language difference does not always use the term style explicitly, but it often addresses the struggles of linguistically-diverse students to preserve their own voices in the face of pressures toward linguistic conformity. A progressive theory and pedagogy of style encourages students to write their voices into the language of the academy, making academic style itself more diverse and dynamic. We can think of language difference as modifying the idea of style as deviation from a norm. Recent work by authors such as Min-Zhan Lu, Bruce Horner, and Suresh Canagarajah encourage teachers to recognize deviation itself *as* a norm of language practices. In this sense, there is always a stylistic component to writing, a choice, and a degree of agency—even in sameness.

Basic writers in particular form a diverse student population that needs an approach to style that values the languages and dialects they bring into the academy. Their styles of writing are often the most at odds with the demands of Standard English and academic writing. Rhetoric and composition has evolved to better meet their educational needs and is, in fact, challenging conventional thinking about the academic styles by which writing teachers judge their linguistic performance. The current conception of basic writers can be traced back to the landmark book *Errors and Expectations*, in which Mina Shaughnessy performs error analysis on student texts to illustrate their attempts at reasoning through conflicting codes and conventions. Shaughnessy's book garnered national attention and shifted scholarly discourse away from the correctness model of the early twentieth century. Shaughnessy revealed the logic behind students' error patterns, dislodging the prevalent perception of them as arbitrary and random.

Shaughnessy's lasting contribution to basic writers was to propose that they are not simply "bad students," but are writers trying to make decisions about discourse conventions of which they had incomplete knowledge. Although her pedagogy focuses on the acquisition of Standard English and academic writing, she nonetheless maintains that style varies among different codes and conventions, "none of which is inferior to others but none of which, also can substitute for the others" (121). Unlike later work on basic writers, Shaughnessy's book does not explicitly treat the other dialects of students as a stylistic resource for their writing. Laura Gray-Rosendale has historicized Shaughnessy's work on this issue, performing a close reading of *Errors and Expectations* to show latent though intentional gestures toward dialogic and poststructural theories of language that were, in her era, still new and not widely accepted. Gray-Rosendale concludes that Shaughnessy herself may have been less inclined to accept the dominance of Standard English and academic writing than her book reveals.

Regardless, teachers may learn from Shaughnessy that "errors," whether mechanical or stylistic, are not all arbitrary or random. Errors often reveal a great deal about a writer's struggle to reconcile competing rules and conventions. A teacher's job is not to condemn students for such problems, but to give them the knowledge they need to make more informed decisions. Subsequent generations of basic writing scholars, such as Min-Zhan Lu and Bruce Horner, advanced pedagogies that place more value on students' other languages and dialects, showing that error does not simply need to be "corrected," but instead discussed in a way that does not presume the superiority of dominant conventions. We might say that Shaughnessy ultimately wanted students' styles to conform to academic discourse, whereas later generations of basic writing scholars called into question the privileged position of academic style itself.

Not all writing teachers openly accept the idea of equality among dialects and registers of English, and so resist them as stylistic resources. A minority of scholarship has, for some time, maintained the superiority of Standard English and academic discourse. Such positions on style are fundamentally about the mastery of standard forms of English and, as such, they are more allied with the dominant public on style than any counterpublics within composition. According to them, only when a writer can demonstrate a superior command of conventions can that writer be permitted to exercise linguistic choice. As one of these conservative voices, Thomas J. Farrell's 1983 *CCC* article, "IQ and Standard English," sought in a more controversial way to reveal the cognitive deficiencies of Black English by analyzing what he argued were incomplete or fragmentary rules owing to its ostensibly oral nature. Those who make such arguments not only reject the dialogic and heteroglossic qualities of language, but also close off dialect and vernacular as a stylistic resource for students. Farrell's view was challenged by a range of compositionists, including Karen Greenberg, Patrick Hartwell, Margaret Himley, and R. E. Stratton. Work by linguists such as Geneva Smitherman also further undermined the view of non-standard Englishes as deficient through in-depth analysis of their rule structures.

Nevertheless, opposition to such work survived in basic writing scholarship for several more years, evidenced by Donald Lazere's partial defense of Farrell in a 1991 *Journal of Basic Writing* article, "Orality, Literacy, and Standard English." Lazere questions the transferability of dialectology to composition, since its foundational research by William Labov centered on oral rather than written discourse (89). In Lazere's view, the misappropriation of sociolinguistics fails to disprove the position that "restriction to Black English or any other oral language with a nonscholastic vocabulary and syntax *is* an impediment to successfully dealing with the complexities of college-level reading and writing" (93). Lazere goes on to argue, following Lisa Delpit in "Skills and Other Dilemmas of a Black Educator," that language minority students often desire to learn standard codes "in addition to, not instead of—[other] dialect[s]," and often "dislike the current neglect of standard form and mechanics" (94).

Arguments such as Lazere's frame the question as either-or, rather than both-and. No scholarship on language difference argues that we teach only one form of discourse. Work promoting language difference asserts that linguistically-diverse students perform better when they learn to see many types of discourse influencing each other. We learn about and teach many styles, and understand style itself as drawing from many types of language. Academic style possesses norms, but we do not have to adhere to all of them all of the time; when we choose to deviate, we might do so because we want to incorporate rules and conventions from vernaculars or dialects that seem better-suited to the ideas we want to express.

During the early 1990s, scholarship emerged that problematized the idea of "error" itself and emphasized the porous nature of academic discourse styles, subverting prior tendencies to think of Standard English and academic writing as unitary or monolithic. This work sought a redefinition of error away from an arbitrary or even reasoned failure to meet norms to a paradigm of linguistic negotiation and hybridity. This definition of linguistic difference builds on definitions of style as deviation from a norm, as articulated by Paul Butler and in line with stylistic studies in general. In a 2000 *Journal of Basic Writing* (*JBW*) article, Patricia Bizzel argues that

> the field of basic writing instruction still relies upon relatively obvious features of student writing as a basis for sorting students.... We quickly read a large number of writing samples ... and the ones exhibiting many features of non-Standard English and non-academic discourse forms lands their authors in basic writing classes, where their writing "problems" are supposed to be addressed. (5)

Bizzell's arguments in "Hybrid Academic Discourses" and "Basic Writing and the Issue of Correctness" look to then-recent publications by Keith Gilyard, Geneva Smitherman, and Victor Villanueva as examples of "'hybrid' forms of academic discourse" that draw on multiple codes in order to produce a unique academic style particular to that author's negotiation of conventions, including Standard English (5-6). In the second of these essays, Bizzell extends her initial idea of hybridity to recognize "the profound cultural mixing that has already occurred in the United States" (9).[36] In effect, Bizzell argues that academic discourse has always been a blend of other styles.[37] Although addressing basic writing, Bizzell's combustion of the "myth" of a static academic discourse anticipates a similar case by Matsuda, who exposes the "myth of linguistic homogeneity" and introduces the metaphor of linguistic quarantine to describe composition practices toward second-language writers in particular ("Myth" 637).

The mixed discourse approach is complemented by Min-Zhan Lu and Bruce Horner, who published a number of articles questioning the definition of "error" and the extent to which students should be expected to simply concede to academic discourse and written Standard English. They envisioned the possibility of students' language prac-

---

36. It should be noted that Bizzell's notion of hybridity itself, as she acknowledges, is borrowed from Deepika Bahri's scholarship and its diffusion throughout postcolonial studies.

37. In a 2002 issue of *JBW*, Judith Hebb situates hybridity within the orality-literacy binary, arguing that "When viewed along a continuum in which characteristics of oral and written—home and school-languages are mixed, a place will be opened up for hybrid academic discourse that serve both writer and reader" (28).

tices altering written Standard English itself, and called on teachers to attend to the contingent nature of language, along with the fallibility inherent in the idea of language governed by static, inflexible rules. Canagarajah describes this development:

> Teachers of critical writing should consider grammar usage as an activity not of reproducing the rule-governed system but of negotiating from a range of available options to represent the writers' identities, values, and interests in the most satisfactory manner possible. What we may reject as an error may be motivated by serious concerns of values and identity for the student. Rather than imposing uniform usage unilaterally, and thus suppressing the creativity of the student . . . it is important to negotiate the best way in which his or her purpose may be achieved through the range of grammatical resources available. (52)

One of Lu's most cited works from this era includes "Politics of Style in the Contact Zone," in which she proposes stylistic interpretation as an alternative to error analysis in order to understand the linguistic motivations for a student's use of the phrase "can able to." For Lu, Shaughnessy's model is insufficient for discovering the cultural, gendered, and socio-political dimensions of the perceived deviation, as the "error" is only an error insomuch as it departs from standard usage. A typical solution is to advise the student to use either "can" or "is able to." However, this solution misses the student's struggle to account for the difference between the physical ability to do something and the cultural norms that one must confront for permission to do that thing. (In the student's case, her Malaysian family had discouraged her from attending college, despite her intelligence.) For Lu, the student makes a stylistic decision that is carefully negotiated, not a confused error.

More recently, research on language difference embraced deviation and difference as a new norm, and offered the term *translingualism* to describe new discursive practices in which global language users blend codes in their writing. Vershawn Young and Suresh Canagarajah both refer to these new textual practices as "code-meshing." Young first used this term in a 2006 *CCC* article, "Your Average Nigga," in which he discusses African-American students as "natural code meshers" who blend academic discourse with dialect and vernacular

(697).[38] Young contrasts code-meshing with the concepts of code-switching and linguistic pluralism, a phrase used by Keith Gilyard. For Young, these approaches to language difference accept that White English Vernacular, Standard English, and Black English Vernacular are mutually exclusive and that they should be used in different social settings. Code-meshing undermines this opposition, along with "the erroneous assumption that the codes that compose BEV and WEV are so incompatible and unmixable because they're so radically different" (Young 706).

Young elaborates on the term code-meshing in a 2009 *JAC* article as "the blending and concurrent use of American English dialects in formal, discursive products, such as political speeches, student papers, and media interviews" (51). The argument for code-meshing rests on sociolinguistic evidence (discussed in Chapter 7) that Standard English is not different from other varieties of English, but is itself composed of multiple dialects. It is not possible to separate varieties of English in the ways that textbooks and dominant teaching practices attempt, making arbitrary distinctions between appropriate and inappropriate discourse strategies. For Young, code-meshing recognizes the continuum of compatible varieties of English, and it even "has the potential to enlarge our national vocabulary [and] multiply the range of available rhetorical styles" (65). Students already tend to appropriate and mix words, phrases, and syntax as they develop their own unique styles of speaking. It stands to reason that academic writing may need to adapt to this linguistic reality. If students see academic writing as open to stylistic innovation, perhaps they might not dread it.

Canagarajah makes similar arguments in favor of code-meshing in his *College English* essay, "Toward a Writing Pedagogy of Shuttling Between Languages," and the *CCC* essay, "The Place of World Englishes in Composition." In the *College English* piece, Canagarajah declares that teachers "must consider [textual deviation] as a strategic and creative choice by the author to attain his or her rhetorical objectives" rather than as "unconscious error" (591). To illustrate, Canagarajah analyzes the research articles of a Tamil scholar who makes different stylistic decisions that deviate from American academic expectations

---

38. Young references an earlier work by Kermit Campbell, titled "Real Niggaz," that does not use the term code-meshing but that, nonetheless, analyzes African-American students' diverse linguistic performances in academic papers, blending slang and formal Standard English.

(e.g., thesis statement, citation, sign-posting, rigid linear structure) in order to craft a civic ethos that is more suited to his readership. The analysis of a second article, published years before, shows that the scholar is capable of producing more standard conventions when needed. Canagarajah hopes to convince teachers that "students should not treat rules and conventions as a given," but instead "think of texts and discourses as changing and changeable" (603). The *College English* article asserts this same point with a more specific argument in favor of allowing students to use their various Englishes in final drafts of papers. This approach contrasts with one described by Peter Elbow in "Vernacular Literacies" to allow deviations in drafts for the sake of editing them into Standard English later on. For Canagarajah, students need more affirmation, because "To use a language without any personal engagement, even for temporary and utilitarian reasons, is to mimic not speak" (597).[39]

From a translingual lens, promoting style must see other Englishes as part of students' stylistic repertoire, as something they can practice using in their writing as they develop their voices.[40] A 2011 *College English* article by Lu, Horner, Trimbur, and Royster builds on prior work in language difference to affirm the recent understanding of difference as a norm. A later 2011 *CCC* article by Horner, Lu, Donahue, and NeCamp makes a similar case for seeing language practices—such as code-switching, code-mixing, code-meshing, and borrowing—as increasingly normal for speakers of multiple languages. Min-Zhan Lu and Bruce Horner's 2013 *College English* article reveals the presence of agency and difference even in the ostensible production of sameness or adherence to stylistic conventions ("Translingual Literacy"). All three articles define deviation as a normal practice, suggesting that there is no longer a "Standard English" or a set of stylistic conventions to begin with—if there ever truly was such a standard outside of rulebooks. Whether style is defined as deviation and difference,

---

39. A variety of positions on the appreciation of linguistically diverse teaching and writing appears in two recent collections: *Code-Meshing as World English* (contains original essays) and *Cross-Language Relations in Composition* (contains some original and many previously-published articles).

40. Canagarajah's 2013 book, *Translingual Practice*, makes the case for this new term given the monolingual historical contexts in which terms describing bilingualism or multilingualism emerged.

risk, voice, or as the manipulation of grammar, it has always involved informed decision-making between ever-shifting rhetorical situations.

Seeing style as translingual benefits all students, including those seen as either monolingual or less linguistically-diverse because they grew up speaking the prestige variety of English. Globalization is already immersing us in linguistic environments, where we encounter varieties of languages far different from what we are familiar with. We can help students see such global difference as exciting, and potentially transformative to the ways they write and speak. If teachers initiate students into a tradition of style that values the development of an authentic voice, and because voice itself is polyphonic (composed of many other voices), then teachers are preparing students to appropriate and adapt new words, phrases, and structures of language for their own writing. The wider their repertoire, the closer students approach the classical ideals of copiousness and facility with language—the difference from classical style being that their copiousness is drawn from many cultures.

Style, Voice, and Feedback in Second Language Writing

The last section showed that style changes at a conceptual level when working with linguistically diverse student populations, because writers negotiate multiple varieties of the same language as well as altogether different languages. Scholarship on second language writing approaches this student population somewhat differently from work in rhetoric and composition on language difference. Second language (L2) writing research focuses more on differences across languages rather than varieties of a single language, and it tends to treat style equally as a matter of divergence from and accommodation to norms. Multilingual writers are directly confronted with the reality that different languages afford different possibilities for stylistic expression. They also contend with the fact that different languages give rise to different conventions and attitudes about what constitutes an effective style.

Ilona Leki, Alister Cumming, and Tony Silva give a brief overview of stylistic issues in L2 writing in *A Synthesis of Research on Second Language Writing in English*, covering articles on the subject appearing over the past two decades. This body of research suggests that second language writers perform style differently from native speakers, in ways that go overlooked. For instance, Indrasuta ("Narrative Styles") and also Stalker and Stalker ("Acquisition"), observe no intentional use of stylistic patterns from the target language, although second language students may transfer stylistic conventions from their first language in a way that readers fail to recognize. Reynolds ("Linguistic Correlates") notes a tendency among second language writers to rely on what appear as more objective and less overt characteristics of style, rather than overt metaphor or turns of phrase. A comparison of first language (L1) to L2 writers by Maier in 1992 concluded that L2 writers struggle to negotiate between registers such as casual, personal, formal, and professional because of their unfamiliarity with different text types in the target language. The last article by McCarthey, Guo, and Cummins indicate that second language writers adapt to the stylistic expectations of local language use, rather than developing what we might call a "unique voice" or a set of language choices that mark them as distinct. In short, the conservative view is that second language writers try to blend in rather than stand out.

This research asks us to question the idea of style as always a clear deviation from a set of norms, or voice as individual expression. Many L2 writing scholars have explored the use of voice in multilingual contexts, and the *Journal of Second Language Writing* devoted a special issue to the topic in 2001—inspired by an earlier article by Vai Ramanathan and Dwight Atkinson on the problematic use of voice in L2 writing contexts ("Individualism" 45). In this issue, Paul Matsuda makes a compelling case for approaching voice with L2 students not as the expression of a true self, but rather as the acquisition of and experimentation with linguistic resources writers encounter ("Voice in Japanese" 35). Moreover, Matsuda advises teachers to resist stereotypes of other cultures as somehow resistant to voice and style, illustrating particular discursive features of Japanese that permit the expression of voice, including "variations in personal pronouns and sentence-final particles. . . which simply are not available in English" (40).[41] Matsuda's point converges with research cited above that L2 writers have a sense of voice and style, though it may be difficult to convey in English

---

41. Matsuda defines "sentence-final particles" as "morphemes that can be attached at the end of a sentence" to stress different meanings (48). For example, particles such as *desu* and *masu* mark formality (48). These particles are part of discursive conventions, but can be negotiated and re-purposed as well.

and often manifests in subtle negotiations of norms rather than obvious deviations. If we use such lenses of voice and style, we might find relevant textual features in any multilingual writer. Likewise, an understanding of voice as the result of stylistic and grammatical choices could help teachers and scholars better identify the presence of style in multilingual writers, and to help them "develop a personal repertoire of discursive features and strategies in the [target] language," including conventions and norms, so that they can learn to negotiate different sets of conventions while still remaining intelligible (51). Understanding the nuances of voice and style in multilingual contexts may also generate interesting perspectives in the debate on error feedback in second language writing.

College writing teachers unused to working with multilingual students may take for granted that they should provide a substantial amount of feedback on grammar and style on students' papers. They may see corrective feedback as unproblematic. Richard Haswell's minimal marking paradigm has become standard practice in training instructors, and many of us may accept the negotiation models outlined by Horner and Lu, and echoed by Kevin J. Porter in "A Pedagogy of Charity." If there is occasional discussion on the issue in major composition journals, then there is more uncertainty on the same issue among scholars in ESL and second language writing. Theories of Second Language Acquisition (SLA) may explain the difference, as discussed by Charlene Polio in a 2012 issue of *the Journal of Second Language Writing*, while also helping to specify certain conditions under which feedback can be effective. Because some college L2 students are still acquiring English, their teachers express much more caution about the impact error feedback can have on the development of their language abilities. Stephen Krashen originally argues that language monitoring and learning (e.g., attention to rules, line-editing) can interfere with the natural acquisition of a language.

Contemporary debates about error feedback began as early as 1996, when J. Truscott advocated abolishing corrective feedback on L2 student writing for reasons similar to Braddock, and later to Hillocks: that it often inhibits writing development, causing more long-term harm than good. Over the next ten years, studies appeared regularly in the *Journal of Second Language Writing* and in various monographs and collections, each conducting studies that reached different conclusions about the value of feedback. A 2008 article by J. Bitchener, appearing in a special issue of the *Journal of Second Language Writing* on error, sketches the decade-long debate before describing a study in which four groups of students were given different types of feedback. Students who received direct, corrective feedback on their use of articles ("a" and "the") showed measurable improvement between a pre-test, immediate post-test, and delayed post-test, over and above a group receiving no corrective feedback. However, Truscott and A. Y. Hsu's study in the same issue contests such conclusions, and the authors provide their own study, in which two groups of students show little to no difference in error reduction on subsequent assignments after one group received direct, corrective feedback, while the other did not. Although the group receiving corrective feedback revised that specific paper, the students did not transfer any "lessons" from one paper to the next any differently than the non-feedback group. Truscott's point is that L2 students progress at their own rate regarding mechanical errors.

Ken Hyland and Fiona Hyland explore prior studies on this matter in detail in their 2006 edited collection, *Feedback in Second Language Writing*, as does Dana Ferris in an accessible introduction to L2 writing in *Teaching College Writing to Diverse Student Populations*. Christina Casanave's *Controversies in Second Language* also contains a chapter overviewing the debate on error feedback. Among them all is a consensus that marking every error in L2 writing has an undesirable effect on student writing that discourages them from the necessary linguistic experimentation—including explorations of style and voice—that accompanies learning. This basic view informs Lu and Horner's pedagogy, and is also echoed in Suresh Canagarajah's *Critical Academic Writing for Multilingual Students*, an early book that presents a premise similar to the language-shuttling model, specifically aimed at Teaching English as a Second Language (TESOL) scholars and L2 writing teachers.

As discussed in the introduction to this book, many teachers still correct stylistic and grammatical "errors" in student writing, and feel pressure to grade writing harshly for repeated mistakes. A common misconception is that multilingual students only learn to write well with a great deal of explicit feedback. Research shows that teachers need to provide feedback on a continuum, according to individual student's needs—there is no "one size fits all" approach to providing stylistic and grammatical feedback the writing of language learners. Based on current research, perhaps the best course of action is to provide some feedback on these issues for multilingual writers, with knowledge that style itself is socially determined, that too much correction can stymie the development of their voices, and that language learners may fare as well or better if they are simply allowed to try on the voices and styles they encounter in their reading.

Women's Writing and Breaking Rules

Prescriptivism in style has also undergone criticism by feminist, poststructuralist theorists. Similar to hybrid academic writing, Helene Cixous's *ecriture feminine* (women's writing) promotes styles of writing resistant to conventions of linearity, cohesion, objectivity, skepticism, clarity, and directness deriving from masculine assumptions and perceptions of reality. Women's writing enables escape from these phallogocentric constraints, and allows writers to search for alternate modes or styles of expression. It flouts rules from the level of punctuation and syntax to that of textual structure and organization (e.g., thesis statements, paragraphs). Cixous maintains that as a practice, women's writing is not exclusive of gender, and she refers to James Joyce and Jean Genet as examples of male writers who are not bound by phallogocentric discourse. One may also think of Gertrude Stein and—more recently—Gloria Anzaldua and Adrienne Rich as exemplars of feminist styles. A similar position is also made by Virginia Woolf, who made the case for a feminine sentence "of a more elastic fiber than the old, capable of stretching to the extreme, of suspending the frailest particles, of enveloping the vaguest shapes" (204-205).

Julia Kristeva indicates poetry and poetic discourse as another linguistic code that provides alternative routes beyond phallogocentric discourse. Moreover, Kristeva's theories of feminine *juissance*, the semiotic, and *chora* outline ways of expression that employ silence and non-linguistic signs, including pre-verbal utterances. Kristeva reveals the limits of language and the need for such non-linguistic modes of meaning production—ones that have been marginalized and excluded by masculine forms. The act of transposition enables movement through and between these different languages and non-verbal modes of expression. Despite such gestures toward a feminine style, feminist scholars have also expressed ambivalence about defining it. Both Cixous and Kristeva resisted the idea of codifying alternative practices, as it would go against the very idea of operating outside of traditional language boundaries. Sara Mills provides a thorough account of these issues in her book *Feminist Stylistics,* including a synthesis of research over gendered differences in spoken discourse. (Also see the section on stylistics in the next chapter).

The movements and shifts narrated in previous chapters defined eloquence in style according to a specific set of standards that most often originate from a privileged class of male theorists. These prescriptions have enjoyed a status as "the" way to write stylistically engaging prose. Such principles still dominate public discussions about style and the way it should be taught in higher education. A major part of Paul Butler, T. R. Johnson, and Tom Pace's project has involved reviving style to counteract these phallogocentric norms. Mainly, they point to the sophists as counter-models, and these parallel those of feminist poststructuralists. Susan Jarratt's work on the sophists directly connects early, pre-classical Greece and Cixous's theory of women's writing. Jarratt shows how both rhetorics employ paradox, non-linearity, emotional utterance, and experimentation in discourse that are discouraged under Aristotelian conceptions of style. In a 1985 issue of *College English*, Pamela J. Annas applies feminist theories of language to the teaching of style in college writing classes, specifically a course designed for women writers that encourages risk-taking over conformity to the correctness model. Citing Robin Lakoff's early work in feminist linguistics, Annas describes women writers as bilingual, as always navigating conventions in the ways that Kristeva describes via the act of transposition.

Feminist rhetorical pedagogies, such as Krista Ratcliffe's rhetorical listening, point our attention to how language choices that are often identified with style reflect larger cultural logics, specifically ones that either mask or reveal race and gender. Ratcliffe defines style as "(un)conscious sentence-level choices with both personal and cultural functions" that students can "learn to recognize and employ," along with the "tropological functions of language" (143). By "tropological," Ratcliffe means how individuals use terms like "white" and "female" or "feminine" to figuratively represent various objects, behaviors, and attitudes. Ratcliffe asks students "to think about how whiteness as a trope plays out in US culture, including in their lives" (144). These cultural items that "white" often acts as a trope for include golf, classical music, suburban living, and polo shirts (150). When people describe these as "white," they make a stylistic choice that reveals cultural attitudes.

Ratcliffe's use of style as an analytical tool for observing racial and gender issues differs from the standard conception of style as means of expression, further highlighting the inventive potential of style. Here, style becomes epistemological, a way of learning about culture and grounding discussions about language in tangible experiences. The appendix to *Rhetorical Listening* includes part of a syllabus in which students spend several weeks analyzing works stylistically (including use of tropes, figures, and schemes such as parallelism) in order to uncover how the author constructs and defines gender and race. The authors assigned include Lillian Smith, James Baldwin, Nikki Giovanni, Adrienne Rich, and Greg Jay. The book provides specific lesson plans for each week, listing steps for pairing up students to explore how each author's language use might indicate constructions of race and gender (175–186).

This basic idea seems to drive research on sentence-level issues in hybrid academic writing, language difference, creative writing, and postcolonialism. Scholarly and pedagogical projects on style can benefit from considering such stylistic experimentation, as theorized by feminist poststructuralists, but also as manifested in iconoclastic writers and poets. Namely, feminist theories of style can help us think radically and question the explicit and invisible rules that might hinder our abilities to convey non-phallogoentric ideas. These theories can liberate our thinking and foster greater creativity in terms of what style can do, how we can teach it, and how we might engage in public debates about style and grammar.

STYLE, ACADEMIC GENRES, AND WRITING ACROSS THE CURRICULUM (WAC)

The last chapter examined style from the perspectives of voice, grammar, and language difference. All of these understandings of style must take genre into account as informing a writer's language choices. Work by Amy Devitt, Charles Bazerman, Anis Bawarshi, Mary Jo Reiff, and Carolyn Miller define genre as a set of socially-determined conventions that arise over time as writers produce similar types of texts in typified situations. There are numerous examples of genres in our academic and everyday lives. We see clearly defined genres in novels, plays, and poems. We may not always be aware of magazine ads, billboards, and public service announcements as genres, but all of these examples function as types of texts that are governed by conventions that have formed over time. These conventions include expectations about style. We expect precise meter and rhythm in certain types of poetry, for instance, and commercial slogans often use the stylistic features of poetry to sell products.

Recently, composition scholars have connected genre with style and grammar. In the collection, *The Centrality of Style*, Zak Lancaster brings together studies in genre theory with aspects of rhetorical grammar and systemic functional linguistics (SFL)—in particular, SFL's attention to field (an author's topic), tenor (the relationship of writer and speaker), and mode (language choices). Lancaster uses this framework for "tracking the choices that speakers/writers make to encode attitudinal meanings, adjust degrees of evaluations, and contract and expand" their discourse (201). These choices contribute to a sense of the writer's style and, over time, they accumulate across authors and texts to shape a genre's stylistic expectations. A functional approach to style hinges on considering writers' choices, with special attention paid to the possible grammatical alternatives available for expressing their ideas. Paul Butler's earlier 2007 *Rhetoric Review* article, "Style in the Diaspora of Composition Studies," links genre and style, proposing a more complicated understanding of pronouns in a stylistic analysis of a syllabus discussed by Anis Bawarshi in *Genre and the Invention of the Writer*. Like Lancaster, Butler also employs SFL, drawing on Halliday and Hasan's definition of pronouns in *Cohesion in English* in order to show how a teacher switches between "you," "I," and "we" at various points to construct a power dynamic between instructor and pupil. At times, "we" invokes the spirit of cooperation, while other times signaling a more hierarchical "we," in which the students are a dependent but not equal part of the pronoun. When a teacher uses "I," it is often to assert the power of the instructor rather than responsibility. In turn, "you" often indicates the responsibilities or duties of students. Butler hypothesizes that such a dynamic could be reversed if the teacher included more discussion of how "you" (the students) will evaluate "I" (the instructor).

Butler's specific example of the difference between exophoric (situational) and endophoric (textual) references in pronouns may not do complete justice to his point. In fact, it is possible to summarize his analysis (as I have done) with a simpler understanding of pronouns, as performed originally by Bawarshi. Butler's extended analysis of the same syllabus and its pronouns shows that style is a matter of concern to genre theorists. Readers may more readily accept Butler's argument that being clearer about when we use style can help bring together the various areas of composition, and begin to provide us with a set of common terms—even if those terms include words like exophoric.

Mikhail Bakhtin focuses on the relationship between genre and style in "The Problem of Speech Genres." Bakhtin stresses attention to stylistics as part of genre analysis, and maintains that any kind of stylistics must be "based on a constant awareness of the generic nature of language styles" (66). He goes on to declare, "Where there is style there is genre. The transfer of style from one genre to another not only alters the way a style sounds, under conditions of a genre unnatural to it, but also violates or renews the given genre" (66). Two other major points Bakhtin makes are that different genres tolerate different levels of stylistic innovation, and that the problems otherwise skilled writers and speakers encounter can derive partly from their lack of familiarity with new genres.

From Bakhtin's theory of genre and style, we can produce four main points: Genre can determine a writer's style, the extent to which a writer is able to craft a distinctive voice, and even affect a writer's ability to compose. Finally, styles can cross genres in ways that change both the text and the genre itself. These ideas apply directly to discussions of style in academic writing in this chapter. When scholars on language difference argue in favor of altering the norms of academic discourse by encouraging students' use of non-standard dialects and vernaculars, they forward the fourth idea from Bakhtin's work on speech genres. They also recognize that students' performance issues may not derive from their language inability in general, but from their struggles to construct a definitive voice for themselves within a strange and intimidating genre that is referred to broadly as academic discourse, one that favors the stylistic traits of Standard English or White English Vernacular (WEV).

Some research on academic writing and WAC attends to the relationship between genre and style. As Charles Bazerman et al. state in their book, *Reference Guide to Writing Across the Curriculum*, WAC "opens up the issue of differences of situations and styles and forms of presentation," with careful attention to how writing is conceived of and imparted within particular programs and departments (88). An especially good example is Susan Peck MacDonald's analysis of the stylistic conventions in psychology, history, and literary studies in *Professional Academic Writing in the Humanities and Social Sciences*. MacDonald argues that larger goals and agendas in these respective fields determine preferences in sentence structure and word choice. Chapters 6 and 7 of her book focus on the tendency of writers in psychology to use an epistemic, synoptic style of writing that enables them to make broad, synthetic claims about trends across individual studies. This style is characterized by a greater tolerance for nominalization, passive voice, and abstractions. By contrast, historical and literary academics tend to use active constructions and more particular words that psychologists would find subjective or overly personal. MacDonald recommends making the relationship between purpose and style clearer to college writing students, even in first-year courses, and exposing them to research in their majors that they can then analyze and imitate in order to understand more fully how style shifts between fields.

Greg Myers's essays, "Stories and Styles in Two Molecular Biology Articles," "The Pragmatics of Politeness in Scientific Journals" (*Applied Linguistics*, 1989), and "The Rhetoric of Irony in Academic Writing" (*Written Communication*, 1990) study the stylistic traits of scientific writing that promote the appearance of consensus, irony, and deference in an effort to subdue contention and conflict. Another important text to stylistic issues in WAC is Jack Selzer's 1993 edited collection, *Understanding Scientific Prose*. The collection includes approaches to textual analysis informed by linguistics and pragmatics. All of the work on style and genre in this section acknowledges that while we can attribute disciplinary conventions with particular styles, those styles are still contingent and emergent. A recent article by Andrea Olinger stresses this point in her discourse-based interviews of three scientific writers, showing how "distinctly individual knowledge permeates disciplinary writing and how that writing comes to be perceived as writing 'in the style of the discipline'" (473). The three writers interviewed in the study showed differences of opinion regarding what constituted an appropriate style in their field, and they even changed their own minds on such issues over time.

English for academic purposes and English for specific purposes have emerged as fields in which a great deal of work is done on the intersections between style, grammar, voice, and genre. Research appears in the *Journal of English for Specific Purposes* and the *Journal of English for Academic Purposes*—both present analyses of specific conceptual and stylistic aspects of academic discourse, as well as the use of such knowledge in the instruction of advanced second-language learners. Ken Hyland's 2000 book, *Disciplinary Discourses*, examines global and local structures, including linguistic features of academic prose at the sentence level. Hyland in particular has published a large body of work on stylistic strategies and their grammatical counterparts in academic writing, including hedging, boosting, and circumlocution. Academic genres and their connections with style are also explored in great depth in Anis Bawarshi and Mary Jo Reiff's 2010 *Genre: An Introduction to History, Theory, Research, and Pedagogy*.

Style, Digital Genres, and Multimodality

If Bakhtin had lived to see the Internet, perhaps he would have written "The Problem of Digital Genres." No digital stylistics has come about, per se, but some scholarship has begun identifying style as a point of inquiry in digital and multimodal writing. Much of what the last section posited about the relationship between style and genre applies to digital rhetoric, an area that studies how forms such as blogs, wikis, tweets, and text messages have undeniably impacted literacies and composing processes. Just as older genres such as the poem and various types of academic research have distinct stylistic expectations, so do these newer genres. As David Bolter and Richard Grusin explain in *Remediation*, in fact, these newer genres often remediate or alter older ones, appropriating many of their conventions (including stylistic preferences). For instance, email now serves many of the same rhetorical purposes as memos did a few decades ago. From Bolter and Grusin's work, we can extrapolate that as newer genres remediate older ones; they borrow and adapt stylistic traits. Consider that professional emails, much like memos, are defined at least partly via their tendency toward the plain style—literal language, formal diction, and short simple sentences.

Some genres constitute a more complicated remediation, such as the blog—a genre that certainly has a range of distinctive stylistic conventions. Carolyn Miller describes blogs as a kind of remediation and synthesis of earlier genres, ranging from the captain's log to the daily journal and to Renaissance-era commonplace books; yet, it is profoundly more public than any of these genres, owing to its appropriation of features from newspapers and websites. The paradox of the blog is that it is both personal and public, an observation by Miller that indirectly invites study from stylisticians.[42] Bloggers most often identify self-expression and disclosure as their primary rhetorical motives, but their audience ranges from personal friends and colleagues to complete strangers. Following Bakhtin's analysis of speech genres, we would agree that speakers already use different styles in different social, private, and professional situations. Blogs fuse these different situations into one, prompting writers to draw on different styles within a single string of text.

David Crystal makes a similar observation about the style of blogs in *Language and the Internet*. Here, Crystal describes the blog as a genre that invites use of oral linguistic styles in writing, nearly rejoicing that it is "as close to the way writers talk as it is possible to get," adding that "the style drives a coach and horses through everything we would be told in the grammatical tradition of the past 250 years about how we should write" (244–45). In other words, bloggers often feel freed from the stylistic constraints of Standard English, and are more willing to experiment and take risks. Part of the reason for the presence of vernacular speech in blogs lies in their lack of editorial oversight. As Crystal explains, bloggers have complete control over their content, and can publish whatever they want to say (sometimes to their detriment). There are no copyeditors and censors to please. For Crystal, this situation is unprecedented. No prior genres have granted individual writers such direct, immediate access to such a wide range of audiences.

According to Jason Tougaw, the generic flexibility of the blog can help students learn to develop a voice that blends personal and academic writing. Recognizing the openness of blogs to multiple discourse styles, including the vernacular, Tougaw assigns his writing students at Princeton to write about their dreams in a series of blogs. He analyzes a few entries in "Dream Bloggers Invent the University" for their blends of academic and personal voice. One student often begins sentences with statements of uncertainty, before sliding into more confident, academic interpretations of his dreams. Phrases used

---

42. In *Rhetorical Style*, Jeanne Fahnestock briefly discusses blogs as a prime example of double-voicing, given that they continually synthesize information and discourse from other sources.

by the student include "Several things I can guess are," "I think," "I am also not sure about," and "Maybe." These phrases contribute to a more personal, inquisitive voice when they preface such statements as "it is an embodiment of my suppressed refusal of normal surroundings around me or mere product of my imagination" (qtd. in Tougaw 256). By close-reading passages from these blogs for their personal-academic voices, Tougaw shows how students implicitly harness the interactive and liberating features of blogs to craft voices for the discussion and analysis of dreams that do not merely mimic the conventions of the academy. Stylisticians such as Butler and Holcomb may resist Tougaw's preference for research on voice over a more rigorous stylistic analysis, given Butler's critique of Bawarshi outlined in the last section. However, his reading of students' voices as facilitated by blogging is an important step toward creating a stylistics of digital genres.

The features of blogs identified by Miller, Crystal, and Tougaw apply in other digital genres, especially social media sites like Facebook and Twitter. Social media users often employ vernacular speech patterns, and appear more willing to write in personal voices or styles that disrupt the norms of Standard English. Such sites serve as a significant catalyst of stylistic innovation and experimentation. The conventions of Facebook encourage users to express opinions or insights in memorable ways, and the fact that we compete for attention with hundreds of other friends prompts us to draw on our linguistic resources to craft the most interesting and memorable sentences we can.

The same premise drives activity on Twitter, in which the character limit functions as a further occasion to experiment with spelling, punctuation, and spontaneity in language in order to convey ideas and information in the most efficient but memorable manner possible. The 140 character limit forces users to employ creativity in conveying information, whether they are news flashes, anecdotes, or complaints.[43] As Chris Vognar writes for the *Dallas Morning-News*, "I've found that paring down my tweets has made my prose leaner. I chop out more adverbs than I used to" ("Twitter's Character Limit"). Vognar interviews a range of authors and poets who have used Twitter for literary purposes, and who praise its influence on their style. The memoirist and poet Mary Karr tweets lines from famous poets while meshing them with her own voice:

---

43. It is worth noting that William Carlos Williams's poem, "The Red Wheelbarrow," meets Twitter's character limit.

> Shelley on Keats, dead at 25: "Clasp with thy panting soul the pendulous earth." Like earth's a bauble swinging from a chain, keeping time.

Karr blends Shelley's voice with her own, and thus appropriates a line from his poetry as an utterance, while also navigating Twitter's character limit by drawing on at least three genres—the newspaper headline, the poem, and the casual remark. The statement "Shelley on Keats, dead at 25" plays on famous headlines such as "Ford to New York: Drop Dead," conveying, in just a few words, a complex set of relations between the poets Percy Shelley and John Keats. Karr then selects a representative line from Shelley that conveys the sentiment. She then integrates that line into her own metaphor by beginning the next sentence with the word "Like," smoothing over the period and forging a connection between these two utterances, making them virtually part of the same statement. Understanding short poems or meditations like Karr's through Twitter illustrates all the meaning one can create with 140 characters, and prompts analysis of a digital genre's remediation of other genres and mediums. Teachers may devote a class period or more to discussing these issues—including how a poem or a line from a novel changes meaning when taken up in another, digital genre.

In addition to fostering attentiveness to style, students can also use Twitter critically to examine how rhetorical ecologies and media converge in manageable ways. The tweet blends voices, genres, and styles, but also links pathways to other texts and spaces through hyperlinks, hashtags, and re-tweets. The hashtag, for example, enables users to quickly search and survey hundreds of tweets on the same topic. Typing "#Occupy" or "#Libya" into Twitter's search box generates pages of results that show how politicians, celebrities, and ordinary citizens worldwide who have shared information or opinions on the given topic, so long as they add a hashtag to the end of their tweet. Users can also gather information such as dates and times of posts, as well as how many times a post has been re-tweeted, as an indicator of audience reception. Studying aggregates of these tweets provides a snapshot of everyday, vernacular discourse.

Internet memes are also an interesting phenomenon to study from a stylistic perspective. As a cultural studies term, the "meme" was originally coined by Richard Dawkins, who borrowed the concept from evolutionary biology to describe the circulation of ideas, images, and phrases in popular culture. The emergence of the Internet meme "Philosoraptor" illustrates the blurred lines between "error" and stylistic innovation. The web series "Know Your Meme" attributes the first-known use of the term to a ten-year-old who posted on an educational website that "I like the philosoraptor because it spits an acidy type of substance in its victims' eyes . . . this dinosaur is da bomb."[44] A classical rhetorician might describe the invention of the word "philosoraptor" as a kind of *metaplasm*, specifically *antisthecon*, where a rhetor substitutes a syllable or letter for another to achieve an effect.

As a genre, meme generator sites impose a number of stylistic constraints and conventions that inform the rhetorical decisions of users—the spatial limitations of the image box and the precedent of prior meme captions. In the case of the "Philosoraptor" meme, all captions are expected to parody the conditional phrase structure of analytical philosophy, the "If p, then q" construction. For instance, in one caption, the Philosoraptor asks: "If 'pro' is the opposite of 'con,' then is progress the opposite of congress?" As another recent meme caption reads, "If guns don't kill people, people kill people, does that mean that toasters don't toast toast, toast toasts toast?" This caption promotes gun control through an ironic analogy with something mundane, one that also toys with language by using the same word as a subject, verb, and object. The unexpected repetition is all the more effective because it is memorable.

Many of the memes available through websites facilitate stylistic experimentation that is closely affiliated with code-meshing, as well as a similar linguistic act that linguists refer to as *calquing*, or "loan translations" of words and phrases from one linguistic code to another (Richardson 250). The "Crafty Interpreter" meme features captions in which users blend English, Russian, Spanish, Chinese, and French in order to make puns or to highlight and parody the difficulties of intercultural communication. The meme "Joseph Ducreux," a character based on a portrait artist from the court of King Louis XIV, serves a similar purpose. The character is explicitly described by *Memegenerator.net* as someone who "translates current sayings [often from vernacular dialects] into the verbiage of his time" by "rewording current slang, sayings, or catchphrases into ye olde speak" of the eighteenth century. When users caption this meme, they are code-meshing. The results may be humorous, but they are also socio-linguistically significant.

---

44. Technically, the child seems to mean dilophasaurus.

At first, memes may appear to possess only entertainment value. However, they fulfill a number of goals for bridging academic and vernacular styles. In my own teaching, I have introduced students to some basic principles of style, and then illustrated them through the Internet meme. Students work separately and in small groups to study the ways users adapt these memes for a variety of socio-political agendas. I encourage students to consider the relationship between content and stylistic aspects of the captions, how diction and figures of expression animate the messages expressed, and how the spatial dimensions of the macro image template have a bearing on these decisions. Students must often employ abbreviations and text-speak to fit their captions into the template. Finally, they compose short reflections on their language choices. Such use of style inspires creativity and generic inter-animation, bringing together many genres and modes of discourse.

The rise of new media has also led to conceptions of style beyond the idea of textual literacy as sufficient alone. Style has always possessed a visual component, as far back as Aristotle's discussion in *Poetics* of the purpose of style to make readers feel as if they are seeing what they read, accomplished through *enargeia*, or vivid language. The proliferation of digital genres and design choices pushes composers toward even deeper engagement with the multimodal elements of style. These new design choices necessitate reinventing frameworks for talking about style. In *The Centrality of Style*, Moe Folk proposes style as technical prowess, difference, and subservience regarding the manipulation of text and graphics for rhetorical effect. She also synthesizes multimodal rhetoric with classical style when analyzing a web text retelling of "Little Red Riding Hood" by a Swedish design student. Folk shows how classical devices such as synechdoche, metonymy, and metalepsis can operate visually as well as verbally. In the same way that words and phrases substitute for larger ideas, images serve a similar symbolic function. The design student employs visual metonymy and synechdoche when zooming in on Red Riding Hood's feet to indicate walking and when focusing on widened eyes and twitching noses to amplify emotions (Folk 223).

Richard Lanham and, later, Collin Gifford Brooke offer perhaps the most substantial alternatives to linguistic definitions of style. In *The Economics of Attention*, Lanham discusses digital media as prompting a kind of revolution in how we view language, looking *through* it (the conventional reading) but also *at* it for meaning, given the range of choices that graphic designers now enjoy regarding text font, color, size, spacing, and other manners of manipulating words in relationship to images. Words always possess a visual element, but Lanham argues that new media confronts us with this fact like never before. In *Lingua Fracta*, Brooke introduces the term *perspective* to Lanham's conception of style, defining it as "an emergent quality of a specific interaction among user, interface, and object(s), drawing on each without being reducible to any of those factors" (140). To illustrate, Brooke analyzes the interface of *World of Warcraft*, a popular online game that requires users to link the style of the interface itself with their gaming strategies. Users have to look "through" the action bars and status icons to feel immersed in the world of the game, but they also have to look "at" these displays to play the game. Furthermore, users also have the option of adjusting their perspective between more "first-person" views *through* the eyes of their characters, and more "third-person" views in which they can see their character move around the landscape.

An even more striking example might involve the recent phenomenon of the "selfie." Because social media sites now permit users to upload and manipulate their own photographs, they now experiment with style linguistically while also making decisions in the at/through/from continuum when they post images. Ostensibly, simple decisions such as whether or not to include oneself in a photo qualify as stylistic. In social media, uploading a self-portrait has become known as a "selfie," and it is not always as trivial as it sounds. Consider the stylistic decisions made by *Buzzfeed.com* writer Matt Stopera, who took a "selfie" with a lion to emphasize the cowardliness of hunter Melissa Bachman, who was banned from South Africa after she posed next to a lion she had stalked and killed: "Just to show you how incredibly difficult it is to hunt a lion . . . here's a selfie I took next to one" (2014).

Stopera's article fits into the genre of the photo-essay, and so we cannot account for its style simply by analyzing his language choices. Here, Brooke's at/through/from apparatus is helpful, pushing us to see how vital the "selfie" is to Stopera's verbal argument that, despite the stereotype of lions as ferocious animals, it would not be heroic or even difficult to shoot one with a modern rifle. Stopera made a stylistic decision to include himself in the photograph, his head unexpectedly jutting in sideways with a somewhat comical expression on his face. Even his use of the term "selfie" is as a stylistic choice meant to amplify the mutual attitude of nonchalance between people on safari and the lions who, at one point, lounge in the shade of Stopera's van. He invites readers to look *through* the medium of the photograph to see the lounging lion, but also *at* the photograph itself and his authorship of it. As such, the photograph not only provides visual evidence for his claim, but also influences the tone of the piece. It is the half-serious style of the "selfie" and its brief caption that mock Bachman more than any particular construction of words. Stopera's "selfie" epitomizes style as the management of language as well as visual perspective.

In *Toward a Composition Made Whole*, Jody Shipka articulates the need to think of composing as a practice that always integrates non-alphabetic modes, as teachers may forget such modes in their awe over new technologies. In these terms, a text is anything that produces meaning for an audience, and can be as simple as an overhead transparency or a set of instructions with accompanying diagrams. As one example, Shipka describes a dance designed and performed by a student named Muffie, who engages a wide range of modes and sign systems that include "*listening* to the song she had selected for the performance, *writing* out project notes, *drawing* up a solo chart, *watching* the classroom footage, and *reading* the in-class writings" (80). It is this navigation of different ways of producing meaning that Shipka highlights. Each decision to take up a new genre or mode, and its particular execution, ultimately constitutes a kind of stylistic decision that goes beyond the textual frameworks of grammar and classical rhetoric. Here, a new set of terms may be less important than an appreciation for how these discrete choices contribute to the larger rhetorical effect of the performance.[45] Shipka's pedagogy reflects similar mindsets in a range of composition textbooks, including Bartholomae and Petrosky's *Ways of Reading: Words and Images*, Wendy Hesford and Brenda Brueggemann's *Rhetorical Visions*, Lester Faigley's *Picturing Texts*, and Donald and Christine McQuade's *Seeing and Writing*.

---

45. Derek Mueller takes a similar approach in a 2012 *Kairos* article, explaining how his students transformed a three-paragraph passage of their choice through the use of digital genres such as the tweet, the web comic, imagtext triptych, or a conventional semantic analysis.

Style in digital rhetoric and multimodal composition is a matter of the interplay of genres and language; it is also the manipulation of modes that are not explicitly textual. Today, writers use multiple styles while moving through a number of genres, many of them digital. Increasingly, the stylistic decisions they make have visual dimensions that function as part of the rhetorical situation. As they navigate these spaces, writers cross-pollinate by using elements of each style in new situations, inevitably changing these genres as they compose. Some of these genres remediate older genres, just as email has adapted the rhetorical purposes and overall style of the memo and as the blog has pulled from a rich collection of antecedent genres. Each of these forms has its own linguistic and visual stylistics, some of them more flexible than others. Nonetheless, these genres and their constraints foster innovation, as we saw in the discussion of Mary Karr's tweet about Keats and Shelley. Understanding style in digital environments reinforces what this chapter asserts about the continual evolution and proliferation of style.

Conclusion

The last several chapters traced the major strands of thought regarding the role of style in rhetorical discourse and writing instruction. While rhetoric and composition may stand at odds with public conversations about writing and style, teachers and researchers can work with one another to form counterpublic discourses in which style is valued as more than the transmission of meaning. A dialogic conception of style that values polyvocality and the negotiation of norms is best-suited to help students learn to write well. Also, grammar does not have to pose a threat to a writer's sense of ingenuity or limit his or her linguistic resources if we place it in service of rhetoric. At this point, we should stop to review the major conceptions of language explored in the last three chapters, and summarize their implications for the study and teaching of style:

1. Linguistic theories of style tend to emphasize its structural qualities and focus on grammatical choices, as seen in the discussion of Williams, Kolln, and Christensen in Chapter 5.

2. Classical theories of style prioritize study of figures, schemes, the value of imitation, and the use of *progymnasmata*.

3. Dialogic theories of style define a writer's voice as a synthesis of other voices, and see style as multiplicitous.

4. Feminist theories of style, such as Cixous's and Kristeva's, advance women's ways of writing that resist and subvert dominant, patriarchal systems of meaning while inscribing linguistic choices with gendered qualities.

5. Sociolinguistic theories view style as a series of choices and identity performances made between languages and social languages (e.g., dialects, registers) that either accommodate or resist group norms.

At one point or another, most scholars of rhetoric and composition have drawn from these theories and the methodologies informing them to make claims about writing, or simply to write. These theories and methodologies do not work in opposition to one another. In fact, they overlap in many ways. The section on postmodern imitation and classical rhetoric observed commonalties between Bakhtin's theories and the classical tradition on writers' innate tendency to imitate and appropriate aspects of others' styles. Likewise, we can use the language of grammar to analyze the stylistic moves of any writer or speaker as they make language choices within and across varieties of English. We would characterize all of these theories as inventive, positioning style as an integral part of writing and vital to meaning, not as an ancillary or after-the-fact consideration of editing or polishing discourse once it has been fully formed. The next chapter presents different methods of research and how they have already begun informing theories of style. It also considers the potential of research in related fields to strengthen the approaches to style laid out here.

7 Researching Style: Methods in Rhetoric, Composition, and Related Disciplines

When researchers analyze patterns of language for their larger meanings, they are conducting stylistic analysis. One of the great but frustrating things about academia is that several names can exist for a similar activity across different disciplines. Thus, there are at least four different terms for the study of language patterns: stylistics, rhetorical analysis, discourse analysis, and genre analysis. Teachers and researchers in rhetoric and composition will likely recognize the term *rhetorical analysis*, but those who do not study style may be unfamiliar with the discipline of European stylistics or the method of discourse analysis, as it is mainly used by sociolinguists but is becoming increasingly popular in related disciplines.

This chapter briefly outlines how style is studied within rhetoric and composition, and explains how other approaches can strengthen our understanding of style and lead to innovations in research and teaching. In particular, this chapter describes how American stylistics faded during the 1970s, only to return within the last several years through work by Butler, Pace, Johnson, and other scholars discussed in the section on style's revival in Chapter 4. This chapter also builds on discussions of language difference started in Chapter 6, revealing its connections to areas such as sociolinguistics, dialectology, and world Englishes. The methods of research, and insights from these areas, help diversify style by outlining their study of language practices in other varieties of English across the US and worldwide.

RHETORIC AND COMPOSITION

Let us begin with approaches to style within rhetoric and composition. A variety of research methods exist here, as originally outlined in Gesa Kirsch and Patricia A. Sullivan's 1992 book, *Methods and*

Methodology in Composition Research. Research on style within the field draws on most, if not all, of the research methods identified in this book. Although twenty years old now, Kirsch and Sullivan's book is still largely accurate in terms of the methods of inquiry: theoretical and meta-theoretical (e.g., North, Miller, Sanchez, Dobrin), historical (e.g., Enoch, Gold, Connors, Crowley), feminist (e.g., Schell and Rawn, Ballif, Jarratt, Hawhee), and ethnographic (e.g., Rose, Carter, Brandt, and Sternglass). The rest of this section briefly explains how researchers approach style from these various standpoints.

Theoretical approaches to style make explicit assertions about its role in writing and rhetoric. In short, they offer a theory of style and then seek to explain its validity. Aristotle promotes a theory of style when he advises plain language with minimal use of metaphor and other figures, asserting that the plainest style is the most suitable to his view of language as representative of thought. If we agree with Aristotle's theory of language as a vessel for meaning, it follows that all language should be plain when attempting to convey information. Although the sophists did not advance an explicit theory of style, Chapter 2 of this book considers work by T. R. Johnson and Susan Jarratt, both of whom construct a theory of style from sophistic texts that oppose Aristotle's. When contemporary scholars such as Paul Butler and Catherine Prendergast advance a view of style as deviation from norms, they advance a theory of style as the expression of individuality that contrasts with those of most handbooks, including Strunk and White's, that theorize style as putting oneself in the background. Theoretical approaches to style often turn to histories, analysis of public discourse, or discussions of pedagogy to elaborate on their theories. For example, Chapter 6 describes how Canagarajah and Lu theorize style as the negotiation of linguistic difference, and then employ literary analysis of student texts as persuasive evidence.

An historical approach to style, as Chapter 2 illustrates, often focuses on interpretations of major figures, treatises, movements, documents, or institutions in a given time period. Historians interested in style ask questions about what educators of a given period say about style and its teaching, the role it played in actual educational practices, and what alternative views existed. Alternative historians seek out voices not represented in the classical tradition or in dominant histories. Such historians endeavor to recover styles and theories about style that are not contained in treatises—such as literary texts or other records. For example, an alternative historian would analyze poetry by Sappho and fragments of Aspasia to construct an implicit theory of style, or perhaps an enactment of style that subverts more dominant, masculine styles.

Histories of style can examine any time period. In many ways, Butler's work takes an historical approach by describing the "exodus" of style into several specializations within rhetoric and composition and, thus, its dissolution as a distinct form of research by itself. Robert Connors was nothing if not an historian, and his examination of late nineteenth an early twentieth century handbooks, textbooks, and other materials illustrate how style became associated with correctness and grammar at elite institutions such as Harvard. A more recent historical perspective on style appears in Tara Lockhart's 2012 *College English* essay, "The Shifting Rhetorics of Style." The article examines the evolution of Cleanth Brooks and Robert Penn Warren's treatment of style over several editions of their textbook, *Modern Rhetoric*, a book that ultimately seemed to "eschew style in ways that parallel broader trends in the field as it moves from the 1970s to the 1980s" (Lockhart 19). In addition to her analysis of all four editions of *Modern Rhetoric*, Lockhart also examines reviews of various editions of the textbook and correspondence between Brooks and Warren.

Historians focusing on the nineteenth and twentieth centuries often focus on archives and special collections housed at universities, as well as government agencies, professional organizations like NCTE, or non-profit organizations like the YMCA. Newspapers, manuals, transcripts, conference proceedings, or virtually any other record is of value to historians if it reveals contexts relevant to their projects. For anyone interested in pursuing these engaging issues, research begins with published or collected primary and secondary documents, and then proceeds to archival work, as described in Alexis Ramsey et al.'s collection *Working in the Archives*, as well as Kirsch and Rohan's *Beyond the Archives*.

Feminist approaches to style, also covered in Chapter 6, emphasize the use of language as a means to circumvent or disrupt dominant or phallocentric assumptions. Feminist scholars can take an historical approach, recovering texts from marginalized voices in a given historical period and showing how they push back against theories of style such as Aristotle's. They might also take a literary and/or theoretical approach like Cixous, writing in a style that deviates from prevalent attitudes about what is "acceptable" or "clear." Feminist approaches to style are especially known for their performative approach, advocating subversion of masculine styles, including admonitions by Strunk and White to be clear and concise, while also performing subversion through active deviation in their own writing. No doubt such methods have influenced work in other areas of our field, evidenced by writers such as Geneva Smitherman and Vershawn Young, who argue in favor of blended Englishes while blending the conventions of academic prose with AAVE. Feminist scholars can also advocate for pedagogies that encourage students to become more aware of how dominant conventions work to suppress individual expression through language choices, helping them discover means to write their ways through and beyond these dominant conventions.

No precise ethnography on writing styles has been published in rhetoric and composition; however, such a work is interesting to hypothesize. An ethnographic approach to style would seek to understand what students themselves think about it, and how it surfaces in their daily literate practices. Some central questions for an ethnography of style would ask to what extent writers' own attitudes and behaviors confirm, contradict, or question our current theories and pedagogies on this subject. Like Marilyn Sternglass in the ethnography, *Time to Know Them*, researchers might interview students or writers at various points over a single semester about their language choices as they move from classroom spaces to social and online ones.

The information students provide about differences and overlaps between style in their academic and social lives could illuminate how students negotiate the desire for expression with demands for clarity and adherence to a single set of standards. An example of the kind of information an ethnography of style could gather appears in Rebecca Lorimore Leonard's 2014 *College English* piece, "Multilingual Writing as Rhetorical Attunement." One multilingual writer Leonard interviewed, Alicia, describes her negotiation of stylistic preferences between Spanish and English:

> When I think of writing in Spanish in comparison to English, we were encouraged to use longer sentences because you sound more sophisticated and like you know what you're talking about. That was very interesting process switching to English because it's the complete opposite. Chop chop chop,

extra words extra words. No need. Where are your periods
and sentences? (241)

Alicia goes on to describe the emergence of her own multilingual stylistic aesthetic as she adjusts to shifting preferences between these two languages for shorter and longer sentences. Ultimately, when writing in English, Alicia balances the expectation for shorter sentences with her own tendency to write "a lot of sentences that could be three, four lines long," because "I like them that way. They make sense to me" (241). According to Leonard, Alicia and many other Spanish students in her study demonstrate a preference for "longer sentences, fewer periods, and more coordination," and believed it contributed to an intelligent, mature voice (241).

Interviews, field notes, and observations like those described above are the primary means by which ethnographic researchers gather information. Researchers would then interpret this data and explain its significance to current research and teaching methods about style. Ethnographers might also conduct more formal background research, seek records and transcripts from students' online activities, papers they write for various classes, and any other data that might help illuminate how they negotiate different language norms. Such basic methods are described in Wendy Bishop's book, *Ethnographic Writing Research*. Elizabeth Chiseri-Strater's chapter on ethnography in *Exploring Composition Studies* also outlines the primary methods and goals of ethnographic research, and references foundational texts such as Shirley Brice Heath's *Ways with Words*, Beverly Moss's *A Community Text Arises*, and Ellen Cushman's *The Struggle and the Tools*. As Chiseri-Strater describes, these main goals involve gathering information about aspects of literacy as they occur inside and outside classroom spaces.[46] To achieve such goals, ethnographies can target populations other than students—for the sake of learning more about the role of style in various workplaces, social spheres, and other extra-institutional contexts. Ethnographies by Moss and Cushman, as well as Deborah Brandt's work on literacy sponsors in *Literacy in American Lives*, and Graham Smart's exploration of workplace literacies in "Reinventing Expertise," provide examples of such spaces.

---

46. A recent turn toward critical ethnography, advocated by Stephen Brown and Sidney Dobrin in *Ethnography Unbound*, also calls for researchers to acknowledge their roles in these ethnographies and employ them in helping to contest or transform material conditions.

Quantitative methods have gained traction since admonitions from Richard Haswell, Richard Fulkerson, and Chris Anson, who all urgently pleaded in three separate articles for more replicable, aggregative, and data supported (RAD) research in rhetoric and composition. Such methods drive a good deal of research published in the journals *Written Communication, Journal of Writing Research,* and *Research in the Teaching of English.* A 2012 *CCC* article by Susan Lang and Craig Baehr advocates for using data-mining to support writing and writing program research as a way of strengthening our theoretical knowledge and intuitions gleaned from practitioner lore. A later section of this chapter explains the methods of corpus research, a particular type of data-mining used by sociolinguists to analyze stylistic elements of language use in a variety of settings. As the next sections show, quantitative methods often inform research in linguistics and sociolinguistics, producing findings that can—like the other methods described here—inform the ways in which rhetoric and composition scholars define, teach, and discuss style.

Stylistics

Stylistics involves the analysis and interpretation of literary and non-literary texts for the methods by which addressors communicate with addressees. Although stylistic analysis goes back to the classical era, the appeal to scientific terminology originated with Roman Jacobson's "Closing Statement: Linguistics and Poetics," presented at the Style in Language Conference of 1958. There, Jacobson urged attendees to draw on structural linguistics to move beyond the simplistic, subjective descriptions of prose in literary analysis. Many scholars publishing critiques of literary analysis in composition, such as Milic and Ohmann, became proponents of stylistics. The early project also involved M. A. K. Halliday, who used formal grammar to parse literary texts such as William Golding's *The Inheritors.*

Early stylistics followed the New Critical distinction between literary and non-literary texts, presuming form and content as inseparable in the latter, but not in the former. Moreover, literary texts possess an inherent style apart from readers' interpretations and expectations. The goal of early stylistics was to subject texts to mechanical analysis, producing statistical data on ratios of different syntactic structures.[47] Stylistics made a dramatic shift from this method as the result of three events: Derek Attridge's retrospective on Jacobson's closing statement, Stanley Fish's condemnation of stylistics, and Michael Toolan's partial redemption of stylistics in response to Fish. All three essays denied Jacobson's attempt to erase readers, taking issue with the tendency of Chomskian linguistics to ignore the socio-political dimensions of structures in language. Specifically, Fish alleges an over-reliance on generative grammar in the work of Ohmann and Halliday. Doing so was "predictable" (107) in Fish's view, because stylistics always privileged abstract structure over real-word context. Rather than dismiss stylistics altogether, Fish states an alternative: "In the kind of stylistics I propose, interpretive acts are what is being described; they, rather than verbal patterns arranging themselves in space, are the content of the analysis" (110).

In the introduction to *The Stylistics Reader*, Jean Jacques Weber observes that the discipline flailed slightly in the wake of Fish's critique, as many others followed. Rather than fade altogether, stylistics re-invented itself and ultimately accepted the role of readers in the formation of textual meaning and form, just as Fish encouraged. Thus, several areas of stylistics emerged that Weber uses to structure his anthology: formalist stylistics (analysis of high literature), functionalist stylistics (analysis of everyday texts), affective stylistics (focus on readers' response to stylistic moves), pedagogical stylistics (approaches to teaching style), pragmatic stylistics (style used in social situations), critical stylistics (the role of style in power dynamics), and feministic stylistics (the role of style in constructing gender).

In an *Introduction to Stylistics*, Peter Verdonk defines these areas succinctly and offers a view of style and its study as the "distinctive expression in language and the description of its purpose and effect" (4). Over the next hundred pages, Verdonk unpacks this definition by introducing fundamental terms, including internal foregrounding (the linguistic choices authors make to emphasize information), semantics (formal meaning), and pragmatics (contextual or social meaning). For contemporary stylisticians, any text—whether a road sign or a novel—contains internal and external factors that weigh on the au-

---

47. Ohmann published representative essays taking this approach, including "Speech Acts and the Definition of Literature," "Speech, Action, and Style," and "Instrumental Style: Notes on the Theory of Speech and Action."

thor's style. Semantics is concerned with textual and internal elements such as grammatical construction, sentence length, and use of stylistic devices. Pragmatics is concerned with contextual elements. Verdonk lists seven:

1. text type or genre;
2. topic, purpose, and function;
3. temporary and physical setting;
4. social, cultural, and historical setting;
5. identities, knowledge, emotions, etc.;
6. relationships between speaker and hearer or author and reader; and
7. associations with other text types. (19)

Moreover, pragmatic stylistics does not consider language as representational, as much as indicative and indexical. Language proceeds via *deixis*, or the process by which speakers and writers orient their addressees to aspects of place, time, and identity. One recent and well-known example of pragmatic approaches to style published after Verdonk's book is Norma Mendoza-Denton's 2005 book, *Homegirls*, a book that analyzes the style-shifting used by adolescent women in Latina youth gangs in Los Angeles. Mendoza-Denton demonstrates the various ways that linguistic choices contribute to her subjects' performance of identity, and also how socio-cultural circumstances determine those choices and identities.

All of these perspectives (e.g., linguistic, pragmatic, and literary) help stylisticians grapple with what Verdonk refers to as "the central issue that stylistics is concerned with: how far can we adduce textual evidence for a particular interpretation, and how far can we assign significance to particular textual features" (31). How stylisticians frame these questions, and what types of texts (genres) they interpret, depends on whether their readings are informed by literary stylistics, feminist stylistics, linguistic stylistics, or a combination thereof. Many of the terms and topics stylisticians draw on may seem familiar to readers, such as point of view, free indirect discourse, stream of consciousness, and interior monologue. These are but a few of the terms used to analyze the style of a particular discourse. A range of terms for stylistic analysis derive from rhetorical stylistics, going back to figures of thought and expression catalogued during the Roman era. Fahnestock and Bialostosky both show that figures of thought and expression in classical rhetoric describe linguistic phenomenon and often have counterpart terms in these other disciplines. The only difference is that classical rhetoricians catalogued hundreds of such linguistic phenomenon, perhaps more than any other endeavor to study language. As this book frequently demonstrates, it stands to reason that such cross-disciplinary efforts can enrich the study of style.

In the 2005 *Rhetoric Review* essay, "Performative Stylistics and the Question of Academic Prose," Holcomb models the kind of analysis that stylistics conducts, attending to what he refers to as the performative style of Judith Butler. Holcomb examines the stylistic choices made by Butler, and shows how they contribute to her direct attempts to perform a liberal, intellectual identity for her readers. Holcomb identifies the classical figures of *antimetabole, ploche,* and *polyptoton* used by Butler as "cultural forms"—more specifically as "ritualizations of language," the use of which "structures larger movements in the essay" and serves to secure Butler's own status as a radical academic (202). In Holcomb's interpretation, Butler chooses deliberately complicated sentence patterns to showcase her intellect and exaggerate the complexity of her ideas. The style she performs is aimed at securing her own status as a radical public intellectual.

Verndock's book serves as an excellent, short introduction to the topic of stylistics, and it contains an overview and selected passages from landmark books in the discipline, as well as a glossary of terms used by the various branches (literary, poetic, feminist, linguistic, and pragmatic). Some of the books mentioned include Sara Mill's *Feministic Stylistics* (1995), Ronald Carter and Walter Nash's *Seeing Through Language: A Guide to Styles of English* (1990), Elizabeth Closs Traugott and Mary Louise Pratt's *Linguistics for Students of Literature* (1980), Roger Fowler's *Literature as Social Discourse: The Practice of Linguistic Criticism* (1981), and H. G. Widdoseon's *Practical Stylistics: An Approach to Poetry* (1992).

The various areas of stylistics still demonstrate vitality, and work in them appears regularly in the journal *Language and Literature*. Recent special issues included topics in rhetorical, pedagogical, and feministic stylistics, as well as new media studies and internationalization. A 2012 special issue of the journal was devoted to stylistic analysis of crime writing. In one compelling article, Christiana Gregoriou analyzes posts on a discussion thread about the popular crime drama, *Dexter*. Gregoriou looks at the use of allusions, metaphor, comparison, irony, humor, and word choice in posters to show how fans indulge in debates about the ethical quandaries of the show, but ultimately subscribe to its ideology, justifying and forgiving Dexter's murders. The word choice of one poster even implies justification for the show's villains, sexualizing the victims in one season as possible prostitutes who "have a look," and so, as Gregoriou summarizes, "their appearance [is] made into an actual justification for their downfall" (283).

In other issues of *Language and Literature*, Kay Richardson outlines a methodology for studying dialogue in popular film and television, Roberta Piazza studies the relationship of visual cues and narrative styles of voice-over in the films of Italian director Antonioni, and Michael Abbott and Charles Foreceville analyze styles of illustrating emotion through facial expressions and body language in Japanese manga. Dan Shen charted the evolution of traditional and westernized stylistics in China, describing their use in analyzing linguistic choice in translations. Masayuki Teranishi, Aiko Saito, Kiyo Sakamato, and Masako Nasu provide a history of pedagogical stylistics in Japan, attending to its role in English as a Foreign Language instruction as well as instruction in Japanese literature. These recent studies underscore the expanding diversity and potential of stylistic studies in interdisciplinary projects.

A number of comprehensive books exist on stylistics that are accessible to non-linguists and students. These include Lesley Jeffries and Daniel McIntyre's *Stylistics* (2010), a book entitled *Teaching Stylistics* by the same editors, Paul Simpson's *Stylistics: A Resource Book for Students* (2004), Katie Wales's *A Dictionary of Stylistics* (2011), and Elena Semino's and Mick Short's *Corpus Stylistics* (2004). Several more books are published in Bloomsbury's series, Advances in Stylistics. It is hard to ignore the fact that most of these authors are based at research institutions outside the US, namely in Britain. The absence of major voices in stylistics from the US may underscore some of the common themes in this book regarding the history of language and writing instruction at US colleges. It could also be that Fish's words still ring in the ears of many, and that his impact on the way writing and literature is taught in the US has been profound.

Discourse Analysis

Discourse analysis has become an increasingly utilized method of inquiry in many fields, as it overlaps with stylistics and rhetorical analysis. This form of analysis involves the close study of socio-discursive situations that often fall outside the traditional scope of rhetoric and literature—such as conversations, meetings, arguments, email exchanges, and even comment threads on websites. In such situations, language users make stylistic decisions, even if they are not completely aware of doing so. We all use certain stylistic devices when we speak, and we all make conscious or unconscious decisions in sentence construction based on with whom we are speaking. When looking at records or transcripts of such exchanges, a discourse analyst observes how a range of social factors determine our speaking styles. For example, researchers might analyze a graduate student's sentence structure when pointing out an oversight by a professor on his or her thesis committee. Consider the difference between these two statements:

1. I just received your email about my thesis. You didn't actually attach the file with your comments. Please send the email again so I can start revising.

2. Thanks for reading through the latest draft of my chapter. It doesn't look like the file was attached. If you have time, could you send the attachment?

The first statement is not antagonistic per se, but many academics might cringe at the idea of ever sending such an email to someone in such an asymmetric relationship. The graduate student is in a weak position, needing the professor in order to complete the thesis. Unfortunately, a tenured professor is in a much stronger position, being under no obligation to serve on the thesis committee at all, much less provide detailed feedback.

A discourse analysis would examine how the student's language demonstrates a lack of awareness, or perhaps even a deliberate disregard, for these circumstances. For instance, the second sentence is phrased as a declarative statement in the active voice, clearly stating that the professor made a mistake. The third sentence is phrased as a command, albeit prefaced with a courteous, "please." These grammatical-stylistic decisions contribute to a certain tone that might strike the professor as confrontational, ungrateful, or arrogant. By contrast, the second example hedges the statement of fact with the phrase "It doesn't look like," and then judiciously uses passive voice to mask who is at fault. Finally, the second email concludes with a request rather than a command, again hedging with a clause, "If you have time." Thus, through discourse analysis of several exchanges like this one, we could come to understand a great deal about how professors and students communicate with one another in light of their different positions within the context of a particular university, as well as academia more broadly.

We might be satisfied by defining a discourse analyst as an applied linguist who analyzes a wide range of texts, focusing on specific language choices that contribute to an overall meaning or stance. Applying these research methods in classrooms, teachers could show students that they already possess a great deal of innate knowledge about style, that it is not an alien world of grammatical terms, tropes, and figures. If style is ultimately about the manipulation of language, then students have a great deal of practice in altering their styles in the situations that discourse analysis uses as sites of inquiry. The stylistic decisions that speakers use in daily situations are often spontaneous, unplanned, and partly unconscious. Discourse analysis makes their socio-discursive dimensions more apparent, showing that in explicit rhetorical situations, style is not so different from style in ordinary interactions with peers, colleagues, co-workers, clients, professors, bosses, and landlords.

Discourse analysts analyze texts in a range of modes and genres, including corpora, archives, conversations, television, new media, and social media. With oral texts, discourse analysts focus on how speakers deliver information in spurts that are marked according to stylistic choices such as intonation, or the stresses that speakers place on individual words and syllables and the pitches they use when stressing them. When conducting conversation analysis, discourse between speakers is marked and broken up in what James Paul Gee calls "stanzas" because the blocks of texts resemble those of poems. Line breaks occur when analysts detect non-final (/) and final (//) intonation contours. Analysts pay attention to stressed words and pitch glides, in which speakers raise and lower their pitch when pronouncing a single word. Speakers do this both consciously and unconsciously to emphasize information in a sentence that they feel is important to a conversation, speech, or any piece of information they deliver to an audience. Gee routinely refers to the differences in stress, word choice, and grammatical structure in terms of style and "social languages," including varieties of a single language. Different social languages of English would include Appalachian and AAVE, but also academic and specialist versions of languages. Linguists specifically refer to some of these social languages in terms of register.

In a 2009 issue of the *Journal of Sociolinguistics*, Sclafani uses many of these techniques when analyzing two parodies of Martha Stewart. First, Sclafani establishes the discourse patterns Stewart has typically used on television, as they conform to Robin Lakoff's characteristics of Woman's Language (WL):

1. lexical items related specifically to women's interests (e.g., dollop, mandolin);
2. hedges (you could, if you like);
3. hyper-correct grammar (British pronunciation of herb with initial /h/, aspirated intervocalic /t/);
4. super-polite forms (double-thanking guests; i.e., "thank you, thank you very much");
5. no joking;
6. speaking in italics (i.e., using emphatic stress);
7. the use of intensive "so" (these are *so* tasty);
8. empty adjectives (gorgeous, utterly fantastic);
9. wider intonation range; and
10. question intonation in declaratives. (qtd. in Sclafani 617)

Sclafani then analyzes parodies of Stewart's discourse style on the television shows *South Park* and *MAD TV*. Analyzing the parody of *South Park*, Sclafani focuses on the exaggeration of Stewart's intonation, raising her pitch at the end of declarative statements and elongating vowels. Her analysis adds a characteristic not included in Lakoff's list: Stewart's persistent use of the pronoun "we" in an effort to build rapport with viewers. Sclafani also studies Stewart's hyper-pronunciation, conducting a quantitative analysis of the host's enunciation (or fortification) of the consonant /t/ in a ten-minute segment. Her analysis shows, somewhat expectedly, that while the actual Martha Stewart does fortify /t/ a noticeable six percent of the time in the middle of utterances, and twenty-three percent of the time at the end of utterances, the *MAD TV* actress fortifies /t/ one hundred percent and eighty percent of the time, respectively.

True, this particular discourse analysis studies pronunciation as part of a speaker's style, and so we cannot apply it directly to an analysis of prose style. However, the study demonstrates the value of quantitative analysis of aspects of language used for effect. We could conduct a similar analysis of any writer's prose using other linguistic features from Lakoff's list, such as lexical items, hedging, use of intensives like "so," and empty adjectives. In this way, discourse analysis of spoken or written discourse helps researchers understand how such linguistic features indicate positions and relationships with other speakers or audiences (including readers). The quantitative aspects of discourse analysis make it a potentially useful complement to stylistic analysis, as stylistic analysis does not necessarily use the statistical frequency of stylistic traits as evidence to support interpretations of a writer's style. In other words, a stylistic analysis of Martha Stewart and/or parodies of her would discuss the effect of lexical items or empty adjectives in certain instances, but it might not go so far as to quantify such features. As such, discourse and corpus-based analysis may help us learn about writer's styles with a greater degree of accuracy and precision, validating impressions of someone's style with hard data.

An important part of the analysis lies not only in the data, but also in the context. As James Paul Gee notes, there is always a question of framing a transcript or passage of discourse in terms of context, because researchers can always discover more context that may contribute to their understanding of speakers' interactions, affecting the conclusions they draw.[48] This context can include speakers' prior interactions and their relationships (both personal and professional), in addition to social, historical, cultural, and political histories. Researchers know when to suspend their consideration of context when their understanding or interpretations of a particular interaction cease to change upon the discovery of further information.

Rhetorical Analysis

Rhetorical analysis does not preclude stylistic analysis, but the field of rhetoric and composition today usually privileges patterns of argu-

---

48. Several other introductory books exist on discourse analysis and corpus-based analysis methods: Brian Paltridge; David Machin; Ruth Wodak and Michael Meyer; and Norman Fairclough.

ment over patterns of language. In *Out of Style*, Paul Butler asserts that stylistic analysis has been subsumed into rhetorical analysis and, consequently, receives less attention than it could. For Butler, rhetorical analysis may devote passing attention to an author's or speaker's use of a few tropes, schemes, and figures, but it often falls short of fully appreciating the extent to which language choices contribute to more global meanings. For instance, it is almost impossible to conduct a rhetorical analysis of a speech like Martin Luther King's "I Have a Dream" without some attention to King's use of anaphora and metaphor. A thorough rhetorical analysis would ideally make substantial connections between a rhetor's purpose, use of evidence, awareness of audience, and manipulation of language to achieve that purpose.

Despite the wide array of frameworks for analyzing arguments, it is possible to describe a general approach and set of methods, as Jack Selzer does in *What Writing Does and How it Does it*. Selzer defines rhetorical analysis as "studying carefully some kind of symbolic action, often after the fact of its delivery," in order to achieve "a heightened awareness of the message under rhetorical consideration, and an appreciation for the ways people manipulate language and other symbols for persuasive purposes" (281). In *Discourse Studies and Composition*, Jeanne Fahnestock and Mary Secor define some specific questions addressed by rhetorical analysis: "How is the speaker of this text being constructed? How is the audience constructed? How is the argument constructed? And how do these three aspects either reinforce or interfere with each other?" (180).

Regarding methods, rhetorical analysis often proceeds this way: Writers summarize a text's main argument or arguments, and list its major claims. They then lay out the evidence in support of each claim. Their intention in doing this lies in assessing the manner in which an author has successfully engaged different audiences. Many teachers and researchers follow the classical tradition, and divide evidence into *ethos*, *logos*, and *pathos*. Others might follow Stephen Toulmin's method, explained in *The Uses of Argument* as the mapping of an argument into claims, warrants (underlying assumptions), and backing (evidence). Still others may use Lloyd Bitzer's method of analyzing rhetorical situations: occasion (event), exigence (context), and constraints (limits on what can be said). Yet another prominent method of rhetorical analysis lies in Kenneth Burke's pentad, as it guides the analysis of any rhetorical event via act, scene, agent, agency, and purpose (see

Burke's *Rhetoric of Motives*). Finally, many teachers use a version of Roman Stasis Theory, a framework for analyzing arguments and issues according to four questions: conjecture, definition, quality, and policy (see Sharon Crowley and Debra Hawhee's *Ancient Rhetorics for Contemporary Students*). These different approaches complement one another, and rhetorical analysis can draw terminology from each of these.

All of these frameworks necessitate attention to how stylistic decisions help writers and speakers persuade audiences. Style can serve as a major component of any rhetorical analysis, because writers and speakers always amplify their discourse using stylistic devices such as tropes, schemes, and figures—even if they are not trained rhetors or even astutely aware of the devices they are using. As Jack Selzer states, the terms used in classical treatises "have been devised to guide rhetorical performance," but "they have also been used to help analysts understand better the tactics visible in specific instances of rhetoric" (284).

As it is taught today, rhetorical analysis is an adaptation of the classical tradition that often blends terminology used by the likes of Quintilian with the language of modern grammar and linguistics. While Fahnestock and Secor point to tropes and figures as means of amplifying a rhetor's use of appeals, they also maintain that "a rhetorical analysis of style need not limit itself to the classical tradition," given that "contemporary linguistics has addressed . . . less remarkable linguistic choices, like ordinary predication and the choice of agents" (182). A rhetorical analysis might explore a writer's use of *hyperbole* (a classical figure) and sentence coordination and parallelism to show how each serve a larger purpose to ignite certain emotions (*pathos*) in an audience, or to reinforce a logical appeal. Use of parallelism can be described using grammatical terms, but it can also be identified as the classical device, *isocolon*. Whether we use classical or linguistic terminology, or both, is not a major issue. The main point is to tie local decisions to broader, persuasive goals.

Literary analysis and stylistics up through the 1960s and 1970s often treated an author's style as fixed, maintaining that one could identify a distinctive series of stylistic traits to, essentially, fingerprint an author. (In my research, I encountered scores of old dissertations and books beholden to this view.) Today, rhetorical analysis is less concerned with an author's distinct style as if it were "a sort of genetic code," and more with style "as characteristic of a particular occasion for writing, as something that is as appropriate to reader and subject and genre as it is to a particular author" (Selzer 289). To illustrate, Selzer analyzes E. B. White's essay, "Education" (a satirical narrative about school), for its use of parataxis and short, declarative sentences that make it seem "informal and conversational, never remote or scholarly" (290). White's rhetorical purpose seems be to critique education, and is supported by a series of narrative anecdotes about the displeasures of attending school. Selzer shows how White achieves this goal through a relatively plain or middle style. His writing uses parallelism to give the prose a "remarkably concrete, remarkably vivid quality" (290). Other devices such as hyperbole and irony give the essay a mock-heroic tone, and contribute to the author's voice. Nonetheless, the absence of anastrophe and parentheses (inverted sentences and interruptions) immerse readers in a story about the emotions experienced during a day in the life of a schoolboy.

Fahnestock and Secor model the process of rhetorical analysis by using an op-ed piece by Stanley Fish and considering his use of the appeals, examples, and analogies, as well as his amplification of them through devices such as *hypophora* (posing and answering one's own question) and *prosopopoeia* (personification, or speaking the thoughts of an absent or imaginary person). Their sample illustrates how rhetorical analysis of the style of a writer or speaker should include such specific devices or grammatical constructions in order to show how choices at the local level accumulate and contribute to meaning at the global level. As Chapter 5 discusses, Martha Kolln and Laura Micciche argue similarly through the concept of rhetorical grammar. Whenever we study any text for its use of rhetoric, it is important to understand the author's use of language, evidence, and appeals as part of the rhetorical situation.

One key goal of college writing courses is to instill in students the ability to produce rhetorically effective prose that relies, in part, upon appreciating language strategies in other works. Rhetorical analysis orients students to the relationship between authors, audiences, and contexts, and trains students to identify specific techniques that contribute to the overall persuasiveness of texts. As such, appropriate attention to style in rhetorical analysis helps writers see how their overall impressions or reactions to arguments is influenced by the skilled manipulation of discourse—the use of rhetorical devices, control over diction and syntax, and variation in punctuation. Analysis makes the tools and terminology of style accessible, and provides a foundation for discussing the effectiveness of students' writing. More broadly, rhetorical analysis aids critical thinking; its tools enable a sensitivity and awareness in novice writers and experienced researchers. Rather than simply accept claims at face value, we are able to step back and assess a situation, identify motives, and determine the validity of arguments for ourselves.

From Style to Styles: An Overview of Sociolinguistics

We learn from sociolinguistics that our ideas about correctness and standards are not universal, but are relative and contingent. What counts as adherence to conventions or norms in one variety of language can qualify as the deviation from norms in another. This basic principle has already surfaced at multiple points throughout the book, especially in the discussion of language difference and the influence of linguistics on composition in the 1960s and 1970s, provided in Chapter 6. Researchers in language difference have essentially applied findings in sociolinguistics, a field that has traditionally focused on oral language, to writing. In a 2013 issue of the *Journal of Sociolinguistics*, Theresa Lillis indicates work by Suresh Canagarajah in particular as helping to elevate written discourse as an area of inquiry for sociolinguists, and she calls on other researchers to "tackle head on the strongly evaluate/'error' oriented stance that overshadows the languages of description around writing" (427). Forwarding Lillis's call, this section considers a number of subfields of sociolinguistics as a method of inquiry for prose style.

When it comes to style, sociolinguistic evidence shows that there is not just one "best" style that is universal. Even academic style is an evolving blend of conventions influenced by literate and oral discourse practices, other Englishes, and even other languages. Yet, much of what we do as academics, including our teaching, presumes the opposite. Chapter 1 discussed how our pedagogies, reinforced or perhaps prompted by textbooks and handbooks, led to a somewhat monolithic understanding of style based on Standard English. Understanding the methods and insights of sociolinguists encourage even the most conservative guardians of English to concede that more than one style exists, and that a writer's style, or voice, is a blend of many different varieties of English—including different dialects and registers. The more researchers and teachers in rhetoric and composition know about the polyphonic world of English through the eyes of sociolinguists, the more they can know style as heterogeneous, not homogenous.

From a sociolinguistic perspective, style refers to a range of markers and indicators that characterize a speaker's use of language and attitude toward interlocutors within different social contexts. Speakers may shift their styles for a variety of reasons, either to accommodate listeners or to perform certain identities or social roles. Sociolinguistic data shows that other varieties of English, conceived of as different styles of speaking, are not impoverished but are, in fact, rule-governed and dynamic. Many college students try to incorporate oral styles from non-standard languages into their writing, only to be penalized for doing so because they are not reproducing the "correct" stylistic conventions of academic discourse and Standard English. Insights from sociolinguistic research can expand writing teachers' existing notions of style by showing how language users navigate many styles, rather than just the dominant one. Linguistic realities outside of academia are polyvocal, and studying them lends support to views within rhetoric and composition (e.g., pedagogies of language difference, dialogic pedagogies based on the work of Bakhtin) that teachers should negotiate stylistic conventions of academic writing.

Miriam Meyerhoff's book, *Introducing Sociolinguistics*, provides a thorough yet accessible orientation to the field's qualitative and quantitative methods in data gathering, and an analysis of the ways speakers innovate language. Meyerhoff covers the basic strategies of interviewing, discourse analysis, and corpus analysis while also discussing the importance of triangulation, or the use of a variety of methods to confirm data and conclusions reached by studies on the same issue. Triangulating data gives sociolinguists assurance that their insights have validity. These basic methods are used by researchers in areas across socolinguistics, including applied linguistics, dialectology, language planning, and World Englishes.

Meyerhoff includes overviews of foundational studies in the field, their reception over time, and current questions being addressed by contemporary research. Each chapter concludes with a list of recommended readings. The anthology, *The Routledge Sociolinguistics Reader*, serves as a companion sourcebook for *Introducing Sociolinguistics*, and contains a wealth of historical and contemporary research published by key figures such as William Labov, Alan Bell, Howard Giles, Deborah Tannen, and Walt Wolfram. Nikolas Coupland's book *Style: Language Variation and Identity* devotes particular attention to research methods and frameworks by Labov, Bell, and Giles as well as approaches that emphasize individual styles and social performance. The next section highlights major works by such key figures, while mapping various branches of sociolinguistics that have the potential to inform teachers' and researchers' approaches to style. It outlines methods used by sociolinguists to gather and interpret information about diverse linguistic practices. These methods provide useful maps for teachers and researchers who want to see how oral styles may influence the written compositions of students.

Dialectology

Dialectology is simply the study of dialects and the production of knowledge about their lexicons and syntax. Many writers operate in more than one dialect, and their styles in fact consist of layered dialects. Dialectology provides us with a formal method of understanding the structure of different dialects that, in turn, helps stylisticians attend to how writers draw on them when making stylistic decisions. It enriches our analysis of an author's style when we can determine when some of the elements of their prose deploys dialect strategically, rather than using mere idiosyncrasy or figurative language. We can also recognize that what might otherwise be mistaken as "error" is really an author introducing the norms of another dialect for stylistic effect.

The distinctive literary styles of writers such as James Baldwin and Langston Hughes owe, at least in part, to their sophisticated negotiation of AAVE and Standard English. Southern writers such as Ron Rash, Fred Chapel, and Allan Gurganas crafted unique styles or voices by drawing on regional varieties of English. We see similar layers of dialects almost everywhere in popular culture, and sometimes (though rarely) in academic writing. Thus, part of diversifying and renewing style in rhetoric and composition should stem from using what we know about style, and placing it in conversation with what sociolinguists know about dialect.

Three areas of dialectology exist. Regional dialectological was the first, originating with the work of William Labov, who published studies on language variation in St. Martha's Vineyard and the lower east side of New York. These studies relied primarily on interviews with a wide range of speakers in the chosen area, documenting their own reports on the way they pronounced words. Social dialectology (the second branch) emerged soon thereafter, and focused more on observations of speakers in their environments rather than explicit interviews in which they were more aware of their habits. The third branch of dialectology is perceptual, a branch that emphasizes speakers' perceptions about and attitudes toward varieties of a language.

Style-shifting is a key term that refers to the way speakers modify the grammar and pronunciation of their speech for different situations. Most sociolinguists recognize this as a central focus of their work. Labov's foundational study on style-shifting proposed a theory to explain this act as largely unconscious. Subsequent efforts by Howard Giles gave an alternative account of style-shifting, known as accommodation theory (sometimes called speech accommodation theory or communication accommodation theory). According to Giles, speakers may not be able to fully explain their motivations for style-shifting, but certainly make conscious decisions when doing so. These decisions aim to accommodate to their listeners. Alan Bell took this idea further, developing an audience-design model based on the idea that speakers alter their language not only in response to an audience but also to initiate new meanings with interlocutors. Still, Bell's model held that an individual speaker's stylistic shifts never exceed the variation within his or her speech community. Nikolas Coupland's synthesis of research on style and identity performance contests this idea, showing that speakers will often cross the linguistic boundaries of class, ethnicity, and gender in order to perform rhetorical identities and personas.

Although these early studies are foundational, and are still referenced by contemporary studies of dialect, the methods of sociolinguists have evolved over time. Craig and Washington developed a method they call the dialect density measure (DDM), used for their 2006 study of AAVE. The DDM calculates the number of dialect features per unit of communication (independent clause plus modifiers), based on a list of thirty-three features culled from four decades' worth of prior studies on AAVE. For example, two prevalent grammatical features of AAVE are s-absence in third person verbs (e.g., "She go to the store") and copula verb absence (e.g., "She nice"). A 2010 article by van Hofwegen and Walt Wolfram uses this method in a longitudinal study to analyze the frequency of AAVE patterns in thirty-two children at six stages in their language development: forty-eight months, first grade, fourth grade, sixth grade, eighth grade, and tenth grade. The researchers used transcripts from informal and formal interviews, as well as observations with the children at each stage. For example, during the last three stages (grades six, eight, and ten), researchers studied the children as they worked with a peer to complete a problem-solving task. Their findings show that the children's use of AAVE recedes during first and fourth grades, but returns strongly in adolescence, during sixth through tenth grades.

The broad implications of both Craig and Washington's study and van Hofwegen and Wolfram's are that early schooling and socialization in Standard English are responsible for the reduction of AAVE patterns in elementary school. They return later on, when children become older and begin to see the non-standard dialect as a means of asserting a social identity. This kind of quantitative and longitudinal analysis could enhance our understanding of dialect's relationship to style. Aside from the qualitative work of scholars in language difference in the field of rhetoric and composition, we honestly do not know much about students' actual style-shifting in college. If we do hope to invite students to blend or mesh different vernaculars with academic writing, as Canagarajah and Young recommend, then methods such as those used by contemporary dialectologists would yield more specific information about how college writers actually already *do* mesh Englishes inside and outside of the classroom. Knowing this information can give teachers and researchers a baseline for constructing lessons and assignments to help merge their vernacular language practices, and to realize such practices as a stylistic resource for their academic writing.

Knowledge of dialectology and its empirical methods can push teachers and researchers toward approaches to style that go beyond the analysis of traditional texts and the study of treatises and handbooks. Empirical research on language users and how they make stylistic decisions across a variety of languages and dialects shows that style is a matter of lived knowledge. When students make stylistic choices in their papers that deviate from the norms of Strunk and White or the Modern Language Association (MLA), they are not simply indulging idiosyncratic preferences that developed inside a vacuum. A writer's unique style or voice, to use Elbow's terms discussed in Chapter 1 and Chapter 4 of this book, evolves from the synthesis of their written and oral discourse practices, and the latter develops within a rich, heteroglossic world. The most effective ways for students to learn how their linguistic realities may inform their writing lies in these methods.

Dialectology and sociolinguistics have had a profound influence on rhetoric and composition, evidenced in the 1974 statement, "Students Right to Their Own Language," as well as in the more recent trends in language difference and translingualism. For instance, Vershawn Young's term, code-meshing, refers to what sociolinguists refer to as both code-switching and code-mixing. The only difference is that sociolinguists and dialectologists tend to study code-switching and code-mixing in habitual, rule-governed forms, whereas Young and Canagarajah adapt the term to the study of students' perceived deviation from norms in their academic work. We might think of the authors described in the section on language difference in Chapter 6 as bringing the fieldwork of dialectologists into the classroom in order to help students incorporate stylistic norms or preferences from their oral, social realities that are seen as deviations in academic contexts.

Corpus Linguistics and Stylistics

Stylisticians typically analyze single texts or small groups of texts, allowing them to make claims about a particular author's style or stylistic traits that run across a particular set of texts. Whereas stylistics takes a qualitative approach, corpus stylistics takes a more quantitative and empirical approach by analyzing language practices in very large collections of texts. As a resource for the study of style, corpus analysis helps produce hard evidence about the language choices people make in different contexts, especially regarding diction and sentence structure. For example, if we wanted to test an assumption that authors in the sciences use passive voice more often than those in the humanities, we could construct a corpus of journal articles in these fields and calculate the frequency of passive and active constructions, either by hand or by computer. The more times researchers can reach similar conclusions from the same large corpus, or from a different, related corpus, the more validity and scope their claims gain. Corpus size also determines the validity of the evidence: the larger the corpus, the more accurately it represents language use. So, the more journals added to a corpus, and the more samples taken from that corpus, the more accurate the claims about the use of active and passive voice in different fields.

In a special issue of the *Journal of Writing Research* devoted to corpus research, Joel Bloch describes the use of corpus-based methods to develop and use concordances (a list of words or phrases generated from a corpus) when teaching grammatical and stylistic issues to writers, specifically regarding differences in reporting verbs such as "claim," "argue," "mention," and "suggest." Using scientific journals, Bloch develops a small corpus to provide students with ample textual data of how these verbs are used by professional writers in order to help them appreciate the subtle differences between verbs. For example, Bloch finds that authors tend to use verbs like "argue" when paraphrasing the sources they agree with, but use the verb "claim" when summarizing sources they disagree with. Bloch also notes that academic writers use the verb "mention" when describing sources that do not discuss a particular issue with enough depth. In this case, the corpus study helps us understand that these are not idiosyncratic choices made by one or two writers. They are, in fact, part of the unspoken or partially intuited aspects of style that most writers trained in the academy use to implicitly convey different meanings. While teachers *might* think to discuss differences in reporting verbs, and might be able to illustrate them through the analysis of one or two articles, a corpus study shows much more convincingly and specifically how reporting verbs function and how students can use them in their own essays.

The most substantial stylistic study relying on corpus-driven data is Elena Semino and Mick Short's *Corpus Stylistics*. Short and Semino describe an ongoing corpus-based project that analyzes the frequency of speech and thought presentation in three genres of written narrative discourse: novels, news reports, and biographies and autobiographies. Their purpose was to gather statistical information on the frequency of these presentations. For example, they explore how often authors of news stories report speech (i.e., quoting politicians or interviewing eyewitnesses) versus authors in the other two genres. As with Bloch's study on reporting verbs, such information may confirm or alter preconceptions about these components of genres, and therefore help researchers, teachers, and writers understand them more fully. In the case of direct and indirect speech reporting, it is not altogether shocking, but still surprising, to learn that the vast majority of newspaper narratives consist of speech reporting: 17% more so than novels, and 22% more so than biographies and autobiographies. Meanwhile, thought presentation (i.e., when writers explain what they or someone else is thinking) occurs three times as much in biography and autobiography compared to news reports, with 992 versus 306 instances.

There does not seem to be a hard-and-fast rule on corpus size: Just make it as large and representative as possible in light of how much time you want to spend annotating it. The methods described in *Corpus Stylistics* may be helpful to teachers and researchers interested in conducting their own studies, either on a small or large scale. Because individual news reports are much shorter than two-thousand words, Short and Semino sampled four days' worth of standard news reports on a single event, from a handful of national British newspapers. The authors generated a corpus of 120 text samples (based on similar studies), with forty texts in each of their three categories (novels, newspapers, biographies and autobiographies). Each text sample consisted of roughly two-thousand words, usually of entire sections or chapters of novels and biographies or autobiographies. Corpus size can be measured and evaluated by wordage, and this study weighs in at 258,348 words—about a quarter the size of the largest corpora maintained by major research universities in Britain.

The authors subdivided each category into serious and popular works: literary versus genre novels; biographies or autobiographies of politicians versus those of celebrities; and newspapers such as *The Guardian* versus tabloids like *The Sun*. They limited themselves to three main genres because these constitute the main forms of narrative written discourse. For coherence and specificity, they also limited their study to British publications. While it is always possible to expand a corpus, deciding whether to do so depends on time and resources. As the authors explain, they decided to annotate the text samples manually in order to exercise contextual judgment about what qualifies as direct speech or thought reporting, rather than rely on a software program (19-41). Manual annotation is time-intensive, as it requires reading through every text sample and tagging it with appreciations such as DS (direct speech) and DT (direct thought).

Anyone can construct a corpus to analyze a particular set of stylistic features in written discourse, if they are willing to commit the time. For instance, Paul Butler's discussion of pronoun use in a college syllabus that builds upon Bawarshi's original analysis in *Genre and the Invention of the Writer*, shows how a single author uses pronouns such as "we," "you," and "I" to indicate power relationships between faculty and students, at times using "we" in a hegemonic sense—in the way a parent might tell a child, "We're going home if you can't behave," when what is meant is more along the lines of "*I'm* taking *you* home if you can't behave." We could conduct a corpus-based study on this same topic to gather statistical information about how instructors use pronouns in their syllabi for stylistic effect. We might want to know how often instructors use a hegemonic "we," and in what parts of their syllabi they do so. Proceeding from this question, we might collect 120 syllabi from first-year composition teachers at three or four major research universities in the Southeast as a pilot study. We would then devise a set of markers like HP (hegemonic pronoun), FP (first-person pronoun) and SP (second-person pronoun), and then tag each instance of these features in all of the collected syllabi.

Corpus researchers must always be careful about claims they make based on their research, and must resist the temptation to generalize beyond the data. Every corpus has limits. In this case, what we learn about the use of pronouns in college syllabi may only be accurate for first-year composition courses at those particular universities, although they might provide at least some tentative insights into the styles used in first-year writing course syllabi across many institutions. A desire for greater accuracy would encourage us to expand the corpus, adding syllabi from other universities, and perhaps creating categories such as syllabi written by teaching assistants (TAs) versus tenured and untenured faculty. The results could be interesting, perhaps showing whether TAs tend to use pronouns in different ways than other faculty in order to compensate for their more tenuous position in the university or to distance themselves from students, who may not be much younger than them. Regardless, the key is to always be mindful of the size and diversity of the corpus.

Research(es) on World Englishes and Global English

The US is home to dozens of dialects, but globalization has, almost exponentially, multiplied the varieties of English. Elements of style such as diction and idiom vary widely between these varieties of English. The stylistic decisions that speakers and writers make within a single variety of written English (WE), like Singlish (Singapore English), appear normal within the context of that variety. However, Singlish speakers may strike speakers of Standard American English as stylistically unsophisticated, or as somehow speaking in "broken"

English. Understanding style from a WE perspective recognizes, first, that stylistic norms differ, and that this does not make other varieties of English inferior to privileged ones spoken in the US and Britain. Second, research on WE may push teachers and researchers interested in style to acknowledge that linguistically diverse students are far from stylistically disadvantaged. If anything, these students possess a rich set of resources they can tap into when writing for their classes. Their innovations and code-mixing can differ greatly from what many writing teachers think of as style, in the sense of rigid adherence to the norms or preferences of academic writing and Standard English. It is important for researchers and teachers to appreciate that a writer's apparent "error" could in fact be a stylistic decision based on a student's various linguistic influences.

Researchers of WE specialize in how these types of English relate to one another, and how language users negotiate them within different academic, professional, civic, and social spheres. Although English has become a lingua franca, its grammar and vocabulary vary significantly between localities, regions, nations, and cultures. Braj Kachru has been a pioneer in WE, and his original categorization of Englishes according to inner, outer, and expanding circles in the 1982 book *The Other Tongue* remains familiar today, if somewhat contested. The inner circle refers to nation-states where English has an historical presence, and is learned as a first language; while the outer circle as where English is learned as a second language, and functions within that state's government and commerce. An expanding circle is where English is learned as a foreign language, and does not serve a major role in the state's public discourse, though is used for commercial or social purposes. These categorizations have become standard practice, and it appears throughout articles and books published on WE.

Researchers in this area employ a variety of methods, including ones discussed in this chapter: stylistic analysis, discourse analysis, and corpus studies. In a 2006 issue of the journal *World Englishes*, Philip Seargeant observes that while "there is no core methodology by which investigation in world Englishes operates," and it "draws on a range of theoretical traditions," researchers nonetheless share a more or less common endeavor to problematize "the notion of monolithic English and to investigate the social and political implications of the spread of the language around the world" (122–23). For example, Taofiz Adedayo Alabi analyzes the poet Toba Olusunle for his use of

Nigerian poetic conventions to diffuse tension through assonance (the repetition of vowel sounds), and to alternate it with other forms of alliteration, such as consonance (the repetition of consonant sounds). Alabi also examines Olusunle's use of indented triplets to simulate the discursive importance of repetition in Nigerian culture, as it "signals emphasis, warning, and caution of alertness to wage an unflinching war against all odds" (235). In a 2010 article, Angela Tan conducts a discourse analysis of conversations in Singlish in order to classify the word "right" as a discourse marker when speakers seek confirmation of shared knowledge or agreement on a topic. Speakers of Singapore English differ from American English in that they insert "right" into the middle and ends of sentences without concern for grammatical conventions. Gerald Nelson's 2006 corpus-based study of WE identifies an absolute common core of English words among six varieties, using corpora maintained by the International Corpus of English (a project originated in 1990). Nelson generated 40,000-word lists using corpora for Great Britain, New Zealand, India, Singapore, the Philippines, and Hong Kong. The study reveals that these six varieties share roughly 30% of their vocabularies—therefore constituting a core—with the remaining 70% on the periphery.

Research on WE is focused not only on gathering qualitative and quantitative data on stable varieties of English across the world, but also on the different strategies WE speakers use to communicate. Suresh Canagarajah describes this emerging field as focused on varieties of English "with a highly systematized and stable variety of English in postcolonial communities" ("Multilingual Strategies" 24). Translingualists such as Canagarajah distinguish WE approaches to language from their own for this reason. However, investigations in WE often discuss what Canagarajah refers to as pluralingual English (PE), defined as "a communicative practice, not a stable variety" in which speakers of *different* stable forms of WE negotiate rather than correct one another when discoursing (24).

There is a lesson in these strategies for writing teachers: Many teachers and researchers may often think of style as the advanced, sophisticated performances of speakers or writers fluent in one or more languages. Thinking this way, they can overlook or dismiss the opportunity to teach style, as is described in the last three chapters as the negotiation of language difference. One key pluralingual strategy described by Canagarajah is the "let it pass" principle, a term he traces back to a 2007 study by Alan Firth and Johannes Wagner (19-20). Firth and Wagner analyzed transcripts of business calls between a Danish dairy distributor and an Egyptian wholesaler, showing how the two non-native speakers resolved misunderstandings based on a lexical item, "blowing," that the Danish speaker did not understand:

1. A: . . . so I told him not to u: :h send the:: cheese after the- (.) the blowing (.) in the customs
2. (0.4)
3. A: we don't want the order after the cheese is u: :h (.) blowing.
4. H: see, yes.
5. A: so I don't know what we can uh do with the order now. (.) What do you
6. think we should uh do with this is all blo:wing Mister Hansen
7. (0.5)
8. H: I'm not uh (0.7) blowing uh what uh, what is this u: :h too big or what?
9. (0.2)
10. A: no the cheese is bad Mister Hansen
11. (0.4)
12. A: it is like (.) fermenting in the customs' cool rooms
13. H: ah it's gone off
14. A: yes it's gone off
15. H: we: ll you know you don't have to uh do uh anything because it's not (continues). (808)

Firth and Wagner's analysis focuses on how the Egyptian speaker switches from his original description of the cheese (blowing) to the Danish speaker's phrase, "gone off," in order to confirm his meaning. For Firth and Wagner, such moments occur regularly in interactions between non-native speakers, revealing "people who [are] artfully adept at overcoming apparent linguistic hurdles, exquisitely able to work together internationally, despite having what at first blush appeared to be an imperfect command of the languages they were using" (801). Here the idea of "let it pass" means that the speakers work toward understanding, sometimes adopting and appropriating each other's discourse styles—including new lexical and semantic constructions—rather than insist on the other speaker adopting their own respective norms.

Canagarajah applies this idea of "let it pass" to a graduate student in one of his seminars, named Buthainah, who frequently experiments with language in a way that disrupts the assumptions of native speakers about English prose style, frustrating her peers during workshops of essay drafts. For example, the student uses phrases such as "storms of thought stampede" and "an illustration of my literacy development shunt me to continue," as well as the verb "adore"—a verb that native speakers found imprecise or incorrect (41). By contrast, Canagarajah interviews the student and applies the "let it pass" principle to her work, concluding that such deviations are "perhaps shaped by the linguistic and cultural influences Buthainah brings with her" (41). As such, Canagarajah encourages teachers and students to consider such deviations for "issues of critical thinking, rhetorical effectiveness, and linguistic creativity, and [therefore] giving less importance to issues of grammatical correctness" (42).

The patterns and communicative practices of those in outer and expanding circles are worthy of stylistic study. First, such studies push research on style beyond a somewhat limited preoccupation with polished writing or eloquent speech. A major theme of this book has been moving beyond a view of style as a ready-made product to be analyzed, and toward a treatment of style as a series of dynamic interactions in real-world situations. Studies such as Firth and Wagner's present that reality in global contexts. Style can be a work in progress, an improvisation between different varieties of a language to produce meaning. If style also embraced spontaneity and risk in language, then studying the lexicons and syntax of WE varieties, as well as how speakers experiment with them in discursive interactions, can only widen our own stylistic repertoires and give us more options to choose from in our own writing.

Such an attitude toward language as fluid and open-ended is a primary objective of many researchers in the study of global English. This attitude raises productive questions for the study of style, because it breaks down traditional binaries in classical approaches, as when Quintilian warns rhetors against barbarisms—or the use of foreign linguistic features (e.g., words, spellings, pronunciations) in Latin. Many of us may see "proper" style in modern English as similarly threatened by the proliferation of English varieties that conflict with our own, but given the shifting multilingual realities of discourse, global English is a frontier for research in style if seen as a rhetor's manipulation and exploration of options grounded in one set of conventions, and yet still receptive to others from around the world.

As this chapter has shown, style manifests in a variety of research areas within rhetoric and composition and related disciplines. Style has often served as a topic of historical inquiry, but it can also be a subject of theoretical and ethnographic studies that generate information about writing and writers. It plays a somewhat familiar role in rhetorical, stylistic, and discourse analysis; and yet, each mode of analysis explored here examines language choices in different ways, opening possibilities for interdisciplinary inquiries into the function of style in persuasive writing, a range of literary and non-literary texts, oral discourse, and a number of situations that are less explicitly persuasive.

Style also becomes a matter of concern for research in sociolinguistics and World Englishes, whose methods of studying variations in diction and syntax across multiple Englishes contributes to the revival of stylistic studies in our own discipline. Dialectology, a branch of sociolinguistics, has already impacted rhetoric and composition by charting the rule-governed systems of other vernaculars in order to challenge the myth of a single, standardized English. The use of features from these social languages constitutes stylistic decisions. Finally, corpus studies offer methods of both corroborating and overturning teachers' and researchers' ideas about style through empirical evidence based on the analysis of large bodies of texts. The questions and methods of these areas differ in significant ways, but they are not mutually exclusive. As style continues its return from the margins, researchers are crossing disciplinary boundaries and conducting inquiries into language that expand existing knowledge about what style is and how it functions in discourse.

8 Teaching Strategies and Best Practices

The most effective teaching strategies for style no longer rest on rote exercises and drills. Teachers now focus on style "for emphasis of ideas, for readability and visual impact" (Vaught-Alexander 546) in order to present possibilities for students, rather than to impose restrictions. Contemporary scholars recommend the language of grammar not merely to observe conventions and parse sentences, but to explain how writers can achieve a style or voice through syntax and to show how style often entails the use of grammar for rhetorical effect. (This was noted the discussion of stylistic grammars in Chapter 5.) Still, a great deal of ambivalence exists among scholars about the role of grammar (e.g., mechanics, punctuation, usage) and style in writing instruction. This chapter briefly outlines persistent anxiety about style and stylistic grammars before presenting teaching methods that may allay these fears, especially in a handful of textbooks that take a progressive, dynamic approach to style.

Arguments against grammar instruction in particular often assert that it is obsolete for the field of rhetoric and composition, suggesting that writing pedagogies should focus attention elsewhere. For instance, Keith Rhodes warns that "the average first-year composition course is already much more deeply mired in a grammar pit than it ought to be," and that "the still-emerging discipline of composition will never get a chance to do the full range of good that such a discipline could" as long as public discourse about writing portrays composition as a gate-keeping course (523). Rhodes maintains that books often touted by grammarians as evidence in support of grammatical instruction are, in fact, widely misread. These books include Rei Noguchi's *Grammar and the Teaching of Writing*, Susan Hunter and Ray Wallace's *The Place of Grammar in Writing Instruction*, and Constance Weaver's *Teaching Grammar in Context*. According to Rhodes, no such text "offers any real support for grammar lessons" (524); instead, they either make tentative claims with heavy qualifications or, in the case of Weaver, actively discourage writing teachers from explicit focus on grammar, in favor of context-based approaches.

As Chapter 5 notes, a handful of scholars resist the rhetoric of fear surrounding such sentence-level issues as grammar. Martha Kolln adamantly objects to the definitive tone of the 1963 Braddock Report in a 1981 issue of *CCC*, stating that grammar is ubiquitous in writing instruction. Moreover, she raises the point that "explicit" attention to grammar can mean many things to many different teachers and researchers. (Her textbook, *Rhetorical Grammar*, is described in this chapter's overview of linguistic orientations to style.) Like Kolln, Laura Micciche promotes a rhetorical orientation to grammar in her 2004 article, "Making the Case for Rhetorical Grammar," mentioned in Chapter 5. Micciche illustrates the pedagogical dimensions of this approach through a number of analyses conducted with students, one of them of George W. Bush's 2002 speech to the UN that urges the invasion of Iraq. Micciche recounts analyzing parts of Bush's grammar with students, closely attending to qualifying words and phrases such as "likely," as well as ambiguous verb phrases such as "UN inspectors *believe* Iraq has produced two to four times the amount of biological agents it declared" (qtd. in Micciche 725). Bush and his speech writers carefully choose words to make uncertain indications of biological weapons appear as evidence. The speech does not lie, per se, but it leverages half-truths for as much persuasive power as is possible. Micciche's students analyze such patterns as parallelism and asyndeton in a range of texts, and then practice imitating those patterns in their own writing. For this purpose, Micciche recommends that students keep a commonplace book to record instances of interesting language that may influence or guide their own composing. This chapter follows Kolln and Micciche's line of thinking regarding teaching practices and textbooks, identifying how various compositionists recommend teaching style or the rhetorical use of grammar, as it may help students develop their own voices. This chapter also aims to provide a gathering and overview of teaching materials and textbooks available that address style and grammar.

An essay by Patricia Licklider offers what is currently a consensus among composition scholars on teaching sentence-level issues. As she states, so-called explicit focuses through lectures, drills, and exercises have made no quantifiable impact on the quality of student writing. Thus, contemporary pedagogies have all but abandoned these avenues, moving toward mini-lectures, attention to sentence-level issues during the revision and feedback process, and collaborative models. These approaches enable teachers to devote individualized attention to the various aspects of student writing. As Licklider says,

> I seldom teach grammar to an entire class since usually only some students need help with a particular grammatical concept. Rather, I work with students one on one or in small groups . . . . Occasionally, I may "go public" with a grammatical concept if it has ramifications that everyone in a class would find useful. (564)

Likewise, older, sentence-level rhetorics may be brought back to life in contemporary classrooms by using more progressive pedagogies. For instance, Nicholas M. Karolides adapts sentence-combining and Christensen rhetoric for classroom use, with special attention to Bonnie Jean Christensen's *The Christensen Method: Text and Workbook* (1979), Frank O'Hare's *Sentence Combining: Improving Student Writing without Formal Grammar Instruction* (1973), and William Strong's *Sentence Combining: A Composing Book* (1983). Echoing critics of these sentence-combining methods, Karolides describes these methods and exercises as theoretically sound, and yet "stilted and stiff . . . given both my interactive teaching style and the nature of college students" (538). Rather than throw the baby out with the bathwater, Karolides explores "a more open approach in which the writers decide how and what to combine rather than following the dictates of cues" (538). This more open approach invites students to generate their own kernel sentences, and prompts them to work in groups to complete exercises, rather than independently from an exercise book (542). To illustrate, Karolides first describes giving students a basic sentence such as "He smiled to himself as he ran," and then asks students to add a participial phrase. In response, they generate sentences such as the following:

> anticipating seeing his girlfriend
>
> hearing the shouts from the stands
>
> imagining the surprise of his parents (542)

The class might then proceed by generating similar kernel sentences, and expanding them through the addition of noun phrases, adjective phrases, or absolute phrases. This approach specifically adapts Christensen Rhetoric, in which teachers are encouraged to introduce the concept of expanding base clauses by tacking on modifiers, while leaving the actual creation and expansion of sentences up to interactive discussion and collaborative activities (something Christensen does not do). Karolides offers a few example sentences that students can study and imitate. Consider the sentence:

1. He dipped his hands in the dichloride solution and shook them,
2. a quick shake,
3. fingers down,
4. like the fingers of a pianist above the keys. (545)

Here, each modifying phrase adds new detail and information to the main clause. Karolides recommends analyzing such sentences with students to help them understand how they can use similar constructions to improve their own writing. These dynamic approaches take into account criticism leveled against sentence-level rhetorics during the 1980s, as well as the line of studies against explicit instruction in grammar. Writing teachers today would be wise to keep these critiques in mind as they craft their own lesson plans, activities, and assignments: Avoid the temptation to dictate all aspects of lesson plans. Give students a genuine opportunity to experiment with units of grammar, and resist the urge to immediately correct their possible mistakes as they do.

Sharon Myers's 2003 article, "Remembering the Sentence," also reanimates sentence-combining pedagogies from a lexical perspective. Myers's use of alternative theories of grammar conflict with Chomsky's by giving attention to "knowledge about the idiosyncrasies of words" and their morphologies (617). Myers quotes Eve Clark, that "the lexicon and syntax" of a language is "intertwined . . . each word carries with it a specification not only of its meaning (or meanings) but also its syntax, the range of constructions in which it can occur" (qtd. in Myers 617). According to Myers, sentence-combining pedagogies are effective not only because they expose students to the variability of word order, but also because they expose them to academic vocabulary and chunks of words that appear frequently in academic writing corpuses. For example, consider how words such as "analyze" and "complicate" might be altered when combining and rewriting sentences. Knowing a word in all its possible forms enables a wide range of stylistic variation on the same idea. For example:

1. This paper analyzes Obama's rhetoric. It complicates previous perceptions of Obama as a far-left liberal.

2. Obama's perception as a far-left liberal is complicated by this paper's analysis of Obama's rhetoric.

3. Although he is perceived as a far-left liberal, analyzing Obama's rhetoric might complicate that picture.

4. Having analyzed Obama's rhetoric in a recent speech, one might encounter complications to the perception of him as a far-left liberal.

These variations combine two simple sentences, and gesture toward the range of options students have even in supposedly rule-governed academic discourse. They also illustrate how words—in this case "analyze" and "complicate"—can be modified to fit different syntactical arrangements and how their position in sentences can shift depending on how writers wish to phrase information.

Uniting sentence-combining pedagogies and corpus linguistics in this way, Myers proposes the use of concordances to help students acquire the academic chunks that experienced writers unconsciously integrate into their prose. In other words, chunks or stock phrases often supply academic writers with a ready-made vocabulary that is already accepted within a given discourse. Examples of chunks include common phrases such as those I have just used: "complicate the perception that" or "challenge the perception of." Even more common chunks might include "It is likely that" or "According to this view." (Some readers may think of Gerald Graff and Cathy Birkenstein's templates in *They Say/I Say*. These templates rely on a similar premise.) Concordances are simply lists of such phrases and the frequency with which they appear in different collections of texts, such as journals in a given field.

Ultimately, students wishing to acquire an academic style must balance a desire for expression with the need for disciplinary acceptance. Although the last chapter devoted a great amount of attention to difference and deviation, we can never completely do away with style as the accommodation of norms. Lexical grammar and the study of concordances at least avoids the trap of conforming to arbitrary rules, and instead helps students appreciate how the use of chunks can improve their styles and still permit a degree of flexibility and voice, if used appropriately. Students can then combine these stock phrases with their own writing in a variety of ways (as shown through the example about Obama's speech). Myers explains that this approach works especially well for English as a Second Language (ESL) students because it provides structure and an empirical reference of commonly appearing words and phrases with which native speakers are already familiar.

These approaches to style and grammar can be further re-animated by applying recent work on language difference, including translingualism and World Englishes, as described in the last two chapters. For example, consider the phase "talking with a girl." In American English, it has only one literal meaning. In Jamaican English, however, the phrase serves as a euphemism for sex. At the 2012 Watson conference, I attended a presentation in which a WE researcher described the interactions between an American teacher and Jamaican student who had written in a paper that "I started talking to this girl and she got pregnant." This sentence is grammatically correct, but it may strike American readers as stylistically incoherent. How does talking to someone lead to pregnancy? The presenter did not criticize the teacher for lack of familiarity with Jamaican English idioms, but argued for awareness of global Englishes that call for negotiation, instead of correction.

My own reading of this moment sees it as an opportunity to discuss the writer's style. Rather than changing this somewhat charming sentence, alternatives might include the use of semantic items in different combinations of sentences that use clauses or phrases to define what "talking to a girl" means. For example, the writer might experiment with syntax by writing: "So I started talking with this girl, what Americans would call 'going steady with,' and then she got pregnant." The writer maintains the student's original choices, and American readers are invited to appreciate such phrases stylistically—as part of the writer's voice, and thus important to the content. Ultimately, the student might learn that he can craft a unique style by experimenting with American and Jamaican English. Thus, a stylistic approach to World Englishes promotes the strategic use of linguistic resources, seeing how a decision to use one set of conventions in a different context is itself creative and expressive.

T. R. Johnson and *The Rhetoric of Pleasure*

Chapter 2 presented T. R. Johnson's historical views on the role of pleasure in debates on rhetorical style, and his argument there contains the inception for his more pedagogical project. Johnson argues in his 1999 *JAC* article, "Discipline and Pleasure: 'Magic' and Sound," that English departments too often celebrate their own disciplining mechanisms and ability to inflict pain as proof of their legitimacy as a discipline. This tendency is symptomatic of a larger academic suspicion of pleasurable writing or discourse with roots in the Platonic-sophistic split, one that directly impacts students, since they are usually the first victims of the need to prove our disciplinary status through the regulation of writing. In his book, *The Rhetoric of Pleasure*, Johnson refers to a study showing that as much as 85% of students associate academic writing with dread, rules, mistakes, sterility, and the impersonal (62). In light of this information, Johnson asks, "How do we create [a] . . . classroom in which convention appears flexible, negotiable, and open to address?" (449). The question echoes Lu and Horner's approach to style through language difference, though Johnson turns to the classical tradition for solutions.

Johnson's *The Rhetoric of Pleasure* offers an answer to this question, and includes detailed accounts of his own approach to teaching style that are accompanied by students' reactions to the material. The pedagogy offered here avoids treating stylistic devices as a body of knowledge or characteristics of finished writing, and sees style via process pedagogies as Lenora Woodman argued for in a 1982 issue of *JAC*. As Johnson states, his approach "advocates multiple drafts, and, at the same time, considers the ways the formal feature of finished products—stylistic figures, schemes, tropes—can actually play a powerful role in the drafting and revising process" (25).

When introducing stylistic devices from the classical tradition, Johnson refrains from testing students on such devices, and instead explains that they should "try to use at least two of these when you write your short homework papers", and that "you will be required to use eight of them in your longer essay assignments" (38). Johnson's philosophy focuses on what style can offer students, encouraging them to take more pleasure in their writing. Moreover, Johnson carefully distinguishes literary training from more general composition courses, stating that "my goal is not simply to get them to produce heavily stylized language, such as we might find in the Bible or Shakespeare, but rather to practice these devices as a kind of interim measure toward listening to and thinking about their prose more carefully" (40).

As Johnson admits, his students are not initially receptive to the idea of style. Many are intimidated by the Greek and Latin names, and also by the sheer number of devices. A majority of students resist the difficulty and "hassle of dealing with language as carefully as I required" (42). An inductive approach to style appears to dissolve some of the tension, as Johnson leads them through exercises that follow different schemes without identifying the device by name. For instance, here is how he teaches students chiasmus (reverse word order) on the day that first drafts of a major paper are due: First, students identify a compelling passage in their paper and articulate a contrary thought or emotion. Then, as he narrates,

> I gave them some time to think, and then I said, "Now, try putting the two terms of this conflict together under a single label, a label that pins down not their opposition, but the connection between them, the thing they share." Again, I gave them some time to think and said, "Now that you've got this term that binds them together, jot down what you think might be the opposite of this term." I then asked them to retrace these steps and come up with a sentence in which the two key terms of the first half of the sentence were repeated in reverse order in the second half.... Needless to say, they struggled. After a few minutes, though, several of them were ready to share their attempts, and, as we jostled these examples to fit the form, more of the students began to catch on. The students soon began to bring an extraordinary energy to this task.... One student, Jessie Courville, said that working on her chiasmus was triggering so many new ideas and possibilities for her paper that she felt as if her mind was about to "boil over." (43)

It may be difficult to replicate the enthusiasm that Johnson attributes to most of his students. However, Jessie's experience, in which a stylistic device "triggers" new ideas, illustrates precisely the connection between style and invention that classical rhetoricians and more contemporary theorists, such as Christensen, have always sought.

Johnson follows this activity with a major writing assignment that asks students to analyze the endings of two essays and to compare them in terms of the writers' styles, specifically what rhetorical devices are used and how they contribute to the authors' tones or voices. This major paper also requires students to use eight rhetorical devices in their own writing. The paper is designed to push students to see the relationship between style at the sentence-level and the larger emotions or moods they help generate in a piece of writing. Once they complete first drafts, students then spend time in peer review workshops, focusing on content as well as style. At one point, Johnson distributes a single student's paper to the class for group work, and has each group review a different paragraph and present suggestions. During class discussion, the various groups debate the essay's degree of focus, regarding its tendency to shift away from key themes at the end of each paragraph, and whether or not this needs revision.

Johnson's book integrates style into every stage of the writing process, not merely the end. Teachers might think of several methods to accomplish this that build on Johnson's work. For instance, they might ask students to routinely incorporate different stylistic devices into their papers, and to keep a journal on how such experimentation affects their thinking about their topics. Asking students to recast conflicting sources or positions on an issue in a research-based paper via *antithesis* or *paronomasia* might help them see the two competing ideas more starkly. Such realizations can lead to an evolved research question, the realization of a need for more research, or a stronger thesis statement. If students are required to use stylistic devices in their papers, then directions for peer review could encourage students to focus primarily on how their use of style creates a voice that strengthens or weakens their overall persuasiveness.

A pedagogy that revives style also revises the idea of play, magic, and wonder—notions that Johnson returns to throughout the book. Thus, *The Rhetoric of Pleasure* joins other contemporary works that encourage a reorientation of style away from correctness and conventions, showing the practical steps that teachers can take to reinstate the sentence in the field. This conception of style as possibility and play is conducive to the way sentence-level issues are approached in a range of other fields that inform teaching materials and textbooks. The next several sections of this chapter explore textbooks taking progressive approaches to style. They are organized according to three main disciplinary orientations: linguistics, classical rhetoric, and mixed approaches.

Textbooks: Linguistic and Sociolinguistic Approaches

A number of textbooks employ grammatical terminology to explain aspects of style for college writing students, all of which fall into the category of stylistic grammars, explained in Chapter 5. These books employ the language of grammar directly in order to account for style in professional and student writing. They often directly state their debt to linguists and linguistic frameworks, as Virginia Tufte does when referring to Chomsky's transformational-generative grammar. Exposure to basic sentence types or patterns, as they provide much of the content for her book as well as Martha Kolln's *Rhetorical Grammar*, come directly from Chomsky's foundational work. As Tufte acknowledges, sentence patterns or "kernels" are responsible for language's "incredible versatility as a creative resource" (10).

Martha Kolln's *Rhetorical Grammar* is entirely devoted to sentence-level issues, and emphasizes the impact of grammatical decisions on audiences in different situations. As discussed in prior chapters, Kolln approaches grammar rhetorically, explaining parts of speech as tools for constructing effective sentences. As Kolln states in the introduction, her book takes a "functional point of view . . . that [grammar] can be taught and learned successfully if it is done in the right way and in the right place, in connection with composition," rather than "for remedial purposes," and therefore as "a Band-Aid for weak and inexperienced writers" (xii). The book is divided into five parts. The first part begins with basic elements of sentence structure that Kolln terms "slots" (e.g., subject, predicate, clause) and basic sentence patterns. Each chapter introduces new patterns and terms, such as conjunctions, complex and compound sentences, coordination, subordination, and parallel structure. The second part builds on these basic terms, and introduces strategies for sentence cohesion, rhythm, tone, and diction. The third and fourth parts focus on particular aspects of voice and style, such as verb choice and stylistic variation through the use of absolute phrases and free modifiers. The final part provides an overview of punctuation, followed by a much-needed glossary of grammatical terms.

Kolln's *Rhetorical Grammar* is well-known because of her plain-spoken views on the importance of grammar in writing instruction during the 1980s, and also because of its depth and specificity. However, teachers may want to preview a variety of other linguistic or grammatical approaches to style before adopting this book. Kolln's discussion of grammatical concepts and sentence structure, even after helpful definitions, may alienate students. Consider her description of a particular sentence as having "a participial phrase as the posthead-word modifier" (212). Kolln's framework of slots to describe sentence parts such as subjects and predicates can seem unnecessarily complicated and cumbersome for teachers who are simply trying to introduce basic grammatical terms to first-year writing students. In many ways, the book is incredibly demanding in its expectation for readers to carry forward terminology from one chapter to the next, wading through dense analyses of relatively short passages. As such, *Rhetorical Grammar* may work best for intermediate and advanced writing courses and for teachers who already have a relatively strong foundation in grammar. That said, the book might work well as a teacher's reference for any course, given its comprehensive coverage of sentence structure, punctuation, and diction.

Some textbooks informed by linguistics express a need to radicalize academic writing style. In one of the most recent books, *The Well-Crafted Sentence*, Nora Bacon defines style as both "a range of voices" and as series of qualities that make one work "distinct from the work of any other writer" (6), and also as the ability to write clearly and concisely. Speaking about academic writing in particular, Bacon maintains that "it's time that we raised our expectations for style in academic writing" to not merely include clarity and accuracy, but also "grace, rhythm, wit, and power" (15). To accomplish a clear but distinct voice in academic writing, Bacon identifies the need for "mastery of sentence structure [grammar] to imagine a range of options for expressing an idea" (11). As such, the book is organized into separate chapters about clauses and modifiers, active voice, sentence coordination and parallel structure, different types of phrases and free modifiers, appositives, and sentence variety.

Each chapter defines these grammatical terms and explains how they can assist writers in developing a sense of style. In Chapter 8, Bacon defines an appositive phrase as "a noun phrase that appears in a sentence next to another noun phrase referring to the same person or thing" (125). She explains how appositives supplement information in sentences, help identify people efficiently, define terms, provide examples, and help to restate ideas. The chapter provides examples of each application:

1. I'd like you to meet Jerry Allen, my brother-in-law from Texas. (Supplementing information)
2. Sir Frederick Ouseley, a former professor of music at Oxford, for example, "was all his life remarkable for his sense of absolute pitch." (Identifying people)
3. Gordon B, a professional violinist who wrote to me about tinnitus, or ringing in his ears, remarked matter-of-factly that his tinnitus was "high F-natural." (Defining terms)
4. The pitch is bundled in with other attributes of the note—its timbre (very importantly), its loudness, and so on. (Filling in examples)
5. Fought in April 1862, Shiloh marked a new departure in warfare, a level of death and destruction previously unknown and unimagined. (Renaming with a twist)

Each chapter also concludes with a set of exercises that ask students to identify syntactical structures in passages, and then to use these patterns to rewrite or combine sentences. In Chapter 8, Bacon gives students five sets of sentences to combine by using appositive phrases. Although similar to books discussed later in this section, Bacon's book stands out in its use of essays (included in the back of the book) that model the sentence structures and their contribution to each writers' voice. Every chapter identifies several examples from these texts, and analyzes them for their use of sentence structures for rhetorical effect, thus contributing to that writer's distinctive style or voice. Bacon includes a table indicating how each essay corresponds to various chapters on aspects of syntax. For example, a passage from Barack Obama's speech, "A More Perfect Union," illustrates effective use of clauses, sentence coordination, and parallel structure. David Sedaris's "Genetic Engineering" demonstrates effective use of verbal phrases. Amy Tan's "Mother Tongue" demonstrates effective use of adjectival phrases. Oliver Sacks's "Pap Blows His Nose in G: Absolute Pitch" demonstrates effective use of appositive phrases, as shown above.

In *Style: Lessons in Clarity and Grace*, Joseph Williams and Greg Colomb acknowledge the influence of linguists such as Halliday and

Chomsky. This book conveys a progressive attitude compared to many other textbooks devoted to issues at the sentence and paragraph levels. The authors downplay the importance of correctness, instead promoting choice. Authors choose between "better and worse," not between "right and utterly, irredeemably, unequivocally Wrong" (11). Effective style is not about observing arbitrary rules such as beginning sentences with "but" or "and," but in understanding when to do so and what impact doing so will have on different types of readers. The authors also recognize that "Standard forms of a language originate in accidents of geography and economic power" (12), leaving writers in the position of needing to learn dominant rules to achieve "selective observance" (13) and apply them for their own purposes. In turn, the book relies on an understanding of clarity not in the Aristotelian sense of conveying ideas in the plainest language possible, but in a pragmatic and ethical sense, where writers try to imagine and reproduce the effects that professional writing has on them as readers. In other words: Write for others the way you want others to write for you.

The authors encourage stylistic complexity rather than grammatical correctness, saying "Your readers want you to write clearly, but not in Dick-and-Jane sentences" (43). Thus, each chapter presents different aspects of style and grammar in terms of the constant tension between clarity—a judgment made by readers rather than a timeless quality of the writing itself—and the writer's desire for self-expression. As they maintain, "like the word *clarity*, the words *choppy* and *disorganized* refer not to the words on the page, but to how we *feel* about them" (67). In addition to sentence-level aspects of style, the book offers a lesson in global-cohesion, for instance, describing effective paragraphs in two parts: issue and discussion. In the issue part of paragraphs, authors introduce a "promise," and then deliver on it through explanation, support, or specification in the discussion part.

These twelve lessons include analysis of passages and a plethora of short exercises asking students to rewrite and edit prose. Each lesson follows a pattern: first, introducing a principle; providing illustrative examples and analysis; and then staging a series of revision activities. The end of the third chapter, on the importance of clear subjects and active verbs versus confusing nominalizations (noun-ified verbs like "investigation"), presents the following sequence of sentences, and asks student to "Analyze the subject/character and verb/action":

> There is opposition among many voters to nuclear power plants based on a belief in their threat to human health.
>
> Many voters oppose nuclear power plans because they believe that such plans threaten human health. (33)

In the first sentence, the verbs "oppose" and "belief" appear in a nominalized form, making the sentence somewhat static and unclear. The second sentence presents the character—in this case, voters—as the main subject and relies on active verbs rather than static ones, such as "is." Once students grasp this concept, they can move on to a more complex exercise that asks them to choose verbs from a list to compose sentences in active and nominalized forms, and to consider the effects of each sentence as they revise back and forth (34).

Every lesson presents part of a graduated sequence of exercises that prompt students to compose and revise rather than simply regurgitate rules or identify stylistic and grammatical errors. The exercises encourage students to learn style in the context of their own writing. The book also includes an appendix that students will find accessible and straightforward about punctuation and source citation, in which Williams and Colomb explain conventions in everyday language.

An outgrowth of a previous textbook, titled *Grammar as Style*, Tufte's textbook, *Artful Sentences*, takes an almost identical approach to Kolln's, with two significant differences: one lies in Tufte's abundant attention to literary prose throughout, and the other in her focus on "syntactic symbolism" in the fourteenth chapter.[49] *Artful Sentences* may work best as supplemental or recommended material for an advanced writing course in fiction or creative non-fiction, but especially in workshop-based courses with self-motivated students. The prevalence of literary analysis and the absence of exercises may make it less appealing for first-year composition instructors. Though the book is not a difficult read, it does not often make direct references to concrete writing situations that first-year students and teachers often look for. Such contexts need to be supplied by teachers or students.

Tufte's central principle for much of the book rests on sentence types and slots, and she describes them in much the same way as Kolln

---

49. Tufte's *Artful Sentences* is similar in content and structure to her earlier textbook, *Grammar as Style*. I discuss *Artful Sentences* because it is more widely available for purchase by students. *Grammar as Style* is available in libraries, but appears to be largely out of print and in limited availability.

and Williams. Tufte's book draws on more than a thousand literary authors in order to illustrate these types and slots. The examples are also often accompanied with brief, almost perfunctory stylistic analysis that focuses on the use of rhetorical devices in particular sentences, such as metaphor, metonymy, and parallelism. In the first chapter, Tufte synthesizes discussion of four sentence types, reading them "in context" to explore such stylistic qualities (19). For instance, she attributes the power of Thomas Merton's writing to the placement of "forceful, violent verbs that contribute to the loud excess" (21). Tufte also provides a section devoted to sentences that blend multiple types, as in an excerpt from Jack Finney's *The Woodrow Wilson Dime* that contains a sentence that "has a base clause [technically an intransitive one], with both left-branching and right-branching free modifiers" (33). Tufte explains how such clauses bring a sentence "into a firmer perspective" (33) and, because the terms "transitive" and "intransitive" refer to verb structures in particular, they can describe simple sentences consisting of a single clause, or compound and complex sentences consisting of multiple ones.

Tufte's final chapter explores the concept of "syntactic symbolism," the organization of clauses and sentence patterns to convey an action or experience more viscerally to readers. Tufte states that "a syntactic symbol is a verbal, syntactic pattern intended to be read for a nonverbal movement or development of some kind: language arranged to look or sound like action" (271). Here, the sentence types and slots, including all kinds of free modifiers, offer writers ways of choosing and ordering words to achieve a "bringing before the eyes" or, more appropriately, a "bringing before the ears" similar to the vividness that Aristotle discusses in Book III of the *Rhetoric* and in the *Poetics*. Because *Artful Sentences* appears to be geared toward advanced classes in literary writing, few references to classical rhetoric appear in Tufte's discussion of the many techniques that other scholars describe as classical schemes.

Although the book is not necessarily appropriate for a first-year composition course, advanced students may be refreshed that the book refrains from condescending directives and its tendency point to "quick tips." Finally, the book contains passages from linguistically diverse authors, including Sandra Cisneros, Gloria Anzaldua, Chinua Achebe, Julia Alvarez, Jamaica Kincaid, and Maxine Hong Kingston. Rarely, though, does it apply linguistic analysis to the translingual features of these texts, showing how the writers negotiate the syntactical and stylistic expectations of two or more dialects or languages. As noted throughout the reference guide, such analysis would need supplemental material and preparation by the teacher.

Donna Gorrell's *Style and Difference* describes a writer's style as the negotiation of, adherence to, and deviation from conventions in grammar, syntax, and punctuation. On the one hand, writers need to observe principles of sentence coordination, subordination, variety, and rhythm. On the other, writers need not observe arbitrary rules from lore about beginning sentences with conjunctions, ending them with prepositions, using contractions, or splitting infinitives. Gorrell's book is divided into five parts: In the first part, Gorrell overviews many similar elements of grammar as Kolln, Tufte, and Williams. Part two of *Style and Difference* stands out from these previously-discussed texts by explaining nine different myths of usage. For instance, Gorrell examines passages from contemporary writers effectively use passive voice. Gorrell also interrogates myths about comma splices and sentence fragments, again providing numerous examples of published writers who violate these prescriptions.

The most striking myth Gorrell deflates concerns pronoun agreement. As she states, the argument against using "they" as a singular referent "overlooks the history of *they* usage, it also overlooks the historical and current acceptability of another pronoun, you, that has both singular and plural senses" (141). As Gorrell explains, the *Oxford English Dictionary* lists several uses of "they" as a generic singular pronoun before 1850, when Britain passed a law requiring "he" as the only acceptable singular pronoun. Another striking chapter encourages writers to use first- and second-person pronouns like "I," "us," "we," and "you" for rhetorical effect, while another encourages students to write in sentence fragments.

Gorrell explains the acceptability of these stylistic decisions while describing their rhetorical effects. For example, fragments are not simply permissible—they can be used to draw attention to ideas, ease transitions between paragraphs, and break complex sentences up into manageable bits (127–129). As observed by many writing teachers, students often write awkward and wordy sentences when trying to observe many of these prescriptions and, as such, feel needlessly anxious and uncomfortable when writing academic papers. Parts three and four of *Style and Difference* discuss conventions of grammar and punctuation that still permit some decision making. As Gorrell states, "punctuation marks [are] a feature of style. Some people use more commas than other people do, but in general we use fewer commas today than in times past" (182). Writers might choose to combine two clauses with a comma and a coordinating conjunction. They might choose to combine these same two clauses with a subordinating conjunction. They might combine them by making one a free modifier, or even combine them without a comma at all. Consider variations of a sentence Gorrell uses from Rachel Carson's *The Sea around Us*:

1. The gases began to liquefy, and Earth became a molten mass.
2. The gases began to liquefy. Earth became a molten mass.
3. Because the gases liquefied, Earth became a molten mass.
4. The gases began to liquefy, making Earth a molten mass.
5. Earth began to liquefy; Earth became a molten mass.[50] (qtd. in Gorrell 185)

Different writers and readers prefer different variations, and these are but a few possibilities. The main point is that these sentence variations are all grammatically correct and, for Gorrell, knowledge of punctuation enables rhetorical strategy and decision-making, not merely accuracy.

To instill this mindset in students, Gorrell provides a few exercises at the end of each chapter. Many of them are short, and involve either analysis or revision of passages. Several times, Gorrell presents a passage from a contemporary work of creative non-fiction, with punctuation marks and other features numbered, asking students to make arguments for why the author chose a particular type of clause, comma, semicolon, or period over another option. I have had some success with these types of exercises in my own teaching, having students work in groups to analyze paragraphs from a variety of readings. For instance, we recently performed an in-class close reading of parts of Clifford Geertz's "Notes on the Balinese Cockfight," focusing on the author's use of subordinating clauses and modifying phrases to add narrative detail. Teachers can take this approach with almost any

---

50. The variations on this sentence are mine. Gorrell only uses the original sentence to illustrate how punctuation contributes to style by helping to mark clause boundaries: "The gases began to liquefy, and the Earth became a molten mass" (qtd. in Gorrell 185).

work of literary or academic writing. It is not so different from what the Greeks and Romans did—presenting model texts for analysis before exercises in imitation.

Matthew Clark's *A Matter of Style* states up front that it presumes a degree of basic knowledge about style and grammar; it does not provide exercises like many other textbooks. However, its strengths lie in providing clear explanations of the effects of grammar on style, and in offering abundant examples from literary fiction and academic prose. Clark writes without the methodical structure of Kolln and Williams, analyzing passages without stopping to explain terms such as adverbial phrase, prepositional phrase, or subordinate clause. For example, he critiques a passage from Charles Dickens's *Bleak House*, in which the subject and predicate are interrupted by subordinate clauses:

> The difficulty that I felt in being quite composed that first evening, when Ada asked me, over our work, if the family were at the house, and when I was obliged to answer yes, I believed so, for Lady Dedlock had spoken to me in the woods the day before yesterday, was great. (qtd. in Clark 21)

Although Clark recognizes that the passage is technically accurate, in terms of grammar, he explains how the "verb phrase 'was great' is too far from its subject" (21). There is no real definition at all of subjects, predicates, or clauses—Clark makes clear that he is writing for an advanced audience. As such, he is more interested in diving directly into possible revisions that solve this stylistic dilemma. Rather than providing one possible revision, he offers two that readers might find clearer:

1. The difficulty that I felt in being quite composed was great that first evening . . .

2. That first evening—when Ada asked me over our work . . . for Lady Dedlock had spoken to me in the woods the day before yesterday—the difficulty that I felt in being quite composed was great. (21)

The first revision makes a simple change in moving the phrase "was great" to the main clause, making the sentence a cumulative one: a main clause with several modifying phrases added to provide more detail without confusing the main idea. The second revision relies on punctuation, fencing off more detailed information with dashes so that readers can more clearly identify the introductory clause and the main idea before the first dash and after the second.

Attention to prose rhythm sets Clark's book apart from most others. Thorough but concise, Clark begins with an enumeration of poetic and prose meters and a brief history of theories of prose rhythm in English. Ultimately, he advises readers that while these terms can be somewhat helpful, "I am not sure . . . that a theory of prose rhythm is possible" because "one has to [also] consider the lengths of words, phrases, clauses, and sentences," among many other variables (31). Nonetheless, the book provides a few examples to help attune students' ears to how these variables work together, as in an analysis of the opening passage from Don Delillo's *White Noise* that describes college students on move-in day. In addition to its metrical elements, Clark shows how lists of items such as "boxes of blankets, boots, and shoes, stationery and books, sheets, pillows, quilts," and so on are marked by a "careful balance of longer and shorter phrases, as well as rhythmic variation created by the lengths of different words and word combinations" (33). In the vein of Fahnestock, the book also examines passages for style at the paragraph level, as Clark focuses on the strategy of repetition to create links and signposts that give paragraphs coherence. For example, he discusses a paragraph from Alasdair MacIntyre's *After Virtue* for its repetition of key terms such as "moral," "contemporary," "disagreement," and "interminable" to generate coherence between the central ideas of paragraphs (138).

A Matter of Style might also fit with books influenced by classical approaches to style. Clark devotes two chapters to figures of speech, taking more time to define devices such as *polyptoton* (using a word in different grammatical forms), *polysyndeton* (overuse of conjunctions), and *asyndeton* (absence of conjunctions). He illustrates these devices through discussions of passages. For instance, Nabokov uses polyptoton in *Ada* when he writes "the collected works of unrecollected authors (55). Anne Rice uses asyndeton in *Interview with the Vampire* when she writes, "It took a moment for the boy to wipe his forehead and his lips with a handkerchief, to stammer that the microphone was in the machine, to press the button, to say that the machine was on" (60).

Altogether, what Clark's book may lack in terms of definitions, exercises, and activities, it makes up for in terms of voice and an abundance of examples. Clark demonstrates a deep sense of the history of style, and he often includes relevant historical context that rounds out each chapter. For instance, discussion of George Saintsbury's *History of English Prose Rhythm* does more than enough to outline the problems of thinking about prose style merely in terms of meter, as described above. Students may appreciate Clark's ability to balance terminology, history, and illustrative analysis, and *A Matter of Style* would serve as a suitable book for teachers who want to learn more about style and are interested in developing their own exercises and short writing assignments based on the book's numerous passages and accompanying analysis.

Approaches Informed by Classical Rhetoric

The fourth edition of Edward Corbett's textbook, *Classical Rhetoric for the Modern Student*, co-authored with Robert Connors, remains a rich text for use at the undergraduate and graduate level. *Classical Rhetoric for the Modern Student* is an appropriate textbook for a range of advanced undergraduate and introductory graduate courses on rhetorical theory; though, the book is ideal for courses emphasizing historical contexts. (It contains an entire chapter on histories of rhetoric through the twentieth century.) Corbett and Connors's approach suits teachers of rhetoric who have knowledge of the subject in its Greco-Roman contexts, and who want to attune their students to the role of style among the other canons.

The first three chapters of the book cover invention and arrangement, with a substantial fourth chapter devoted to style. At the outset, the authors not only reject a view of style as mere ornament of thought, but they also reject any interpretation of classical rhetoricians to that effect. As they state,

> It is difficult to determine just which school of rhetoric gave currency to the notion that style was ornament or embellishment, like tinsel draped over the bare branches of a Christmas tree, but it is certain that none of the prominent classical rhetoricians—Isocrates, Aristotle, Demetrius, Longinus, Cicero, Quintilian—ever preached such a doctrine. (338)

Such a doctrine is damaging to students, the authors claim, and the broader goal of the chapter is to redefine the relationship between grammar, usage, and style in order to help students gain control over their writing at the sentence level. What follows may be a refreshingly clear consideration of the difference between grammar and style, replete with concrete examples.

The authors explain that grammar deals with what is possible or impossible in a language, while rhetoric (and style) provides a method for judging the effectiveness of different grammatical organization of the same words. For instance, the sentence "He already has forgiven them for leaving, before the curtain fell, the theatre" is grammatically accurate but stylistically awkward and confusing (341). The authors set usage apart from grammar, and trace it back to George Campbell's definition of "good usage" as following what was reputable, national, and present. It is usage, and not grammar, that precludes "dialectical words, technical words, coinages, and foreign words" (346), and so is an aspect of writing that requires judgment and experience rather than persistent adherence to rules.

The authors warn against a preoccupation with usage, admitting that "If American schools had been as much concerned with grammar, logic, and rhetoric, as they have been with 'good usage,' the quality of student writing today might be better than it generally is" (348). The authors elaborate on style in terms of diction, rhythm, sentence patterns, and figures of thought and expression. This portion extends for roughly fifty pages, as the authors introduce various sentence types, simple techniques for marking stresses in prose for euphony, and a condensed catalogue of stylistic devices. Although this section is thorough, it remains focused on how these various methods help students study and learn from professional writers in order to improve their own compositions.

Corbett and Connors's textbook contains an entire chapter guiding students through a series of imitation exercises. In the 1971 *CCC* article, "The Theory and Practice of Imitation in Classical Rhetoric," Corbett explains and rationalizes the classical approach to imitation that led to this chapter. In the article, Corbett defines the triadic theory of classical writing education as consisting of imitation, practice, and theory. Students first desire to imitate (*imitatio*) certain arts or sports, acquiring basic skills. They then engage in practice (*exercitatio*) to improve those basic skills, and finally set out to learn the theories (*ars*) that enable mastery. Although "not many records of imitative practices in Greek and Roman schools are extant," Corbett manages to construct a set of teaching practices for imitation by turning to sixteenth and seventeenth century texts that describe imitation exercises (245). These exercises consisted of Analysis and Genesis. First, the instructor led students through "a close study of the model to observe how its excellence follows the precepts of art" (245), an activity sometimes referred to as prelection. Quintilian describes the same process in *The Orator's Education* at length (2.5.6–16). The close analysis could move sentence-by-sentence—similar to the explication conducted in rhetorical analysis or close readings today—or it could explicitly focus on a single key feature of a model (figures of thought, for example) that students would emulate. Afterward, students moved to the Genesis stage to measure or copy the passage exactly, emulate a model's form, paraphrase it, or set out to write something more loosely inspired.

Corbett presents his own version of an imitation pedagogy that involves three stages: First, students copy passages from their own selection or from a selection of models provided in the textbook. Second students imitate the patterns of model sentences. Third students introduce variations on these sentences by recombining clauses. The textbook then provides a list of reminders to students, such as: "You must do this copying with a pencil or pen"; "You must not spend too much time with any one author"; "You must read the entire passage before starting to copy it"; and "You must copy the passage slowly and accurately" (425). The ultimate goal of the three-phase sequence is "to achieve an awareness of the variety of sentence structures of which the English language is capable," and to venture beyond the safe but limiting structure of short, simple sentences (443). Corbett concludes the chapter on style by stating that analysis and imitation of professional writers "can make you aware of the variety of lexical and syntactical resources which your language offers" (447).

Echoing Quintilian, Corbett warns students about "servile imitation" and issues a series of cautions about these exercises regarding "spend[ing] too much time with any one author," as it would inhibit "developing one's own style by getting the 'feel' of a variety of styles" (425). The ideal for Corbett is to copy a passage a day for a month or more. Examples of the second and third exercises especially contest the notion that imitation does not engage invention. For example, the sentence imitation exercises only require students to imitate the form. Students must supply the *content* of the sentences:

> Model Sentence: I went to the woods because I wished to live deliberately, to front only the essential facts of life, and see if I

could learn what it had to teach, and not, when I came to die, discover that I had not lived.

Imitation: I greeted him politely, although I planned to challenge him repeatedly, to assess his reduction, to test whether he could discriminate what was expedient in each situation, and, after I had probed him thoroughly, to announce that we had no place for him in our organization. (555)

The difference in content between these two sentences shows an ability to imitate with a difference. Corbett encourages students to engage in wordplay by imitating and improving on the model passages, rather than conforming to them.

The depth and breadth of Corbett and Connors's discussion of grammar, usage, and style is often meticulous, if not dense, and it focuses on history as much as practical writing advice and assignments. The chapter on imitation may appeal to composition teachers, given its practical orientation, with an adequate though not overwhelming contextual explanation about the importance of imitation in the classical tradition. Nonetheless, the model passages include only a few multilingual authors, and none of them demonstrate a great degree of multilingual or multidialectal prose. The monolingual dimension of these passages somewhat contradicts the critiques of usage elsewhere in the book. As such, this book may function much better in training teachers, orienting advanced undergraduate and graduate students to the importance of style, and serving as an aid or supplement, rather than as a primary textbook in introductory level undergraduate courses.

In 1999, Corbett and Connors published a much shorter textbook, titled *Style and Statement*, covering much of the same territory on style, but without discussion of the other canons. The book breaks style down into sub-components: grammatical accuracy, diction, clause and sentence types, prose rhythm, and figures of speech. Here again, the authors explain where grammar and style overlap and depart—grammar dealing with what is possible, and style dealing with what is rhetorically effective. (Again, they show that sentences can be grammatical accurate but not stylistically appropriate, depending on readers' tastes.) In the section on rhetorical figures, the authors provide a lengthy list of devices with definitions and examples. The book does not provide many exercises, other than the description of a project in which students analyzed published essays for sentence and paragraph length, comparing them to their own writing (34). A follow-up exercise asks students to count sentences according to simple, compound, complex, and compound-complex, again making comparisons to their own writing. Almost half of the book is dedicated to imitation, including model passages from a slightly more diverse body of writers, ranging from Washington Irving and Jane Austen to M. Scott Momaday, James Baldwin, Alice Walker, Richard Rodriguez, and Toni Morrison. The setup is simple: Students first copy passages by hand, analyze them, and then imitate the sentence patterns. Teachers interested in taking a classical approach to style, but are hesitant to adopt all of classical rhetoric into their courses, may appreciate this shorter book, and find it a useful supplement to other readings.

Sharon Crowley and Debra Hawhee's textbook, *Ancient Rhetorics for Contemporary Students*, rivals Corbett and Connors's in terms of historical depth, but it employs the *progymnasmata* as well as imitation exercises. In general, the book is an appealing alternative to Corbett and Connors's book. Crowley and Hawhee write in a more inviting voice, and often make more of an effort to relate principles of classical rhetoric to contemporary politics and popular culture. The book treats all five canons of rhetoric, with an entire chapter devoted to style, and another to imitation. The authors provide an overview of the history of style, noting its emergence as early as the Homeric era and its later classification into four virtues (correctness, clarity, appropriateness, and ornament). The most thorough treatment regards the virtue of appropriateness in terms of *kairos* (rhetorical time). As they state, for Roman rhetoricians (namely Cicero), "propriety was not something that can be made into a list of hard and fast rules. Cicero defined propriety as 'what is fitting and agreeable to an occasion or person'" (253). They go on to say that "Cicero favored a situational propriety, one that comes closer to the Greek notion of *kairos*" as employed by the sophists (254). They quote Cicero at length from *De Oratore* on the different uses of style for "deliberative speeches, panegyrics, lawsuits and lectures, and for consolation, protest, discussion and historical narrative, respectively" (3.5.211–212).

More so than in other classically oriented textbooks, Crowley and Hawhee emphasize the proto-generic aspects of classical style. Neither Cicero nor Quintilian exhaustively defined the corresponding mixtures of style to different types of speeches and texts, but that was because, even within these proto-genres, one had to attend to the kairotic configuration of audience, situation, and speaker. No precise understanding of genre as rhetorical situations typified over time emerged in classical Greece (see Miller "Genre as Social Action"). The closest notion was the three levels of style, as discussed in the second chapter of his book.

Crowley and Hawhee manage to accomplish a great deal of what Corbett and Connors do, but in fewer pages. The chapter on style contains definitions and examples of figures of thought and expression, illustrating with examples from antiquity as well as contemporary articles on topics like social media that are of interest to students. The authors also devote attention to the relationship between stylistic devices, grammatical parts of speech, and aspects of voice, such as the rhetorical effects of using first versus second or third person. The authors discuss how manipulating diction and syntax can achieve different levels of distance or intimacy within texts, making language direct or indirect, implicit or explicit, and objective or emotional.

Every chapter is accompanied by one of the *progymnasmata*, designed specifically to scaffold and rehearse the treatment of the other canons. Therefore, *Ancient Rhetorics* is successful in its synthesis of style and invention. While it discusses the terminology of style in a single chapter, it engages issues such as clarity and expression early on, and the progression of exercises invites experimentation with amplification and use of different figures as students hone their rhetorical skills by responding to prompts about contemporary, socio-political issues. For example, the second chapter includes a discussion of the exercise *chreia* (anecdote), and gives several steps based on Aphthonius's manual for expanding a brief account of a moment from history or poetry:

- Begin with praise of a famous speaker or doer of deeds.
- Explain or paraphrase the famous saying or action.
- Supply a reason for the saying or doing.
- Compare and contrast the famous saying or doing to some other speech or event.
- Add an example and support the saying or doing with testimony.
- Conclude with a brief epilogue. (53)

Some exercises provide students with more contemporary material for amplification; for example, the third exercise at the end of the second chapter:

3. Choose a song lyric by your favorite musical artist and cast it as a *chreia* (remember that the distinguishing mark of *chreia*

> is that the saying is attributed to a particular person or group of people—this could well apply to a band). Then amplify the lyric according to Aphthonius's instructions. (54)

Most of the original exercises in the classical handbooks ask students to amplify, shorten, or paraphrase passages from classical literature. Adapting them as Crowley and Hawhee do mainly involves substituting the source material. Instead of asking students to paraphrase famous Athenian speeches or passages from epic poems, teachers might ask students to choose material from their own daily readings and experiences. The exercises of narrative, fable, *chreia*, and description are especially conducive to such experimentation. The exercises provide the framework for amplification, style manuals provide lists of tropes and figures to experiment with, and students may provide idioms and proverbs from their own cultural and linguistic backgrounds.

The only drawback of the textbook is the same one that affects many others—the somewhat national and monolingual approach. The authors draw largely from socio-political debates and readings from the US, without much of a global perspective that would prompt students to negotiate other cultures and languages. Nonetheless, teachers can augment the chapters as discussed above with readings, passages, and discussion topics that attend more directly to language difference as a source of style.

Writing teachers looking for an appropriate text on style for first-year composition may find Holcomb and Killingsworth's *Performing Prose* more approachable, more affordable for students, and easier to integrate into a syllabus. One of the most recent textbooks on style, *Performing Prose* is written for advanced undergraduate and graduate students and scholars; however, it is easily adaptable to a first-year writing course. The authors draw largely from classical rhetoric, but also from sociolinguistics and performance theory, and they explain basic principles and provide a brief historical context. For instance, they reference work by linguists Geoffrey Leech and Michael Short to distinguish between stylistic variance and stylistic value and to reconcile tensions between form and meaning. Stylistic variants refer to "alternate expressions for roughly the same thing," and values refer to "the consequences (what is gained and lost) by choosing one alternate over another" (2). Writers balance variant and value when writing for different rhetorical situations that have their own unique configurations of time, place, audience, and purpose. In some cases, rephrasing a sentence does not significantly alter the meaning; in other cases it does. Holcomb and Killingsworth advise teachers and students to negotiate the two.

The third chapter in particular engages the dynamic between convention and deviation in a way that promises to enlighten students and teachers. Working with the idea of style as deviation from a norm, the authors develop an understanding of how norms emerge within communities of writers and readers. These norms are summarized as five "conventions of readability" about prose:

> It is active.
> It flows.
> It organizes for emphasis.
> It uses familiar language.
> It is concise (41).

Holcomb and Killingsworth's explanation for each of these conventions does not insist on adherence, but instead intends to help students decide how to deviate from these norms in effective, rather than random or arbitrary, ways. The authors provide an example from James Watson and Francis Crick's Nobel Prize-winning essay on DNA, illustrating how "The authors preserve many key features of scientific style, notably the technical terminology and frequent use of the passive voice," meanwhile making unconventional moves such as "the use of first-person plural" and a "greater frequency of action verbs" that "adds a sense of urgency and excitement to the presentation" (51). The authors are careful to point out that such style gained them fame but also infamy, as other scientists responded negatively, seeing such direct, enthusiastic language as egotistical.

Discussions and exercises treat style as a set of tools that enable choice within different rhetorical conventions, rather than imposing a single set of conventions and demanding conformity. Each chapter includes two or three substantive exercises that often involve substantial writing of at least three or more paragraphs. For example, at the end of the third chapter, on deviation and convention, the authors ask students to compare two reviews of the same film regarding how they adhere to or depart from stylistic conventions for the review genre. As they explain, "variations [in style] often depend on the venue in which the review is published: a review appearing in the *New Yorker*, for instance, will likely differ stylistically from one found in *Rolling Stone* or *Entertainment Weekly*" (54). A subsequent exercise asks students to then write their own review based on observations regarding their stylistic analysis of reviews in different genres. The exercise encourages them to "look for opportunities to deviate in terms of either structure or style" (55).

The fifth chapter, on style in the classical tradition, includes exercises that ask students to rank contemporary prose according to Cicero's continuum of plain, middle, and grand styles. Another exercise in the same chapter asks students to imagine themselves as an expert on a topic of their choosing, and have been asked to write three short essays for different occasions: a simple instructional lesson, an entertaining lecture, and an encomium of the subject itself (83). As these examples show, the exercises reinforce a view of style as part of the invention process, often helping to determine the shape of one's prose in response to different rhetorical situations.

In this sense, the textbook a similar philosophy of many others discussed here. However, *Performing Prose* is unique for its attention to what the authors refer to as the textual, social, and cultural areas of style (4). This framework is explained in the introduction, is used to explore style through interactions of writers and readers, and is also used to account for how "verbal patterns . . . circulate in, and gain resonance from, the broader cultural context," becoming "rituals of language" (10), such as the "emphatic repetitions" (9) and sometimes metaphorical language often employed routinely and therefore expected in religious and political addresses. The authors do not cite Bakhtin, but an idea of style as delimited in different ways in different genres appears to drive much of their advice to students and teachers. Holcomb and Killingsworth work from the classical idea of style as entwined with the other canons, especially invention and delivery; as such, they focus on the varying demands for different types (or levels) of style in different rhetorical situations and genres.

Although geared toward upper-level writing courses, Holcomb and Killingsworth's book may be the most suitable of the classically oriented texts for first-year writing courses. At the same time, the book may require some additional planning in order to serve as a successful introductory text for first-year students. Although the chapters themselves are direct, concise, and clear, the exercises often assume advanced literacy and knowledge of genres. Consider the activity from chapter three, in which students are asked to consider the stylistic conventions of magazines such as *The New Yorker* and *Rolling Stone*. While upper-level English majors and graduate students likely read these magazines, or are at least familiar with their conventions, in my experience, first-year college students do not usually read either of these magazines, and probably do not read film reviews. For the exercise to make sense, teachers will need to devote at least two or three class meetings to readings and explorations of the film review genre, assigning reviews from such magazines as readings.

In some cases, I take the general principles and basic ideas behind Holcomb and Killingsworth, and devise my own in-class activities that are more accessible to non-English majors and less advanced students. In one class, I adapted principles and exercises from the third chapter to the conventions of Amazon product reviews—a genre more familiar to young adults. I had students form groups and read conventional Amazon product reviews, and then read satirical reviews of products like Amazon's banana slicer or the Justin Bieber singing electronic toothbrush. Students first analyzed how satirical Amazon reviewers parody the norms of regular reviews. Students then searched the site for other products, and wrote their own satirical reviews. Finally, groups then presented and discussed their stylistic decisions in terms of adherence to and deviation from norms.

Like *Classical Rhetoric and Ancient Rhetorics*, Frank D'Angelo's *Composition in the Classical Tradition* draws on the *progymnasmata*. While the first two books serve as comprehensive rhetorics, and Corbett's curtails discussion of the exercises in favor of imitation, D'Angelo's focuses exclusively on the twelve (or fourteen, depending on the handbook) preliminary exercises used by Roman educators during late antiquity. In the introduction, D'Angelo lays out principles for the exercises, explains their use in preparing students for the three branches of oratory (deliberative, forensic, ceremonial), and discusses how each exercise and accompanying mode of speech is deployed within a particular branch, as well as how the exercises provide training in literary genres. For instance, he explains narrative as preparing students for the narrative portion of deliberative and forensic speeches that "comes right after the introduction and before the arguments" (22)—in turn, these are followed by proposition, confirmation, refutation, and conclusion (themselves subjects of subsequent exercises).

Stressing the relevance of the exercises beyond rhetoric and oratory, D'Angelo points out that while "the exercise in praising and blaming belongs to the ceremonial genre of rhetoric, it is also related to literary forms such as tragedy, epic, elegiac poetry, comedy, satire, and parody" (17). Each chapter explores a different exercise through a brief definition of its purpose, and is followed by model passages, discussion questions, and exercises that prompt students to edit and rewrite short passages using the modes of persuasion from that exercise.

D'Angelo discusses style throughout the textbook, but without a thorough consideration of figures seen in Corbett and Connors or in Holcomb and Killingsworth. D'Angelo's text never introduces or defines any stylistic devices, such as schemes or tropes, and they do not appear in a glossary. This absence may undermine the overall effectiveness of the book, as it frequently asks students in discussion sections to analyze passages for their rhetorical methods. In some cases, such as the chapter on description, it calls on students to "analyze and discuss in class the techniques Homer uses to describe 'The Slaying of the Suitors'" after describing only how the passage "has all of the features of a vivid description of action—motion, direction, and force" (47). The discussion section here contains eighteen questions, six of which ask students to analyze or describes specific techniques. Thus, it seems to assume a great deal of prior knowledge.

Another slight contradiction appears in the choice of model passages. The introduction to the book highlights the multicultural origins of Greco-Roman literature to justify its value and prominence in each chapter. However, the claim that Greco-Roman literature served as a well-spring for other cultures risks the very Eurocentricism and cultural arrogance that it hopes to avoid. Moreover, a majority of the more contemporary passages are pulled from newspapers and, though compelling, do not represent or engage linguistic and cultural diversity as fully as they could. As the discussion of other classically influenced books indicates, this problem runs throughout textbooks advocating classical style. For teachers adopting all or portions of this book, it is easy enough to replace the models with other passages. In this sense, the main value of the textbook lies in its precise and methodical presentation of the exercises and their role in rhetorical training, both in antiquity and today.

Mixed Approaches

Richard M. Eastman's textbook, *Style: Writing and Reading as the Discovery of Outlook*, works from the basic idea that a writer's style indicates an attitude or outlook toward a given subject. Eastman's approach to style links it with invention—he shows how style surfaces in a writer's decisions about how to select and present information. Different interpretations of the same reality lead to different ways of presenting that information; for Eastman, this constitutes a key part of style beyond the level of sentences and passages.

While other textbooks take a bottom-up approach to style, emphasizing how stylistic decisions contribute to an overall tone or voice, Eastman takes a top-down approach, focusing on how someone's stance or perspective on a situation influences their stylistic decisions (e.g., diction, sentence structure, uses of metaphor). The book discusses style in four parts: on the relationship between style and outlook, style and audience, style and language, and style and larger patterns of organization. The first three chapters of Part I show how various outlooks manifest in the selection of details and the presentation of information. As Eastman illustrates, an infantry officer stresses the defensive aspects of a garden, seeing bushes and trees as places to take cover, whereas a civilian might describe the beauty of the flowers and foliage. A student who aces an exam may select and present different details on a test than a student who barely passes. The successful student may choose to talk about his or her score, while the barely successful student may complain about the questions and focus of the test.

The fundamental idea of style as outlook informs Eastman's discussion of audience and language patterns in Part III and Part IV of the book. Writers not only make stylistic decisions from their own outlooks, but also regarding the perceived outlooks of different audiences. Eastman uses the example of explaining vaccines to first graders, who may emphasize pain and promises of health over aspects that adults may find more relevant, such as cost and effectiveness (50). Therefore, the audience's outlook informs the selection and presentation of information, including more micro-level issues of diction and sentence patterns. Eastman's discussion of language patterns and diction covers a lot of the same territory as other books, but the explanation of their importance to outlook makes it unique.

Eastman's sequencing of exercises may require substantial alteration for contemporary college students, especially first-year writers. For example, the preview chapter asks students to "point to exact details of word-choice or sentence structure" (10) when analyzing passages for their outlook, while, several chapters before, Eastman explains such concepts as diction or syntax. If students were able to analyze sentence structure decades ago, today most of them need more orientation to grammatical concepts before they can be expected to do so. Other exercises seem slightly dated. For example, Eastman asks students to visit the vegetable section of a supermarket and write a short description from different perspectives, such as the manager, an elderly couple, or a child (28). Another exercise asks students to combine and rewrite roughly ten sentences from a "paranoid dramatist" in order to convey "an incoherent and highly perturbed state of mind" (29). Yet another exercise asks students to analyze lines from Shakespeare's and Dryden's respective dramatizations of Antony and Cleopatra to discuss the authors' larger outlook on the historical figures (29). In the chapters that focus on grammar, syntax, and paragraph coherence, Eastman asks students to study and imitate passages from James Joyce's *Ulysses*, William Faulkner's *Sound and the Fury*, and Samuel Beckett's *Molly*.

These exercises seem pitched to upper-level English majors, not necessarily college students in first-year composition who are unlikely to have read any of these works, much less find compelling material in the paranoid ranting of a dramatist. As such, contemporary college writing teachers may find the general premise of many exercises useful, but their actual content unsuitable or inappropriate for students or for course outcomes aimed at the acquisition of academic discourse. Rather than dismiss the exercises altogether, teachers might present their basic structure to students and permit them to supply the content. Have students work in groups to identify a popular character and find ten statements the person made, and then follow Eastman's original instructions to organize the statements into a passage that shows the person's outlook on an issue. Instead of going to the supermarket, students might pick a place on their own to write about from three different perspectives. Instead of studying and imitating literary passages, students might work with excerpts from essays and books by public intellectuals who present a more academic outlook on issues of general importance.

For example, I am currently planning for students to study and paraphrase a short op-ed piece on Miley Cyrus written by a sociologist at the University of Washington. Although a great deal of superficial and reactionary coverage emerged from Miley's sexually provocative dress and dance routine at the Video Music Awards in 2013, sociologist Pepper Schwartz discusses the media discourse around it for underlying messages about American sexuality and media representations of children and teenagers. One of my activities involves having students compare the sociologist's outlook on Cyrus's performance to the outlooks of non-academics. This question provides an occasion to see how an academic outlook calls for a more academic vocabulary, complex sentences, and a serious, analytical tone. Contemporizing many of Eastman's exercises can prompt students to understand that even ostensibly superficial issues about celebrities can provide the subject matter of more serious outlooks.

Tom Romano's *Blending Genre, Altering Style* serves less as a textbook, and more as a teachers' guide for creating multi-genre paper assignments. Addressed to teachers, Romano approaches style as the selection and arrangement of genres within a single paper. These genres range from fiction, poetry, and drama to photographs, letters, and recipes. The book provides little information about style in terms of figurative language, rhythm, or syntax. Instead, it devotes chapters to individual genres such as short stories, dialogue sequences, different subgenres of poetry, and model essays. These essays illustrate how authors carry topics and themes across several genres, over eight to twelve pages. One essay Romano provides consists of recipes, diary entries, poems, and conversations written in the form of a screenplay.

The basic idea behind Romano's book is helpful, in that it treats style as a means of negotiating and understanding genres. Yet, the book does not appear to develop links between genre and style. For instance, a short chapter on the conventional research paper merely recognizes the value of the "voice that argues and illustrates and extends thinking in a logical progression of language and ideas . . . the voice that understands the power of thesis statements and knows how to incorporate powerful secondary sources" (88). Romano shares no other thoughts about integrating the conventions of research-based writing with fiction or poetry. None of the model essays attempt such synthesis. Nor does Roman go into depth about how various genres produce their own stylistic conventions.

Teachers need not assign multi-genre papers, per se, in the somewhat flat-footed method Romano explains, with papers stitched together from one- or two-page snippets that emulate other genres. Some students may even find such assignments simplistic and naïve, given their own literacy experiences in cyberspace that has, if nothing else taught, us the blurred lines between many types of texts. Instead, teachers might begin by rupturing the research-based essay, showing how it can take up the conventions of other genres—fiction, poetry, drama—while still sustaining a complex, thesis-driven argument with secondary sources. Jody Shipka's book, *Toward a Composition Made Whole* describes the over-arching project of multimodal scholarship in this regard, encouraging teachers to explore "the ways in which writing intersects and interacts with other semiotic systems," such as the "selfie" described in Chapter 6 (137). A complete composition course should ultimately have students compose multi-genre projects like those Romano describes, but be even more open to "visual, auditory, olfactory, or tactile modes" (138). Shipka describes a range of projects in which students integrate text with these other genres and mediums, including essays inscribed on physical objects like ballerina shoes, board games with advertisements, and comic strips. For each assignment, students complete a "statement of goals and choices" that asks them to reflect on their decisions to incorporate different media (113).

In various classes I have taught, students compose their own versions of *The Daily Show* in response to current events, produced postmodern retellings of fairy tales in the form of graphic novels, and published digital research papers as blogs. Such assignments expose students to different stylistic conventions, and prompt them to reflect on and engage with style through navigating multiple genres and mediums. Through workshops, conferences, and feedback, teachers can help students make local and global decisions about when to employ an objective, analytical tone, versus when to reinforce such analysis with a more personal or outspoken voice.

Lanham's *Revising Prose* engages "bureaucratic writing," a term that refers to wordy sentences often written in the passive voice with an excessive number of prepositional phrases and circumlocutions. In the first three chapters, Lanham constructs what he calls the "paramedic method" for students to use to edit for conciseness and precision (41-42). The method consists of eight short steps that instruct writers to chart and mark their sentences for issues such as "prepositional-phrase strings" that inhibit a writer's rhythm and, in turn, make prose difficult to understand, often clouding even the writer's own thinking about a given issue:

1. Circle the prepositions.
2. Circle the "is" forms.
3. Find the action.
4. Put this action in a simple (not compound) active verb.
5. Start fast—no slow windups.
6. Read the passage aloud with emphasis and feeling.
7. Write out each sentence on a blank screen or sheet of paper and mark off its basic rhythmic units with a "/."
8. Mark off sentence length with a "/."

The rest of the book illustrates how this method can be applied to different types of professional writing, including business prose, legal prose, and technical prose. The end of the book presents roughly thirty "diagnose and repair" exercises in which students apply the paramedic method to problematic passages, and then rewrite them.

Although loosely informed by grammar and classical rhetoric, Lanham admits to sacrificing theoretical accuracy for practicality. According to his own method, when diagramming a sentence, he states that, "I don't claim this division is linguistically correct, whatever that might mean. Just the opposite. It is a quick and easy method any of us can use to chart our own reading of a passage to imagine how our voice might embody the prose rhythm" (45). Thus, the book does not discount other approaches to style and grammar, though it does claim to be the simplest and most effective for making students conscious of the impact writing has at the sentence level.

Many teachers have incorporated the paramedic method into their own teaching and feedback practices without necessarily using the textbook. Because of its simplicity, the paramedic method may appear on almost countless writing center handouts and online tutorials. For instance, the popular Online Writing Lab maintained by Purdue University has kept a page on the method for years. Many of the most experienced writers and editors, especially journalists, readily follow the basic principles of the paramedic method. Yet, the paramedic method is not without its shortcomings. Sometimes writers use circumlocution and indirect language for emphasis. Phrases like "What I mean by that is," or long prepositional chains like "the house at the end of the street on top of the hill across town" add clarity or spontaneity, rather than fog. Moreover, simply shortening sentences can eviscerate a powerful statement. Imagine applying the paramedic method to Martin Luther King's "I Have a Dream" speech, a speech loaded with majestic metaphors that nonetheless rely on long stretches of prepositional phrases. Likewise, passive constructions that use "is" and "was" are sometimes simpler and more straightforward than contorting a sentence around an active verb. Even Lanham might admit that there is nothing stylistically awkward about the sentence, "That house is made of wood," and that it is probably clearer than saying, "Someone made that house out of wood." The difference between foggy, bureaucratic writing and clear, precise writing in these terms lies in knowing when certain constructions work and when they do not. As I tell my students, such judgment takes years of development and feedback that begins in a college composition class, but does not end there.

Noah Lukeman's *A Dash of Style* addresses aspiring creative writers, but its basic principles about punctuation as stylistic tools equally apply to academic writers. Promoting the use of punctuation as an "art form" (1), Lukeman treats punctuation marks in three major sections. The first section covers periods, commas, and semicolons. Lukeman conflates period use with sentence length, advising writers that the frequency of periods reveals the style of a writer or character. Short sentences contribute to a straightforward, crisp, and action-oriented style. Meanwhile, longer sentences imply complexity of thought, depth, and slower internal conflicts. The second section covers colons, dashes, parentheses, quotation marks, and paragraph and section breaks. The third section covers exclamation marks, ellipses, and hyphens.

Exercises at the end of each chapter may be useful to both creative and academic writers, as when Lukeman asks readers to write page-long sentences that may help them "find a new narration style" or "more creative freedom" (41). Other exercises prompt writers to experiment with punctuation marks by rewriting passages from their own work, inserting more commas, removing all commas, extending and expanding sentences, and noting how each punctuation mark affects the rhythm and pace of sentences. Although Lukeman relies on illustrations from literary works, and often refers to novels and short stories in the exercises, the same principles about punctuation for purpose—rather than correctness—may help college students learn to play with the conventions of academic writing. The book frequently reminds readers that there are multiple correct ways to punctuate a sentence, and that writers can develop a voice by exploring the wide range of possibilities.

The main weakness of Lukeman's book is that he rarely defines grammatical concepts such as clauses, phrases, modifiers, or even sentences. The book may be useful for teachers who want to develop a more aesthetic approach to punctuation, one that influences their approach to teaching mechanics or commenting on such issues in student papers. However, other books such as Kolln's, Williams and Colomb's, and Holcomb and Killingsworth's may be more effective as actual classroom texts. Unlike Lukeman's book, these texts take the time to define grammatical terms, and explain more clearly how grammar (not punctuation alone) functions as a component of style.

Final Thoughts on Teaching Style

As this chapter's examination of textbooks shows, style is not a matter of editing or proofing at the end of the composing process. Writers should see style as a valuable means of persuasion and as a method of discovering ideas. The more teachers stress the idea of style as part of writing processes, as an opportunity to develop a voice and an appreciation for difference, the richer that writing will be. There are a number of strategies and techniques to take away from this book:

1. Integrate style into the curriculum at multiple points, and make it an explicit topic by assigning readings and adapting exercises and activities from the books discussed in this chapter.
2. Assign essays, books, and speeches that demonstrate lively academic styles. Try to assign a linguistically and culturally diverse range of authors.
3. With students, analyze the sentence patterns, uses of rhythm, and figurative language in these works.
4. Assign in-class or out-of-class activities in imitation. Give students credit for completing them, but consider commenting or responding rather than "correcting" these compositions. Have them imitate a wide variety of authors.
5. Encourage or even require students to use stylistic devices (e.g., tropes, figures, and schemes) in major assignments.

6. Assign low stakes and high stakes assignments that ask students to compose in a range of genres (e.g., reviews, letters, emails, essays, research papers, editorials, photo-essays). Have them analyze the stylistic conventions of these genres and then experiment with them in their own writing.
7. Encourage special consideration to digital genres and their stylistic conventions. Have students compose tweets, memes, and status updates with attention to their stylistic constraints and possibilities.
8. Assign reflective essays that ask students to discuss their views about style and how other assignments may foster a greater awareness of the rhetorical impact of linguistic choices on their writing.

For those teachers who adopt them, these guiding principles bring style out of the shadows of college writing classes, helping to improve students' writing while also perhaps increasing their satisfaction in producing the academic texts required for success. Teachers may find responding to and evaluating student writing less laborious—less about "correcting errors"—and instead provide comments that help students achieve a balance between convention and expression, or conformity and deviation. Given the long and turbulent history of style, it would be naïve to think that this book will instantly transform teaching practices nationwide. However, even a handful of teachers adapting a handful of these approaches will affirm the message of this book—that style can be inventive and meaningful, and that it merits serious attention from teachers and researchers concerned with the effects of language.

Table 1. Table of Textbooks

Book Title	Linguistic Approach	Classical Approach	Mixed/Other Approach	Exercises/Activities	Course Level (Introductory, Intermediate, Advanced)
Style: Lessons in Clarity and Grace	x			x	Intro/Intermediate
Classical Rhetoric for Modern Students		x		x	Intermediate/Advanced
Style and Statement		x			Intro/Intermediate
Ancient Rhetorics for Contemporary Students		x		x	Intermediate/Advanced
A Matter of Style	x	x			Advanced
Rhetorical Grammar				x	Intro/Intermediate
Performing Prose					Intro/Intermediate/Advanced
Artful Sentences: Syntax as Style	x				Advanced
Composition in the Classical Tradition		x		x	Intro/Intermediate
Revising Prose			x		Intro/Intermediate
The Well-Crafted Sentence	x			x	Intro/Intermediate
A Dash of Style			x		Intermediate/Advanced
Style: Writing as the Discovery of Outlook			x		Intermediate/Advanced

Glossary

This glossary provides a brief but informative series of definitions associated with the key issues explored in this book. It focuses on terms that have been implicitly defined in the text, and does not include concepts or fields that have been explicitly dealt with elsewhere. A complete listing of stylistic terms would not be feasible, and has already been done by contemporary and classical rhetoricians. Teachers or researchers interested in a full description of stylistic devices might consult Richard Lanham's *A Handlist of Rhetorical Terms* or the website *Silva Rhetoricae*, maintained by Brigham Young University. Textbooks described in the previous chapter also include detailed definitions of grammatical terms and parts of speech.

Amplification — Amplifying discourse involves "endow[ing] it with stylistic prominence so that it acquires conceptual importance . . . and salience in the minds of the audience" (Fahnestock 390). The item amplified could be an idea, an image, or word. A range of strategies exist to amplify discourse, including diction, syntax, and simple abundance (e.g., Erasmus's *copia*). Amplification is a broad term under which the use of specific stylistic devices falls, when used to stress the importance of elements within a given text.

Alliteration — The manipulation of sonic textures in language for rhetorical or aesthetic effect is referred to as alliteration. Poets have used this strategy since antiquity in Western and Eastern oral and literate traditions. The older sophist Gorgias is identified as the first rhetorician to use alliteration. Two of the most common alliterative devices are consonance (repetition of consonant sounds) and assonance (repetition of vowel sounds). Although a frequent strategy in literary works, rhetorical texts also often demonstrate a sense of sonic texturing.

Assonance — See Alliteration.

Attic — During the classical Greek and Roman eras, orators could be described as having an "Attic" or mainland Greek style when they spoke plainly, with a minimal amount of ornamentation. An "Attic" style also referred to shorter, less complicated sentences. In *Brutus*, Cicero defines Attic against Asiatic or bombastic rhetoric, as he saw the former as appropriate for younger rhetors or passionate issues, and a hallmark of Asian rhetorical styles. Quintilian sought to complicate the easy distinction between Attic and Asiatic, asserting in Book XII of *The Orator's Education* that many rhetors switch between restrained and expressive styles.

Asiatic — See Attic.

Cumulative Sentence — A cumulative sentence consists of a main clause that branches right with additional phrases and clauses, for example: "The car sped down the street, hitting mailboxes, knocking over trash bins, and nearly ramming a cyclist." Classical rhetoricians traditionally prefer these sentences over periodic ones because they are more direct. Periodic sentences, by contrast, contain clauses and phrases before the main clause, for example: "Hitting mailboxes, knocking over trash bins, and nearly ramming a cyclist, the car sped down the street." Periodic sentences are intended to create a feeling of suspense that, if not managed effectively, can lead to confusion and impatience.

Clause — A unit of language containing a subject, verb, and object. A simple sentence consists of at least one clause, whereas complex and/or compound sentences consist of more than one clause. Writers can alternate their use of clauses within and across sentences to contribute to a distinctive voice or tone in a given text, and to coordinate levels of information.

Code-Meshing — A relatively recent term introduced by Vershawn A. Young and A. Suresh Canagarajah, now used by a number of rhetoric and composition researchers. Code-meshing refers to the general use of more than one social language or register in the same text. Some debate has ensued about the necessity of a new term that synthesizes similar terms from linguistics, including code-switching or mixing (using two codes in the same speech act), lexical borrowing between languages, embedded language (stretches of untranslated discourse within another language), and loan translations (adapting a new word into a language according to its spelling and morphological conventions).

Christensen Rhetoric—Francis Christensen advocated a particular approach to stylistic dexterity in his 1967 book, *Notes Toward a New Rhetoric*, where Christensen resists the contemporaneous approach of sentence-combining that was also prominent during the late 1960s and 1970s. Instead, Christensen saw the key to effective writing in cumulative sentences and the manipulation of detail in paragraphs. For Christensen, writers need add detail and clarification to their sentences by adding successions of clauses and modifiers to their main ideas. Effective paragraphs demonstrate a writer's ability to shift smoothly between levels of generality and specificity, contributing a sense of coherence to writing that might be described as mature or graceful.

Consonance — See Alliteration.

Descriptive Grammar — While prescriptive grammars in English date back to the emergence of usage handbooks during the seventeenth and eighteenth centuries, descriptive grammar emerged as an alternative during the late nineteenth and early twentieth centuries. Prescriptive or school grammars could be said to try to codify language into rules that are either followed or broken. In contrast, descriptive grammars seek to describe language use without making judgments about what is correct or incorrect. Most linguists take a descriptive approach; the grammatical models of English they constructed—such as transformational and functional grammar—supply writers and writing teachers with much terminology that is used to discuss stylistic decisions. If grammar is a matter of exhaustively describing the available options for formulating sentences, then style is a matter of using the language of descriptive grammar to determine the options that are appropriate for given situations.

Error — This is a loaded term with a long history that dates back to Quintilian's enumeration of barbarisms and solecisms, including misspellings and awkward sentence constructions. In the history of the English language, error became especially important during the period of standardization and the evolution of print during the seventeenth and eighteenth centuries. Histories of rhetoric and composition acknowledge that American cultural insecurity and linguistic xenophobia played a role in creating the contemporary notion of error that culminated in the late nineteenth and early twentieth century literacy crises engineered by Harvard University. Researchers in rhetoric and composition have challenged and redefined error at multiple points: sociolinguists point out the socially-constructed nature of error in the field's major journals in the 1950s and 1960s. Mina Shaughnessy's *Errors and Expectations* thoroughly shows that errors are not random, but are instead indicative of a writer's attempts to negotiate conflicting conventions. Bruce Horner and Min-Zhan Lu further Shaughnessy's project by proposing a negotiation model for addressing errors, as opposed to simple correction. Scholarship on error in composition and second-language writing has generally sought to de-stigmatize and pluralize error.

Figures of Speech and Thought — These are rhetorical devices that were defined by classical rhetoricians as the use of language for effect. Figures are different from tropes because they do not necessarily entail metaphorical language. Figures of speech refer to uses of language that alter the expression of an idea, but are not part of structuring of an argument. In *Rhetorica Ad Herennium*, paradox and oxymoron are considered figures of expression. By contrast, personification and division are considered figures of thought. Although important historically, many contemporary rhetoricians question what seems to be an ever-shifting and sometimes arbitrary system of classification. For example, paradox is technically considered a figure of expression; yet, it is not difficult to appreciate it as impacting the content as well as the form of an argument.

Imitation — In classical rhetoric, imitation was the process by which rhetors acquired their own distinctive style. They copied model passages verbatim while also translating works between Latin and Greek. Certain imitation exercises called on students to imitate the styles of famous characters or authors while supplying their own content. During the European Renaissance, students followed a similar curriculum that involved copying and translating between Greek, Latin, and English. Edward P. J. Corbett was at the forefront of a movement to revive classical imitation during the 1960s and 1970s. Corbett laid out a complete curriculum involving imitation in his textbook, *Classical Rhetoric for the Modern Student*. Dialogic and postmodern interpretations of the classical canon stress imitation as an innate discursive act that all language users engage in, regardless of whether they do so as part of a formal curriculum. Writers and speakers always emulate, imitate, and appropriate one another's speech and writing styles. Postcolonial approaches to imitation use the term "mimicry" to describe a subversive form of imitation utilized to contest power dynamics. Recent research in language difference proposed that the apparent adherence to conventions may not passively imitative but, in fact, signifies agency and decision-making that is used to reproduce dominant styles with latent or subtle contextual differences.

Levels of Style — Cicero originally created three general tiers of style: the plain, the middle, and the grand. Each level of style corresponded to a different rhetorical purpose and form of rhetoric. The plain style was appropriate for forensic rhetoric, the middle for deliberative, and the grand for epideictic. Quintilian and Augustine forwarded the three-tiered style, and Augustine adapted it for the purposes of sermonizing. Later, Hermogenes expanded the levels of style to allow rhetors more flexibility for adjusting their use of language to a wider range of rhetorical situations. Hermogenes's seven types of style became popular during the European Renaissance, given the proliferation of genres that exceeded the explanatory power of the original three tiers. Today, rhetoric and composition researchers gravitate further away from tiers and toward genre as a more useful framework for understanding the relationship between language choices and recurring rhetorical situations, such as campaign speeches, eulogies, obituaries, lectures, and op-ed pieces.

Metaphor — Aristotle originally defined metaphor as an apt transference of words from one class to another in order to render ideas more clear or vivid. Aristotle's prescriptions for metaphor stressed clarity, candor, and refrain from far-fetched comparisons. Metaphor is a broad term that can include subtypes such as similes, tropes, and figures of thought and expression. Language that is metaphorical is merely non-literal. Although many theorists discuss metaphor as a tool of ornamentation, a constructivist approach to language holds that metaphors reflect and shape users' perceptions of reality. Research in sociolinguistics and stylistics examined the ways in which widely used metaphors reveal dominant ideologies. For instance, the frequent appearance of war-like metaphors to describe sports highlights American and Western ideological associations between competition and violence.

Meter – Often used as a tool for analyzing verse, meter is a unit of measurement used to describe rhythm via a speaker or writer's use of stressed and unstressed syllables. Four main types of meter exist: anapest (two stressed, one unstressed), dactylic (one unstressed, two stressed), iambic (one unstressed, one stressed), and trochaic (one stressed, one unstressed). Meter can be measured in any form of oral or written discourse, including prose. George Saintsbury articulated a complex theory of prose meter in his 1910 book, *A History of English Prose Rhythm*, offering a variety of meters unique to prose that many theorists dismiss as somewhat convoluted and overly technical. In *A Matter of Style*, Matthew Clark doubts that a complete theory of prose rhythm is possible, and advises writers to attend to syllable variation intuitively rather than systematically.

Periodic Sentence — See Cumulative Sentence.

Progymnasmata — Classical rhetoricians in Greece and Rome based a large portion of their training on a set of fourteen preliminary exercises that bridge rhetorical and grammatical instruction and are organized by level of difficulty. Students completed the exercises in conjunction with instruction in analysis and imitation of model speeches and works of literature. The main goal was to instill in students the ability to amplify discourse to practice writing shorter works that corresponded to the parts of orations: introduction, narration, refutation, and conclusion. The exercises are described in the *Rhetorica ad Herennium* and *The Orator's Education*. Four extant handbooks are translated by George Kennedy in *Progymnasmata: Greek Textbooks of Prose Composition and Rhetoric*.

Prescriptive Grammar — See Descriptive Grammar.

Register — Traditionally, this term is used by different sociolinguists to account for language use in different discursive situations. M. A. K Halliday and R. Hasan's *Cohesion in English* (1976) describes register as language features used for specific purposes and tasks in recurring situations. Formal registers in public and professional settings tend to rely on standard features of a language, while casual registers are characterized by the use of slang and vernacular, and private or intimate registers may be more affected by intonation and nonverbal cues. Increasingly, research in sociolinguistics has used the term register and style interchangeably.

Rhetorical Grammar — This idea was introduced into contemporary rhetoric and composition pedagogy by Martha Kolln, who co-authored a textbook with the same name. More recently, Laura Miccicche revived rhetorical grammar as a tool to synthesize micro- and macro-level discourse, showing how language choices such as diction and syntax contribute to larger rhetorical elements. The last several decades are characterized by tension between pedagogies that privilege either form or content. Rhetorical grammar aims to dissolve the tension and articulate the relationship between style, grammar, and rhetoric.

Rhythm — See Meter.

Annotated Bibliography: Further Readings on Style

This brief annotated bibliography describes some important works that are not directly discussed in this book for various reasons. Many of these works are collections of essays are addressed separately regarding their contributions to the study of style. Because they provide convenient access to some of the most significant positions on style in rhetoric and composition, they complement this reference guide well.

This list excludes some useful resources that are commonly referred to elsewhere, such as Patricia Bizzell and Bruce Herzberg's *The Rhetorical Tradition*, Susan Miller's *Norton Book of Composition Studies*, and John Breteton's *The Origins of Composition Studies in the American College, 1875–1925*. For more information on the classical period and classical rhetorical treatises, see James J. Murphy, Richard A. Katula, and Michael Hoppmann's *A Synoptic History of Classical Rhetoric*, as well as Murphy's *A Short History of Writing Instruction*. Teachers and researchers interested in stylistics should consult the journal *Language and Literature* as well as Bloomsbury Publishing's Advances in Stylistics series, edited by Dan McIntyre.

An extensive list of sources on style and stylistics can be found at Rebecca Moore Howard's collection of bibliographies:

> http://www.rebeccamoorehoward.com/bibliographies/
> style-and-stylistics-sentence-combining-t-units

Readers may also want to consult a separate, crowd-sourced bibliography by Nora Bacon on style models. This resource is also available on Howard's website: http://www.rebeccamoorehoward.com/bibliographies/style-models.

Ballif, Michelle, and Michael G. Moran. *Classical Rhetorics and Rhetoricians: Critical Studies and Sources.* Westport: Praeger, 2005. Print.

Ballif and Moran gathered an extensive collection of scholarly profiles on important figures in the history of rhetoric. Its coverage is deep and broad, including well-known rhetoricians such as Aristotle and Aspasia, but also more obscure rhetoricians, such as Apsines of Gadara and Libanius. Each profile is written by a different specialist in the histories of classical rhetoric. This guide focuses exclusively on Greco-Roman antiquity. Those interested in learning more about classical orientations to style, or mapping out historical research projects on classical style, should consult this book.

Butler, Paul. *Style in Rhetoric and Composition: A Critical Sourcebook.* Boston: Bedford/St. Martins, 2010. Print.

Butler's collection contains five sections on stylistic studies in rhetoric and composition. The first section is devoted to classical sources, including excerpts from Aristotle's *Rhetoric*, Cicero's *Orator*, and Quintilian's *The Orator's Education*. The second section considers the marginalization of style in composition studies, with essays by Robert Connors, Frank Farmer and Philip Arrington, and Mike Duncan. The third section covers debates on style in the discipline, especially those occurring during the 1970s and 1980s. This section includes essays by Francis Christensen, Virginia Tufte, Martha Kolln, and Richard Ohmann. The fourth section addresses pedagogy, with essays by Edward P. J. Corbett, Winston Weathers, and Laura Micciche. The fourth section contains alternative perspectives on style by Geneva Smitherman, Min-Zhan Lu, and Mary P. Hiatt that address issues of language difference and feminist rhetorics. The final section contains contemporary advances in stylistic studies, including work by Butler, T. R. Johnson, Kathryn Flannery, and Farmer. Many of the essays here are cited in this book, and it is a useful gathering of key pieces on the role of style in writing and rhetoric. It may serve as a valuable complement to this reference guide.

Duncan, Mike, and Star M. Vanguri. *The Centrality of Style*. Anderson and Fort Collins: Parlor Press and The WAC Clearinghouse, 2013. Online.

This book is also practical in orientation, outlining a variety of frameworks for incorporating style into first-year and advanced college writing courses. Although the book is divided into two parts—one about the conceptualizations, and one about the practical applications of style—each essay has direct or indirect pedagogical implications. Essays by Denise Stodola and Tom Pace draw specific connections between historical conceptions of style and contemporary teaching. Other essays by Moe Folk, Zak Lancaster, and Luke Redington lay out different theoretical lenses for style, but address their relevance for pedagogy. Crystal Fodrey proposes options for addressing style in creative non-fiction courses, and Jonathan Buehl offers a model of teaching style in the contexts of scientific writing. The collection also contains an essay by Chris Hoclomb and Jimmie Killingsworth, outlining their notion of performative style—also found in their book, *Performing Prose*, discussed in Chapter 8.

Fahnestock, Jeanne. *Rhetorical Style: The Uses of Language in Persuasion*. Oxford: Oxford UP, 2011. Print.

Fahnestock's book covers style from a range of angles, drawing on linguistics, sociolinguistics, literary theory, and rhetorical history and theory. The book is divided into four long parts, with several sections each. The first part covers word choice in style, with attention to the history of the English language and classical orientations to tropes as well as figures of thought and expression. The second part covers sentence structure, construction, and modification. It also includes discussion of loose and periodic sentences, sentence sequences, and prose rhythm. The third part covers the relationship of voice, dialogue, and dialogism to stylistic issues. The final part explores the contribution of micro-level stylistic decisions to overall cohesion and meaning at the level of paragraphs and passages. Fahnestock's treatment of style targets a somewhat advanced audience. Although clearly written, it assumes a basic level of knowledge in style and linguistics that this book tries to provide. It may be a valuable resource for those interested in developing an advanced knowledge of style and as a jumping-off point into research projects.

Gaillet, Lynée L, and Winifred B. Horner. *The Present State of Scholarship in the History of Rhetoric: A Twenty-First Century Guide.* Columbia: U of Missouri P, 2010. Print.

Gaillet and Horner's collection is a set of comprehensive bibliographies on historical eras in rhetoric, moving from antiquity through the twenty-first century. It contains six contributions: a treatment of the classical period by Louis Agnew; a treatment of the Middle Ages by Denise Stodola; a treatment of the Renaissance by Don Paul Abbott; a treatment of the eighteenth century by Linda Ferreira-Buckley; a treatment of the nineteenth century by Gaillet; and a treatment of the twentieth and twenty-first centuries by Krista Ratcliffe. Each entry contains a general description of the time period, with extensive discussion of key primary and secondary sources, followed by a nearly exhaustive list of resources.

Horner, Bruce, Min-Zhan Lu, and Paul K. Matsuda. *Cross-language Relations in Composition.* Carbondale: Southern Illinois UP, 2010. Print.

This book gathers a number of key arguments published in the area of language difference over the past two decades that pertain to the discussion of linguistic diversity and style in Chapter 6 of this book. These key arguments include John Trimbur's historical consideration of English Only attitudes in the US; Min-Zhan Lu's negotiation model for "error" in writing; Paul Kei Matsuda's critique of the myth of linguistic homogeneity in US college composition; Richard Lyon's notion of rhetorical sovereignty in Native American rhetorics; LuMing Mao's articulation of Asian American rhetorics; A. Suresh Canagarajah's exploration of linguistic shuttling and code-meshing; and Anis Bawarshi's synthesis of linguistic diversity and uptake. Many of these essays and positions are addressed in this book, and reading them in conversation with this book promises a more in-depth understanding of a translingual or linguistically diverse conception of rhetorical style.

Johnson, T. R., and Tom Pace. *Refiguring Prose Style: Possibilities for Writing Pedagogy*. Logan: Utah State UP, 2005. Print.

This collection appeared as one of the early calls in rhetoric and composition for a revival of stylistic studies and pedagogy, after Robert Connors's influential "The Erasure of the Sentence," but before Paul Butler's *Out of Style*. It is divided into four parts: the first reflects on the marginalization of style in the discipline; the second offers pedagogical and theoretical considerations of literary style in writing instruction; the third focuses exclusively on pedagogical applications of rhetorical style; and the fourth proposes new definitions and frameworks for style. The primary strength of this collection lies in its arguments and strategies in favor of teaching aspects of style in college writing courses. It is targeted toward a broad audience of beginning and experienced teachers who want to explore options for attending to style.

Olinger, Andrea and Zak Lancaster. "Teaching Grammar-In Context in College Writing Instruction: An Update on the Research Literature." WPA-CompPile Research Bibliographies, No. 24.

This bibliography provides a comprehensive treatment on the question of grammar in writing instruction and its relationship to style. The authors ultimately promote the idea that grammar instruction in context enables students in both first and second-language contexts to develop a critical metalinguistic awareness that aids their literacy development, without perpetuating the correctness model associated with earlier school-based grammars. Their bibliography includes sources in rhetoric and composition as well as linguistics, sociolinguistics, systemic functional linguistics, and second-language writing. The authors also include coverage of sentence-combining, acknowledging that the original approach has pedagogical potential when adapted for more meaningful activities tied to students' actual reading and writing assignments.

Weber, Jean J. *The Stylistics Reader: From Roman Jakobson to the Present*. London: Arnold, 1996. Print.

This collection of readings provides a helpful orientation to analytical approaches in stylistics. Although it is an older collection, the reprinted essays are foundational to understanding more recent work in this discipline. It includes Roman Jakobson's address at the Style in Language Conference in 1958 that inaugurated stylistics as a mode of inquiry, as well as Stanley Fish's critique of stylistics that prompted a turn toward less formal and more interactive models of stylistic analysis. The readings are divided into eight sections: formalist stylistics; functionalist stylistics; affective stylistics; pedagogical stylistics; pragmatic stylistics; critical stylistics; feminist stylistics; and cognitive stylistics. Readers interested in the discussion of stylistics in Chapter 7 of this book will find that the book fairly represents the central projects and purposes of each approach.

Works Cited

Abbot, Don Paul. "The Renaissance." *The Present State of Scholarship in the History of Rhetoric*. Ed. Lynee Lewis Gaillet and Winifred Bryan Horner. Columbia and London: U of Missouri P, 2010. 82–113. Print.

—. "Rhetoric and Writing in the Renaissance." *A Short History of Writing Instruction*. Ed. James J. Murphy. Mahwah, NJ: Lawrence Erlbaum, 2001. 145–72. Print.

Adams, J. N. *Bilingualism and the Latin Language*. Cambridge: Cambridge UP, 2003. Print.

Alberici, Mauro Inguanez. *Alberici Casinensis Flores Rhetorici*. Trans. Henry M. Willard. Rome: Montecassino, 1938. Print.

Alexander, Gavin, ed. *Sidney's 'the Defence of Poesy' and Selected Renaissance Literary Criticism*. London: Penguin, 2004. Print.

Amare, Nicole. "Style: The New Grammar in Composition Studies?" *Refiguring Prose Style: Possibilities for Writing Pedagogy*. Ed. T. R. Johnson and Tom Pace. Logan: Utah State UP, 2005. 153–66. Print.

Annas, Pamela J. "Style as Politics: A Feminist Approach to the Teaching of Writing." *College English* 47.4 (1985): 360–71. Print.

Anzaldua, Gloria. *Borderlands*. San Francisco: Aunt Lute Books, 2007. Print.

Aristotle. *On Rhetoric: A Theory of Civic Discourse*. Trans. George Kennedy. Oxford: Oxford UP, 1991. Print.

—. W. H. Fyfe, Longinus, and Demetrius. *Aristotle, the Poetics: "Longinus," on the Sublime, Demetrius on Style*. Cambridge: Harvard UP, 1973. Print.

Ascham, Roger. *The Scholemaster*. Amsterdam: Theatrum Orbis Terrarum, 1968. Print.

Baca, Damian and Victor Villanueva. *Rhetorics of the Americas*. New York: Palgrave Macmillan, 2009. Print.

Bacon, Nora. "Style in Academic Writing." *The Centrality of Style*. Ed. Mike Duncan and Star Medzerian Vanguri. Anderson: Parlor Press, 2013. 173–90. Print.

—. *The Well-Crafted Sentence: A Writer's Guide to Style*. Boston: Bedford/St. Martins, 2013. Print.

Bahri, Deepika. *Native Intelligence: Aesthetics, Politics, and Postcolonial Literature*. Minneapolis: U of Minnesota P, 2003. Print.

Bain, Alexander. *English Composition and Rhetoric Enlarged*. London, 1908. Print.

Bakthin, Mikhail. *Problems of Dostoevsky's Poetics*. Minneapolis: U of Minnesota P, 2003. Print.

—. *The Dialogic Imagination: Four Essays*. Ed. Michael Holquist. Austin: U of Texas P, 1981. Print.

—. *Speech Genres and Other Late Essays*. Ed. Vern McGee, Michael Holquist, and Caryl Emerson. Austin: U of Texas P, 2010. Print.

Ballif, Michelle. "Re/Dressing Histories; Or, On Re/Covering Figures Who Have Been Laid Bare By Our Gaze." *Rhetoric Society Quarterly* 22.1 (1992): 91–98. Print.

—. *Seduction, Sophistry, and the Woman with the Rhetorical Figure*. Carbondale: Southern Illinois UP, 2001. Print.

Ballif, Michelle, and Michael Moran. *Classical Rhetorics and Rhetoricians: Critical Studies and Sources*. Westport: Greenwood, 2005. Print.

Banks, Adam. *Digital Griot: African-American Rhetoric in a Multimedia Age*. Carbondale: Southern Illinois UP, 2011. Print.

Bartholomae, David. "Inventing the University." *Journal of Basic Writing* 5.1 (1986): 4–23. Print.

Bartholomae, David and Anthony Petrosky. *Ways of Reading: Words and Images*. Boston: Bedford/St. Martin's, 2003. Print.

Bazerman, Charles. "An Essay on Pedagogy by Mikhail M. Bakhtin." *Written Communication* 22.3 (2005): 333–38. Print.

Bazerman, Charles et al. *Reference Guide to Writing Across the Curriculum*. West Lafayette: Parlor Press, 2005. Print.

Beaugrande, Robert. "Generative Stylistics: Between Grammar and Rhetoric." *College Composition and Communication* 28.3 (1977): 240–46. Print.

Bennett, Beth S. "Boethius." *Classical Rhetoric and Rhetoricians*. Ballif and Moran. 86–95.

Berlin, James A. *Rhetoric and Reality: Writing Instruction in American Colleges, 1900–1985*. Carbondale: Southern Illinois UP, 1987. Print.

Bialostosky, Don. "Rhetoric in Literary Criticism and Theory." *The Sage Handbook of Rhetorical Studies*. Ed. Andrea A. Lunsford and Kirt H. Wilson. Thousand Oaks: Sage. 215–26. Print.

Binkley, Roberta, and Carol S. Lipson, eds. *Rhetoric Before and Beyond the Greeks*. Albany: State U of New York P, 2004. Print.

—, eds. *Ancient Non-Greek Rhetorics*. West Lafayette: Parlor Press, 2009. Print.

Bishop, Wendy, ed. *Elements of an Alternate Style: Essays on Writing and Revision*. Portsmouth: Boynton/Cook Heinemann, 1997. Print.

—. "Responding to, Evaluating, and Grading Alternate Style." *Elements of an Alternate Style: Essays on Writing and Revision*. Ed. Wendy Bishop. Portsmouth: Boynton/Cook Heinemann, 1997. 174,77. Print.

—. *Ethnographic Writing Research: Writing it Down, Writing it Up, and Reading It*. Portsmouth: Heinemann, 1999. Print.
Bitchener, J. "Evidence in Support of Written Corrective Feedback." *Journal of Second Language Writing* 17.2 (2008): 102–18. Print.
Bizzell, Patricia. "Hybrid Academic Discourses: What, Why, How." *Composition Studies* 27.2 (1999): 7–22. Print.
—. "Basic Writing and the Issue of Correctness, or, What To Do with 'Mixed' Forms of Academic Discourse." *Journal of Basic Writing* 19.1 (2000): 4–12. Print.
Blair, Hugh, Linda Ferreira-Buckley, and S. M. Halloran. *Lectures on Rhetoric and Belles Lettres*. Carbondale: Southern Illinois UP, 2005. Print.
Bloch, Joel. "A Concordance-Based Study of the Use of Reporting Verbs as Rhetorical Devices in Academic Papers." *Journal of Writing Research* 2.2 (2010): 219–44. Print.
Boethius. "An Overview of the Structure of Rhetoric." Trans. Joseph M. Miller. *The Rhetorical Tradition: Readings from Classical Times to the Present*. Ed. Patricia Bizzell and Bruce Herzberg. Boston: Bedford/St. Martin's, 2001. 488–91. Print.
Borrowman, Shane. "The Islamization of Rhetoric: Ibn Rushd and the Reintroduction of Aristotle into Medieval Europe." *Rhetoric Review* 27.4 (2008): 341–60. Print.
Brandt, Deborah. *Literacy in American Lives*. Cambridge: Cambridge UP, 2001. Print.
Brereton, John. *The Origins of Composition Studies in the American College, 1875–1925: A Documentary History*. Pittsburgh: U of Pittsburgh P, 1995. Print.
Brooke, Collin Gifford. *Lingua Fracta: Toward a Rhetoric of New Media*. Cresskill, NJ: Hampton Press, 2009. Print.
Brooks, Cleanth and Robert P. Warren. *Modern Rhetoric*. New York: Harcourt, Brace & World, 1958. Print.
Brown, Stephen G. and Sidney I. Dobrin. *Ethnography Unbound: From Theory Shock to Critical Praxis*. Albany: State U of New York P, 2004. Print.
Butler, Judith. "A 'Bad Writer' Bites Back." *The New York Times* 20 March, 1999. Web. 6 September 2014.
Butler, Paul. "Style and the Public Intellectual: Rethinking Composition in the Public Sphere." *JAC: A Journal of Rhetoric, Culture, and Politics* 28.1-2 (2008): 55–84. Print.
—. "Revisiting the Evidence: A Reply to Donald Lazere." *JAC: A Journal of Rhetoric, Culture, and Politics* 31.1-2 (2011): 314–22. Print.
—. "Style in the Diaspora of Composition Studies." *Rhetoric Review* 26.1 (2007): 5–24. Print.
—. *Out of Style: Reanimating Stylistic Study in Composition and Rhetoric*. Logan: Utah State UP, 2008. Print.

Camargo, Martin. "Si Dictare Velis: Versified Artes dictandi and Late Medieval Writing Pedagogy." *Rhetorica: A Journal of the History of Rhetoric* 14.3 (1996): 265–88. Print.

Campbell, George. *The Philosophy of Rhetoric*. Ed. Lloyd Bitzer. Carbondale: Southern Illinois UP, 1963. Print.

Canagarajah, Suresh. *Critical Academic Writing and Multilingual Students*. Ann Arbor: U of Michigan P, 2002. Print.

—. "Multilingual Strategies for Negotiating English: From Conversation to Writing." *JAC: A Journal of Rhetoric, Culture, and Politics* 29.1–2 (2009): 711–43. Print.

—. "The Place of World Englishes in Composition: Pluralization Continued." *College Composition and Communication* 57.4 (2006): 586–619. Print.

—. "Toward a Writing Pedagogy of Shuttling between Languages: Learning from Multilingual Writers." *College English* 68.6 (2006): 589–604. Print.

—. "Afterword: World Englishes as Code-Meshing." *Code-Meshing as World English*. Ed. Vershawn Ashanti Young and Aja Y. Martinez. Urbana: NCTE, 2011. 273–82. Print.

—. *Translingual Practice: Global Englishes and Cosmopolitan Relations*. New York: Routledge, 2013. Print.

Carr, Jean F., Stephen L. Carr, and Lucille M. Schultz. *Archives of Instruction: Nineteenth-Century Rhetorics, Readers, and Composition Books in the United States*. Carbondale: Southern Illinois UP, 2005. Print.

Casanave, Christine. *Controversies in Second Language Writing: Dilemmas and Decisions in Research and Instruction*. Ann Arbor: U of Michigan P, 2004. Print.

Chatman, Seymour. "'Style': A Narrow View.'" *College Composition and Communication* 18.2 (1967): 72–76. Print.

—, ed. *Literary Style: A Symposium*. New York: Oxford UP, 1971. Print.

Chiseri-Strater, Elizabeth. "'What Goes On Here?': The Uses of Ethnography in Composition Studies." *Exploring Composition Studies: Sites, Issues, and Perspectives*. Ed. Kelly Ritter and Paul K. Matsuda. Logan: Utah State UP, 2012. 199–210. Print.

Chomsky, Noam. *Syntactic Structures*. 2nd ed. New York: Walter de Gruyter, 1957, 2002. Print.

Christensen, Francis and Bonniejean Christensen. *A New Rhetoric*. New York: Harper & Row, 1976. Print.

—. *Notes Toward a New Rhetoric: Six Essays for Teachers*. 2nd ed. New York: Harper & Row, 1967, 1978. Print.

—. "A Generative Rhetoric of the Sentence." *College Composition and Communication* 14 (1963): 155–61. Print.

—. "Generative Rhetoric of the Paragraph." *College Composition and Communication* 16.3 (1965): 144–56. Print.

Cicero. *On the Ideal Orator*. Trans. James M. May and Jakob Wisse. Oxford: Oxford UP, 2001. Print.

—. *Cicero: Brutus, Orator*. Trans. G. L. Hendrickson, H. M. Hubbell. Cambridge: Harvard UP, 1939. Print.

Cixous, Helene. "The Laugh of the Medusa." *New French Feminisms*. Ed. Elaine Marks and Isabelle de Courtivron. New York: Schocken Books, 1981. 245–64. Print.

Clark, Donald Lemen. "Imitation: Theory and Practice in Roman Rhetoric." *Quarterly Journal of Speech* 37 (1951): 11–22. Print.

—. *John Milton at St. Paul's School: A Study of Ancient Rhetoric in English Renaissance Education*. New York: Columbia UP, 1948. Print.

Clark, Gregory, and S. M. Halloran. *Oratorical Culture in Nineteenth-Century America: Transformations in the Theory and Practice of Rhetoric*. Carbondale: Southern Illinois UP, 1993. Print.

Cole, Thomas. *The Origins of Rhetoric in Ancient Greece*. Baltimore: Johns Hopkins UP, 1995. Print.

Conley, Thomas. *Rhetoric in the European Tradition*. Chicago: U of Chicago P, 1994. Print.

Connolly, Joy. "Fabius Quintilianus." *Classical Rhetoric and Rhetoricians*. Ballif and Moran. 320–30.

Connors, Robert. "The Erasure of the Sentence." *College Composition and Communication* 52.1 (2000): 96–128. Print.

—."The Rhetoric of Mechanical Correctness." *Selected Essays of Robert J. Connors*. New York: Bedford St. Martin's, 2003. 71–98. Print.

Consigny, Scott. "The Style of Gorgias." *Rhetoric Society Quarterly* 22.3 (1992): 43–53. Print.

—. "Edward Schiappa's Reading of the Sophists." *Rhetoric Review* 14:2 (1996): 253–69. Print.

Corbett, Edward P. J. *Classical Rhetoric for Modern Students*. Oxford: Oxford UP, 1998. Print.

—. "The Theory and Practice of Imitation in Classical Rhetoric." *College Composition and Communication* 22.3 (1971): 243–50. Print.

Coupland, Nikolas. *Style: Language Variation and Identity*. Cambridge: Cambridge UP, 2007.

Crowley, Sharon. *The Methodical Memory: Invention in Current-Traditional Rhetoric*. Carbondale: Southern Illinois UP, 2010. Print.

Crystal, David. *English as a Global Language*. 2nd ed. Cambridge: Cambridge UP, 2012. Print.

Cushman, Ellen. *The Struggle and the Tools: Oral and Literate Strategies in an Inner City Community*. Albany: State U of New York P, 1998. Print.

Daiker, Donald, Andrew Kerek, and Max Morenberg. *The Writer's Options: College Sentence Combining*. New York: Harper & Row, 1979. Print.

D'Angelo, Frank. *Composition in the Classical Tradition.* New York: Longman, 1999. Print.

—. "Imitation and Style." *College Composition and Communication* 24.3 (1973): 283–90. Print.

Delpit, Lisa. "Skills and Other Dilemmas of a Progressive Black Educator." *American Educator* 20.3 (1996): 9. Print.

Dominik, William J. *Roman Eloquence: Rhetoric in Society and Literature.* New York: Routledge, 1997. Print.

Donahue, Patricia, Gretchen F. Moon, Mariolina R. Salvatori, and Jean F. Carr. *Local Histories: Reading the Archives of Composition.* Pittsburgh: Pittsburgh UP, 2007. Print.

Dulac, Liliane. "The Representation and Functions of Feminine Speech in Christine de Pizan's *Livre de Trois Vertus*." *Reinterpreting Christine de Pizan.* Ed. Earl Jeffrey Richards. Athens: U of Georgia P, 1992. 13–22. Print.

Duncan, Mike. "Whatever Happened to the Paragraph?" *College English* 69.5 (2007): 470–95. Print.

Duncan, Mike and and Star Medzerian Vanguri, eds. *The Centrality of Style.* Anderson: Parlor Press, 2013. Print.

Eagleton, Terry. "In the Gaudy Supermarket." *London Review of Books* 21.10 (13 May, 1999). Web. 6 Sept. 2014.

Elbow, Peter. "Voice in Writing Again: Embracing Contraries." *College English* 70.2 (2007): 168–88. Print.

—. *Writing with Power: Techniques for Mastering the Writing Process.* New York: Oxford UP, 1998. Print.

—. *Vernacular Eloquence: What Speech Can Bring to Writing.* Oxford: Oxford UP, 2012. Print.

Ellsberg, Michael. "Why Trying to Learn Clear Writing in College is Like Trying to Learn Sobriety in a Bar." *Forbes* July 31, 2011. Web.

Enoch, Jessica. *Refiguring Rhetorical Education: Women Teaching African-American, Native American, and Chicano/a Students, 1865–1911.* Carbondale: Southern Illinois UP, 2008. Print.

Enos, Richard L. *Greek Rhetoric Before Aristotle.* Prospect Heights, IL: Waveland Press, 1993. Print.

—. "Ancient Greek Writing Instruction." *A Short History of Writing Instruction: From Ancient Greece to Modern America.* Ed. James J. Murphy. Mahwah: Lawrence Erlbaum Associates, 2001. 9–34. Print.

Erasmus, Desiderius. *Collected Works of Erasmus.* Ed. Richard Schoeck and Beatrice Corrigan. Toronto: U of Toronto P, 1974. Print.

Fahnestock, Jeanne. *Rhetorical Style: The Uses of Language in Persuasion.* Oxford: Oxford UP, 2011. Print.

—. *Rhetorical Figures in Science.* Oxford: Oxford UP, 1999.

—. "Rhetorical Stylistics." *Language and Literature* 14 (2005): 215–30. Print.

—. "Aristotle and Theories of Figuration." *Rereading Aristotle's Rhetoric*. Ed. Alan Gross and Arthur Walzer. Carbondale: Southern Illinois UP, 2000. 166–84. Print.

Fahnestock, Jeanne and Mary Secor. "Rhetorical Analysis." *Discourse Studies in Composition*. Ed. Ellen Barton and Gail Stygall. Cresskill: Hampton Press, 2002. 177–200. Print.

Faigley, Lester. "Generative Rhetoric as a Way of Increasing Syntactic Fluency." *College Composition and Communication* 30.2 (1979): 176–81. Print.

—. *Picturing Texts*. New York: W.W. Norton, 2004. Print.

Fairclough, Norman. *Critical Discourse Analysis: The Critical Study of Language*. Hoboken: Taylor and Francis, 2013. Print.

Fantham, Elaine. "*Varietas* and *Satietas*: *De Oratore* 3. 96–103 and the Limits of *Ornatus*." *Rhetorica* 6.3 (1988): 275–90. Print.

Farrell, Thomas J. "IQ and Standard English." *College Composition and Communication*. 34.4 (1983): 470–84. Print.

Farmer, Frank. "On Style and other Unremarkable Things." *Written Communication* 22.3 (2005): 339–47. Print.

—, ed. *Landmark Essays on Bakhtin*. Mahwah: Hermagoras Press, 1998. Print.

Fish, Stanley. "What is Stylistics and Why are People Saying Such Terrible Things About It?" *Is There a Text in This Class?: The Authority of Interpretive Communities*. Cambridge: Harvard UP, 1980. 68–96. Print.

—. *How to Write a Sentence*. New York: Harper, 2011. Print.

Flannery, Kathryn T. *The Emperor's New Clothes: Literature, Literacy, and the Ideology of Style*. Pittsburgh: U of Pittsburgh P, 1995. Print.

Fleming, J. David. "The Very Idea of a 'Progymnasmata." *Rhetoric Review* 22.2 (2003): 105–20. Print.

—. *From Form to Meaning: Freshman Composition and the Long Sixties, 1957–1974*. Pittsburgh: U of Pittsburgh P, 2011. Print.

Flesch, Rudolf. "Let's Face the Facts about Writing." *College English* 12.1 (1950): 19–24. Print.

—. *The Way to Write*. Revised ed. New York: Harper & Brothers, 1949. Print.

—. *The Art of Readable Writing*. New York: Harper, 1949. Print.

—. *Why Johnny Can't Read and What you Can Do About It*. New York: Harper & Brothers, 1955. Print.

Flower, Linda and John Hayes. "A Cognitive Process Theory of Writing." *College Composition and Communication* 32.4 (1981): 365–87. Print.

Fogarty, Daniel. *Roots for a New Rhetoric*. New York: Columbia UP, 1959. Print.

Folk, Moe. "Multimodal Style and the Evolution of Digital Writing Pedagogy." *The Centrality of Style*. Ed. Mike Duncan and Star Medzerian Vanguri. Anderson: Parlor Press, 2013. 213–38. Print.

Foster, David and David R. Russell. *Writing and Learning in Cross-National Perspective.* Urbana: NCTE Press, 2002. Print.

Fries, Charles. *American English Grammar: The Grammatical Structure of Present Day American English with Special Reference to Social Differences or Class Dialects.* New York: Appleton-Century Company, 1940. Print.

—. *The Structure of English: An Introduction to the Construction of English Sentences in 1952.* New York: Harcourt Brace. Print.

Gage, John. T. "Philosophies of Style and Their Implications for Composition." *College English* 41.6 (1980): 615–22. Print.

Gaillet, Lynee Lewis and Winifred Bryan Horner. *The Present State of Scholarship in the History of Rhetoric: A Twenty-First Century Guide.* Columbia: U of Missouri P, 2010. Print.

Gazdar, Gerald, Ewan Klein, Geoffrey Pullum, and Ivan A. Sag. *Generalized Phrase Structure Grammar.* Oxford: Blackwell, 1985. Print.

Gee, James Paul. *How to Do Discourse Analysis: A Toolkit.* New York: Routledge, 2011. Print.

Geoffrey of Vinsauf, *Poetria Nova.* Trans. Margaret F. Nims and Martin Camargo. Toronto: Pontifical Institute of Mediaeval Studies, 1967. Print.

Genung, John F. *The Study of Rhetoric in the College Course.* Boston: D. C. Heath & CO, 1887. Print.

Giles, Howard and Peter F. Powesland. *Speech Style and Social Evaluation.* London: Academic Press, 1975. Print.

Glenn, Cheryl. *Rhetoric Retold: Regendering the Tradition from Antiquity through the Renaissance.* Carbondale: Southern Illinois UP, 1997. Print.

—. *Unspoken: A Rhetoric of Silence.* Carbondale: Southern Illinois UP, 2004. Print.

Gold, David. *Rhetoric at the Margins: Revising the History of Writing Instruction in American Colleges, 1873–1947.* Carbondale: Southern Illinois UP, 2008. Print.

Gorrell, Donna. "Controlled Composition for Basic Writers." *College Composition and Composition* 32.3 (1981): 308–16. Print.

—. *Copy-Write: Basic Writing through Controlled Composition.* Boston: Little Brown, 1982. Print.

—. *Style and Difference: A Guide for Writers.* Boston: Houghton Mifflin Co, 2005. Print.

Graff, Richard. 2001. "Reading and the 'written style' in Aristotle's Rhetoric." *Rhetoric Society Quarterly* 31.4 (2001): 19–44. Print.

Graff, Richard, Arthur Walzer, and Janet Atwill. *The Viability of the Rhetorical Tradition.* Albany: State U of New York P, 2005. Print.

Greenberg, Karen, Patrick Hartwell, Margaret Himley, and R. E. Stratton. "Responses to Thomas J. Farrell, 'IQ and Standard English.'" *College Composition and Communication* 35.4 (1984): 455–69. Print.

Greever, Garland and Easley S. Jones. *The Century Handbook of Writing.* New York: Century CO, 1918. Print.

Gregoriou, Christiana. "'Times like These, I Wish There was a Real Dexter': Unpacking Serial Murder Ideologies and Metaphors from TV's Dexter Internet Forum." *Language and Literature* 21.3(2012): 274–85. Print.

Grendler, Paul. *Schooling in Renaissance Italy Literacy and Learning, 1300–1600.* Baltimore: Johns Hopkins UP, 1989. Print.

Gross, Alan and Arthur Walzer, eds. *Rereading Aristotle's Rhetoric.* Carbondale: Southern Illinois UP, 2000. Print.

Hake, Rosemary. "Joseph Williams. Response [to Marie Secor]." *College English* 44.6 (1982) 639–42. Print.

Halasek, Kay. "An Enriching Methodology: Bakhtin's 'Dialogic Origin and Dialogic Pedagogy of Grammar' and the Teaching of Writing." *Written Communication* 22.3 (2005): 355–62. Print.

Halliday, M. A. K. *An Introduction to Functional Grammar.* New York: Routledge, 2004. Print.

Harris, Joseph. *A Teaching Subject: Composition Since 1966.* New Jersey: Prentice Hall, 1996.

Hartwell, Patrick. "Grammar, Grammars, and the Teaching of Grammar." *College* English 47.2 (1985): 105–27. Print.

Heath, Shirley Brice. *Ways with Words: Language, Life, and Work in Communities and Classrooms.* Cambridge: Cambridge UP, 1983. Print.

Hebb, Judith. "Mixed Forms of Academic Discourse: a Continuum of Language Possibility." *Journal of Basic Writing* 21.2 (2002): 21–36. Print.

Hemingway, Ernest. *A Farewell to Arms.* New York: Scribner, 1929.

Hermogenes. *Hermogenes'* On Types of Style. Trans. Cecil W. Wooten III. Chapel Hill: U of North Carolina P, 2011. Print.

Hesford, Wendy S. and Brenda J. Brueggemann. *Rhetorical Visions: Reading and Writing in a Visual Culture.* Upper Saddle River: Pearson/Prentice Hall, 2007. Print.

Hill, Achibald A. "Correctness and Style in English Composition." *College English* 12.5 (1951): 280–85. Print.

Hillocks, George. "What Works in Teaching Composition: A Meta-Analysis of Experimental Treatment Studies." *American Journal of Education* 93.1 (1984): 133–70. Print.

Hirsch, E. D. "Stylistics and Synonymity." *Critical Inquiry* 1.3 (1975): 559–79. Print.

Hirvela, Alan. "Computer-Mediated Communication and the Linking of Students, Text, and Author on an ESL Writing Course Listserv." *Computers and Composition* 34.1 (2007): 36–55. Print.

Hodge, John C. *Harbrace Handbook of English.* New York: Harcourt, 1941. Print.

Holcomb, Chris. "Performative Stylistics and the Question of Academic Prose." *Rhetoric Review* 24.2 (2005): 188–206. Print.

Holcomb, Chris and Jimmie Killingsworth. *Performing Prose: The Study and Practice of Style in Composition*. Carbondale: Southern Illinois UP, 2010. Print.

Holderness, Julia Simms. "Compilatio, Commentary, and Conversation in Christine de Pizan." *Medieval Studies* 20 (2003): 47–55. Print.

Hope. "I like the philosoraptor because…" Comment on Echantedlearning.com. 28 December, 1998. Web. 6 Sep. 2014.

Horner, Bruce. "'Students' Right,' English Only, and Re-Imagining the Politics of Language." *College English* 63.6 (2001): 741–58. Print.

Horner, Bruce, Min-Zhan Lu, and Paul Kei Matsuda. *Cross-Language Relations in Composition*. Carbondale: Southern Illinois UP, 2010. Print.

Horner, Bruce and Min-Zhan Lu. *Representing the Other*. Urbana: NCTE, 1999. Print.

Horner, Bruce, Min-Zhan Lu, Jacqueline Jones Royster, and John Trimbur. "Opinion: Language Difference in Writing: Toward a Translingual Approach." *College English* 73.3 (2011): 303–21. Print.

Horner, Bruce and John Trimbur. "English Only and U.S. College Composition." *College Composition and Communication* 53.4 (2002): 594–630. Print.

Horner, Bruce, Samantha NeCamp, and Christiane Donahue. "Toward a Multilingual Composition Scholarship: from English Only to a Translingual Norm." *College Composition and Communication* 63.2 (2011): 269–300. Print.

Horner, Winifred and Michael Leff, eds. *Rhetoric and Pedagogy: Its History, Philosophy, and Practice*. Mahwah: Laurence Erlbaum, 1995. Print.

Huckin, Thomas, Jennifer Andrus, and Jennifer Clary-Lemon. "Critical Discourse Analysis and Composition." *College Composition and Communication* 64.1 (2012): 107–29. Print.

Hyland, Ken. *Disciplinary Discourses: Social Interactions in Academic Writing*. Ann Arbor: U of Michigan P, 2004. Print.

Hyland, Ken and Fiona Hyland. *Feedback in Second Language Writing: Contexts and Issues*. Cambridge: Cambridge UP, 2006. Print.

Indrasuta, C. "Narrative Styles in the Writing of Thai and American Students." *Writing Across Languages: Issues on Contrastive Rhetoric*. Ed. A. Purves. 206–27. Newbury Park: Sage. 1988. Print.

Isocrates. *Isocrates: With an English Translation*. Trans. George Norlin. Cambridge: Harvard UP, 2000. Print.

Johnson, T. R. *A Rhetoric of Pleasure: Prose Style in Today's Composition Classroom*. Portsmouth: Boynton/Cook, Heinemann, 2003. Print.

—. "Discipline and Pleasure: 'Magic' and Sound." *JAC: A Journal of Rhetoric, Culture, and Politics* 19.3 (1999): 431–52. Print.

Kachru, Braj. *The Other Tongue: English Across Cultures*. Urbana. U of Illinois P, 1982. Print.

—. Yamuna Kachru and Cecil L. Nelson. *The Handbook of World Englishes*. Malden: Blackwell Publishers, 2009. Print.

Keilen, Sean. *Vulgar Eloquence: On the Renaissance Invention of English Literature*. New Haven: Yale UP, 2006. Print.

Kelly, William. *Simple, Clear, and Correct*: Sentences. New York: Longman, 2011.

Kennedy, George A. *A New History of Classical Rhetoric*. Princeton: Princeton UP, 1994. Print.

—. *Progymnasmata: Greek Textbooks of Prose Composition and Rhetoric*. Atlanta: Society of Biblical Literature, 2003. Print.

Kirchner, Roderich. "Elocutio: Latin Prose Style." *A Companion to Roman Rhetoric*. Ed. William Dominik and Jon Hall. Malden: Blackwell Publishing, 2010. 181–94. Print.

Kirkpatrick, Andy and Zhichang Xu. *Chinese Rhetoric and Writing: An Introduction for Language Teachers*. Anderson, SC: Parlor Press and the WAC Clearinghouse, 2012. Print.

Kitzhaber, Albert R. *Rhetoric in American Colleges, 1850–1900*. Dallas: Southern Methodist UP, 1990. Print.

Kolln, Martha. *Rhetorical Grammar: Grammatical Choices, Rhetorical Effects*. Boston: Allyn and Bacon, 1999. Print.

Krashen, Stephen. *Second Language Acquisition and Second Language Learning*. Oxford: Pergamon Press, 1981. Print.

Kumamoto, Chikako. "Bakhtin's Others and Writing as Bearing Witness to the Eloquent I." *College Composition and Communication* 54.1(2002): 66–87. Print.

Labov, William. *Language in the Inner City: Studies in the Black English Vernacular*. Pittsburgh: U of Pittsburgh P, 1973. Print.

—. *The Study of Nonstandard English*. Urbana: NCTE, 1978. Print.

Lancaster, Zak. "Tracking Interpersonal Style: The Use of Functional Language Analysis in College Writing Instruction." *The Centrality of Style*. Ed. Mike Duncan and Star Medzerian Vanguri. Anderson, SC: Parlor Press and the WAC Clearinghouse, 2013. 191–212. Print.

Lanham, Carol Dana. "Writing Instruction from Late Antiquity to the Twelfth Century." *A Short History of Writing Instruction*. Ed. James J. Murphy. Mahwah: Lawrence Erlbaum, 2001. 79–122. Print.

Lanham, Richard. *Revising Prose*. New York: Pearson/Longman, 2007. Print.

—. *Style: An Anti-Textbook*. 2nd ed. Philadelphia: Paul Dry Books, 2007. Print.

—. *The Economics of Attention: Style and Substance in the Age of Information*. Chicago: U of Chicago P, 2006. Print.

Lazere, Donald. "Orality, Literacy, and Standard English." *Journal of Basic Writing* 10.2 (1991): 87–98. Print.
—. "Butler Unclarifies the Issue." *JAC: A Journal of Rhetoric, Culture, and Politics* 31.1–2 (2011): 308–14. Print.
Leonard, Rebecca Lorimer. "Multilingual Writing as Rhetorical Attunement." *College English* 76.3 (2014): 227–47. Print.
—. "Redefining the Legacy of Mina Shaughnessy: A Critique of the Politics of Linguistic Innocence." *Journal of Basic Writing* 10.1 (1991): 26–40. Print.
Locke, John. *An Essay Concerning Human Understanding*. Ed. P. H. Nidditch. Oxford: Clarendon Press, 2011. Print.
Lockhart, Tara. "The Shifting Rhetorics of Style." *College English* 75.1 (2012): 16–41. Print.
Lloyd, Donald. "Structure in Language." *College English* 24.8 (1963): 598–602. Print.
Lloyd, Donald and Harry Warfel. *American English in Its Cultural Setting*. New York: Alfred A. Knopf, 1956. Print.
Lu, Min-Zhan. "Professing Multiculturalism: The Politics of Style in the Contact Zone." *College Composition and Communication* 45.4 (1994): 442–58. Print.
—. "An Essay on the Work of Composition: Composing English against the Order of Fast Capitalism." *College Composition and Communication*. 56.1 (2004): 16–50. Print.
Lu, Min-Zhan and Bruce Horner. "Translingual Literacy, Language Difference, and Matters of Agency." *College English* 75.6 (2013): 582–607. Print.
Lukeman, Noah. *A Dash of Style: The Art and Mastery of Publication*. New York: W.W. Norton, 2006. Print.
Lunsford, Andrea. *Reclaiming Rhetorica*. Pittsburgh: U of Pittsburgh P, 1995. Print.
Lunsford, Andrea, and Lahoucine Ouzgane. *Crossing Borderlands*. Pittsburgh: U of Pittsburgh P, 2004. Print.
Mac Donald, Heather. "Why Johnny Can't Write." *Public Interest* 20 (1995): 3,13. Print.
MacDonald, Susan Peck. "The Erasure of Language." *College Composition and Communication* 58.4 (2007): 585–625. Print.
—. *Professional Academic Writing in the Humanities and Social Sciences*. 2nd ed. Carbondale: Southern Illinois UP, 2010. Print.
Machin, David and Andrea Mayr. *How to Do Critical Discourse Analysis: A Multimodal Introduction*. Los Angeles: Sage, 2012. Print.
Mack, Peter. *Elizabethan Rhetoric: Theory and Practice*. New York: Cambridge UP, 2002. Print.

—. *A History of Renaissance Rhetoric, 1380–1620.* Oxford: Oxford UP, 2011. Print.

Macrorie, Ken. *Telling Writing.* Upper Montclair: Boynton/Cook, 1985. Print.

Maier, Paula. "Politeness Strategies in Business Letters by Native and Non-Native English Speakers." *English for Specific Purposes* 11.3 (1992): 189–205. Print.

Marrou, H. I. *A History of Education in Antiquity.* Madison: U of Wisconsin P, 1982. Print.

Matsuda, Paul Kei. "The Myth of Linguistic Homogeneity in U.S. College Composition." *College English* 68.6 (July 2006): 637–51. Print.

—. "Voice in Japanese Written Discourse: Implications for Second Language Writing." *Journal of Second Language Writing* 10 (2001): 35–53.

McCarthey, S., Y. Guo, and S. Cummins. "Understanding Changes in Elementary Mandarin Students' L1 and L2 Writing." *Journal of Second Language Writing* 14.2 (2005): 71–104. Print.

McEnery, Tony and Andrew Hardie. *Corpus Linguistics.* Cambridge: Cambridge UP, 2012. Print.

McNabb, Richard. "Remapping Medieval Rhetoric: Reading Boethius from a Grassian Perspective." *Rhetoric Society Quarterly* 28.3 (1998): 75–90. Print.

McNeely, Trevor. *Proteus Unmasked: Sixteenth Century Rhetoric and the Art of Shakespeare.* Bethlehem: Lehigh UP, 2004. Print.

McQuade, Donald and Christine McQuade. *Seeing & Writing 4.* Boston: Bedford/St. Martin's, 2010. Print.

Mellon, John. *Transformational Sentence-Combining.* Urbana: NCTE, 1969. Print.

Micciche, Laura. "Making a Case for Rhetorical Grammar." *College Composition and Communication* 55.4 (2004): 716–37. Print.

Milic, Louis T. "Theories of Style and their Implications for the Teaching of Composition." *College Composition and Communication* 16.2 (1965): 66–69. Print.

—. "Metaphysics in the Criticism of Style." *College Composition and Communication* 17.3 (1966): 124–29. Print.

Mills, Sara. *Feminist Stylistics.* New York: Routledge, 1995.

Minock, Mary. "Toward a Postmodern Pedagogy of Imitation." *JAC: A Journal of Rhetoric, Culture, and Politics* 15.3 (1995); 489–509. Print.

Miynarczyk, Rebecca and George Otte. *Reference Guide to Basic Writing.* West Lafayette: Parlor Press, 2010. Print.

Moran, Richard. "Artifice and Persuasion: The Work of Metaphor in *The Rhetoric.*" *Essays on Aristotle's* Rhetoric. Ed. Amelie Rorty. Berkeley: U of California P, 1996. 385–98. Print.

Moss, Beverly J. *A Community Text Arises: A Literate Text and a Literacy Tradition in African-American Churches.* Cresskill: Hampton Press, 2003. Print.

Muckelbaur, John. "Imitation and Invention in Antiquity: An Historical-Theoretical Revision." *Rhetorica: A Journal of the History of Rhetoric* 21.1 (2003): 61–88. Print.

Mueller, Derek. "Tracing Rhetorical Style from Prose to New Media: 3.33 Ways." *Kairos* 16.2 (2012).

Murphy, James J., ed. *A Short History of Writing Instruction.* London: Routledge, 2001. Print.

—, ed. *Medieval Eloquence.* Berkeley: U of California P, 1978. Print.

—, ed. *Renaissance Eloquence.* Berkeley: U of California P, 1983. Print.

Myers, Greg. "Stories and Styles in Two Molecular Biology Review Articles." *Textual Dynamics of the Professions: Historical and Contemporary Studies of Writing in Professional Communities.* Ed. Charles Bazerman and James Paradis. Madison: U of Wisconsin P, 1991. 45–75. Print.

—. "The Pragmatics of Politeness in Scientific Journals." *Applied Linguistics* 10.1 (1989): 1–35. Print.

—. "The Rhetoric of Irony in Academic Writing." *Written Communication* 7.4 (1990): 419–55. Print.

Myers-Scotton, Carol. *Contact Linguistics: Bilingual Encounters and Grammatical Outcomes.* Oxford: Oxford UP, 2002. Print.

Neel, Jasper. *Aristotle's Voice: Rhetoric, Theory, and Writing in America.* Carbondale: Southern Illinois UP, 1994. Print.

Nichols, Eljenholm. "Syntax and Style: Ambiguities in Lawrence's 'Twilight in Italy.'" *College Composition and Communication* 16.5 (1965): 261–66. Print.

Negro, Pescennio F. *Modus Epistola[n]di.* Trans. Konrad Kachelofen. Leipzig: Konrad Kachelofen, 1487. Print.

Newman, Sara. "Aristotle's Notion of 'Bringing Before the Eyes': Its Contributions to Aristotelian and Contemporary Conceptualization of Style and Audience." *Rhetorica* 20 (2002): 1–23. Print.

Obama, Barack. Keynote Address. Democratic National Convention. Boston, MA. 27 July, 2004.

O'Gorman, Ned. "Longinus's Sublime Rhetoric, or How Rhetoric Came into Its Own." *Rhetoric Society Quarterly* 34.2 (2004): 71–89. Print.

Olinger, Andrea, "On the Instability of Disciplinary Style: Common and Conflicting Metaphors and Practices in Text, Talk, and Gesture." *Research in the Teaching of English* 48 (2014): 453–78.

O'Hare, Frank. *Sentence Combining: Improving Student Writing without Formal Grammar Instruction.* Urbana: NCTE, 1973. Print.

Ohmann, Richard. "Literature as Sentences." *College English* 27.4 (January 1966): 261–67. Print.

O'Rourke, Sean Patrick. "Anaximenes, Rhetorica ad Alexandrum." *Classical Rhetorics and Rhetoricians: Critical Studies and Sources*. Ballif and Moran. 19–23.

O'Sullivan, Neil. *Alcidamas, Aristophanes, and the Beginnings of Greek Stylistic Theory*. Stuttgart: F. Steiner, 1992. Print.

O'Sullivan, Patrick. "Homer." *Classical Rhetoric and Rhetoricians: Critical Studies and Sources*. Ballif and Moran. 214–18.

Pace, Tom. "Style and the Renaissance of Composition Studies." *Refiguring Style: Possibilities for Writing Pedagogy*. Ed. T. R. Johnson and Tom Pace. Logan: Utah State UP, 2005. 3–22. Print.

Paine, Charles. *The Resistant Writer: Rhetoric as Immunity, 1850 to the Present*. Albany: State U of New York P, 1999. Print.

Paltridge, Brian. *Discourse Analysis: An Introduction*. London: Continuum, 2006. Print.

Parks, Stephen. *Class Politics: The Movement for the "Students' Right to Their Own Language."* Urbana: NCTE, 2000. Print.

Patterson, Annabel. *Hermogenes and the Renaissance: Seven Ideas of Style*. Princeton: Princeton UP, 1970. Print.

Pernot, Laurent. *Rhetoric in Antiquity*. Trans. W. E. Higgins. Washington DC: Catholic U of America, 2005. Print.

Perotti, Niccolò and Franciscus Rolandellus. *Rudimenta Grammatices*. Treviso: Gerardus de Lisa, de Flandria, 1476. Print.

de Pizan, Christine. *The Treasure of the City of Ladies*. Trans. Sarah Lawson. London: Penguin, 2003. Print.

—. *The Book of the City of Ladies*. Trans. Rosalind Brown-Grant. London: Penguin 2005. Print.

Poulakos, John. *Sophistical Rhetoric in Classical Greece*. Columbia: U of South Carolina P, 2008. Print.

Plato. *The Republic*. Trans. Robin Waterfield. Oxford: Oxford UP, 1998. Print.

—. "Gorgias." Trans. W.R.M. Lamb. *The Rhetorical Tradition: Readings from Classical Times to the Present*. Ed. Patricia Bizzell and Bruce Herzberg. Boston: Bedford/St. Martin's, 2001. 87–137. Print.

—. "Phaedrus." Trans. H.N. Fowler. 138–68. *The Rhetorical Tradition: Readings from Classical Times to the Present*. Ed. Patricia Bizzell and Bruce Herzberg. Boston: Bedford/St. Martin's, 2001. 87–137. Print.

Polio, Charlene. "The Relevance of Second Language Acquisition Theory to the Written Error Correction Debate." *Journal of Second Language Writing* 21.4 (2012): 375–89. Print.

Poster, Carole, and Linda Mitchell, eds. *Letter-Writing Manuals and Instruction from Antiquity to the Present*, Columbia: U of South Carolina P, 2007. Print.

Prendergast, Catherine. "The Fighting Style: Reading the Unabomber's Strunk and White." *College English* 72.1 (2009): 10–28. Print.

—. *Buying into English: Language and Investment in the New Capitalist World*. Pittsburgh: U of Pittsburgh P, 2008. Print.

Quintilian. *The Orator's Education, V.* Books 11–12. Trans. David Russell. Cambridge: Harvard UP, 2002. Print.

Ramanathan, Vai, and Dwight Atkinson. "Individualism, Academic Writing, and ESL Writers." *Journal of Second Language Writing* 8.1 (1999): 45–75.

Ramsey, Shawn. "The Voices of Counsel: Women and Civic Rhetoric in the Middle Ages." *Rhetoric Society Quarterly* 42.5 (2012): 472–89. Print.

Ramus, Peter. *Arguments in Rhetoric Against Quintilian*. Trans. James J. Murphy. Carbondale: Southern Illinois UP, 2010. Print.

—. *Peter Ramus's Attack on Cicero: Text and Translation of Ramus's* Brutinae Quaestiones. Trans. James J. Murphy. Ed. Carole Elizabeth Newlands. Davis: Hermagoras Press, 1992. Print.

Rankin, Elizabeth. "It's Not Just Mumbo Jumbo." *Elements of an Alternate Style: Essays on Writing and Revision*. Ed. Wendy Bishop. Portsmouth: Boynton Cook, 1997. 67–74. Print.

Ratcliffe, Krista. *Rhetorical Listening: Identification, Gender, Whiteness*. Carbondale: Southern Illinois UP, 2005. Print.

Reed, Scott. "'Demetrius' *On Style*." *Classical Rhetorics and Rhetoricians: Critical Studies and Sources*. Ballif and Moran.124–27.

Reynolds, D. "Linguistic Correlates of Second Language Literacy Development: Evidence from Middle-Grade Learner Essays." *Journal of Second Language Writing* 14 (2005): 19–45. Print.

Rhetoric to Herennius. Trans. Harry Caplan. Cambridge: Harvard UP, 1981. Print.

Richards, I. A., and C. K. Ogden. *The Making of Meaning: A Study of the Influence of Language Upon Thought and of the Science of Symbolism*. New York: Harcourt, Brace & World, 1946. Print.

Richardson, Elaine. "African American Language in Online German Hip-Hop." *Code-Meshing as World English*. Ed. Vershawn Ashanti Young and Aja Y. Martinez. Urbana: NCTE, 2011. 231–256. Print.

Ritchie, Joy, and Kate Ronald. *Available Means: An Anthology of Women's Rhetoric*. Pittsburgh: U of Pittsburgh P, 2001. Print.

Rivenburgh, Viola K. "Sentence Structure as Style." *College Composition and Communication* 5.2 (1954). 75–76. Print.

Ritter, Kelly. *Before Shaughnessy: Basic Writing at Harvard and Yale*. Carbondale: Southern Illinois UP, 2009. Print.

Ronald, Kate. "Style: The Hidden Agenda in Composition Classes." *The Subject Is Writing: Essays by Teachers and Students*. Portsmouth: Heinemann, 1999. 167–82. Print.

Russell, D. A. *Greek Declamation*. New York: Cambridge UP, 1983. Print.
Ryan, David Christopher. "Attic Orators: Demosthenes, Aeschines, and Lysias." *Classical Rhetorics and Rhetoricians: Critical Studies and Sources*. Ballif and Moran. 69–73.
Scheel, Eileen, and K. J. Rawson, eds. *Rhetorica in Motion: Feminist Rhetorical Methods and Methodologies*. Pittsburgh: U of Pittsburgh P, 2010. Print.
Schiappa, Edward. *The Beginnings of Rhetorical Theory in Classical Greece*. New Haven: Yale UP, 1999. Print.
Scott, Fred N., and Joseph V. Denney. *Paragraph-Writing*. Boston: Allyn and Bacon, 1893. Print.
Secor, Marie. "A Comment on 'Style and its Consequences' [by Rosemary Hake and Joseph Williams]." *College English* 44.6 (1982): 637–39. Print.
Selzer, Jack. "Rhetorical Analysis: Understanding How Texts Persuade Readers." *What Writing Does and How It Does It: An Introduction to Analyzing Texts and Textual Practices*. Ed. Charles Bazerman and Paul Prior. Mahwah: Lawrence Erlbaum, 2004. 279–308. Print.
Semino, Elena, and Mick Short. *Corpus Stylistics: Speech, Writing and Thought Presentation in a Corpus of English Writing*. London: Routledge, 2004. Print.
Shaughnessy, Mina P. *Errors and Expectations*. New York: Oxford UP, 1977. Print.
Shipka, Jody. *Toward a Composition Made Whole*. Pittsburg: U of Pittsburgh P, 2011. Print.
Smart, Graham. "Reinventing Expertise: Experienced Writers in the Workplace Encounter a New Genre." *Transitions: Writing in Academic and Workplace Settings*. Ed. Patrick Dias and Anthony Paré. New York: Hampton Press, 2000. 223–52. Print.
Smith, Ian. *Race and Rhetoric in the Renaissance: Barbarian Errors*. New York: Palgrave Macmillan, 2009. Print.
Smitherman, Geneva. *Talkin and Testifyin: The Language of Black America*. Detroit: Wayne State UP, 1986. Print.
Sprat, Thomas. *History of the Royal Society*. St. Louis: Washington UP, 1958. Print.
Stalker, J. W., and J. C. Stalker. "The Acquisition of Rhetorical Strategies in Introductory/Paragraphs in Written Academic English: A Comparison of NNS and NSS." *Variations in Second Language Acquisition Vol. 1: Discourse and Pragmatics*. Ed. S. Grass, C. Madden, D. Preston, and L. Selinker. Clevedon: Multilingual Matters, 1989. 144–60. Print.
Stevens, David. "Concerning 'Generative' Rhetoric." *College Composition and Communication* 18.3 (1967): 172–77. Print.
Stodola, Denise. "The Middle Ages." *The Present State of Scholarship in the History of Rhetoric*. Ed. Lynee Lewis Gaillet and Winifred Bryan Horner. Columbia: U of Missouri P, 2010. 42–81. Print.

Stopera, Matt. "Why Killing a Lion is The Most Cowardly Thing You Can Do." *Buzzfeed.com* 18 November, 2013. Web.

Swearingen, Jan. "Song to Speech: The Origins of Early Epitaphia in Ancient Near Eastern Women's Lamentations." *Rhetoric Before and Beyond the Greeks*. 213–26. Ed. Carol Lipson and Roberta A. Binkley. Albany: State U of New York P, 2004. Print.

Thomas, Owen. *Transformational Grammar and the Teacher of English*. New York: Holt, Rinehart and Winston, 1965. Print.

Tibbetts, A. M. "A Comment on Richard Ohmann's 'Literature as Sentences' and Martin Steinmann's 'Rhetorical Research.'" *College English* 27.8 (1966): 634–35. Print.

Timmerman, David, and Edward Schiappa. *Classical Greek Rhetorical Theory and the Disciplining of Discourse*. New York: Cambridge UP, 2010. Print.

Tougaw, Jason. "Dream Bloggers Invent the University." *Computers and Composition* 26.4 (2009): 251–68. Print.

Trimbur, John. "Linguistic Memory and the Politics of U.S. English." *College English* 68.6 (2006): 575–78. Print.

Truscott, John. "The Case Against Grammar Correction in L2 Writing Classes." *Language Learning* 46.2 (1996): 327–69. Print.

Truscott, John, and A. Y. Hsu. "Error Correction, Revision, and Learning." *Journal of Second Language Writing* 17.4 (2008): 292–305. Print.

Tufte, Virginia. *Grammar as Style*. New York: Holt, Rineheart and Winston, 1971. Print.

Ulman, H Lewis. *Things, Thoughts, Words, and Actions: The Problems of Language in Late Eighteenth-Century British Rhetorical Theory*. Carbondale: Southern Illinois UP, 1994. Print.

Vaught-Alexander, Karen. "Teaching Style." *Strategies for Teaching First-Year Composition*. Ed. Duane Roen, Veronica Pantoja, Lauren Yena, Susan K. Miller, and Eric Waggoner. Urbana: NCTE, 2002. 546–49. Print.

Verdonk, Peter. *Stylistics*. Oxford: Oxford UP, 2002. Print.

Vico, Giambattista. *The New Science*. Ithaca: Cornell UP, 1968. Print.

Vognar, Chris. "Twitter's Character Limit Sparks New Style of Short-Form Writing." *Dallas Morning News*. 27 June, 2010. Web.

Walker, Jeffrey. *Rhetoric and Poetics in Antiquity*. New York: Oxford UP, 2000. Print.

Walpole, Jane R. "Style as Option." *College Composition and Communication* 31.2 (1980): 205–12. Print.

Warner, Michael. *Publics and Counterpublics*. New York: Zone Books, 2005. Print.

Webb, Ruth. "The *Progymnasmata* as Practice." *Education in Greek and Roman Antiquity*. Ed. Yun L. Too. Leiden: Brill, 2001. 289–316. Print.

Weathers, Winston. "Teaching Style: A Possible Anatomy." *College Composition and Communication* 21.2 (1970): 144–49. Print.

Whatley, Richard. *Elements of Rhetoric*. Carbondale: Southern Illinois UP, 1963. Print.

Whitehead, Barbara. *Women's Education in Early Modern Europe*. New York: Garland Publishing, 1999. Print.

Whitehall, Harold. *Structural Essentials of English*. New York: Harcourt, 1956. Print.

Wible, Scott. "Pedagogies of the 'Students' Right' Era: The Language Curriculum Research Group's Project for Linguistic Diversity." *College Composition and Communication* 57.3 (2006): 442–78. Print.

Wilkins, John. *An Essay Towards a Real Character: And a Philosophical Language*. London: Printed for S. Gellibrand, 1668. Print.

Williams, James D. "Grammar." *Concepts in Composition*. Ed. Irene Clark. Mahwah: Lawrence Erlbaum, 2003. Print.

Williams, Joseph. *Style: Lessons in Clarity and Grace*. New York: Pearson Longman, 2007. Print.

Williams, Joseph, and Rosemary Hake. "Style and Its Consequences: Do as I do, Not as I Say." *College English* 43.5 (1981): 433–51. Print.

Wilson, Thomas, and Peter E. Medine. *The Art of Rhetoric (1560)*. University Park, Pa: Pennsylvania State University Press, 1994. Print.

Winterowd, W. Ross. "Prolegomenon to Pedagogical Stylistics." *College Composition and Communication* 34 (1983): 80–90. Print.

Woodman, Leonora. "Teaching Style: A Process-Centered View." *JAC: A Journal of Rhetoric, Culture, and Politics* 3 (1982): 116–25. Print.

—. "A Rhetorical Model of Prose Style: Notes Toward a Synthesis of Rhetoric and Poetics." *JAC: A Journal of Rhetoric, Culture, and Politics* 2 (1981): 69–78. Print.

Woodward, William Harrison. *Studies in Education during the Age of the Renaissance: 1400–1600*. Cambridge: Cambridge UP, 1906. Print.

Woolf, Virginia. "Dorothy Richardson." Virginia Woolf: Women and Writing. Michele Barrett, ed. New York: Harcourt Brace Jovanovich, 1980.

Woolley, Edwin C. *Handbook of Composition: A Compendium of Rules Regarding Good English, Grammar, Sentence Structure, Paragraphing, Manuscript Arrangement, Punctuation, Spelling, Essay Writing, and Letter Writing*. Boston: D. C. Heath, 1907. Print.

Worman, Nancy. *The Case of Character: Style in Greek Literature*. Austin: U of Texas P, 2002. Print.

Yearwood, Stephenie. "A Comment on Rosemary L. Hake and Joseph M. Williams' 'Style and Its Consequences: Do As I Do, Not As I Say.'" *College English* 45.6 (1983): 608–10. Print.

Young, Richard, Alton Becker, and Kenneth Pike. *Rhetoric: Discovery and Change*. New York: Harcourt College Publishers, 1970. Print.

Young, Vershawn. *Your Average Nigga: Performing Race, Literacy, and Masculinity*. Detroit: Wayne State UP, 2007. Print.

—. "Your Average Nigga." *College Composition and Communication* 55.4 (2004): 693–715. Print.
—. "Nah, We Straight: An Argument Against Code-Switching." *JAC: A Journal of Rhetoric, Culture, and Politics* 29.1–2 (2009): 49–76. Print.
Zappen, James. *The Rebirth of Dialogue: Bakhtin, Socrates, and the Rhetorical Tradition*. Albany: SUNY P, 2004. Print.
Zidonis, Frank. *The Effect of Study of Transformational Grammar on the Writing of Ninth and Tenth Graders*. Urbana: NCTE, 1966. Print.

About the Author

Brian Ray is an Assistant Professor of English and composition program coordinator at the University of Nebraska at Kearney. His work on style and language issues has appeared in *Rhetoric Review, Composition Studies, Computers and Composition*, and the *Journal of Basic Writing*.

Index

Abbott, Don Paul, 68, 231
Abbott, Michael, 160
Accommodation Theory, 131, 171, 186
Achebe, Chinua, 196
Aeschines, 28
African American Vernacular English, 50, 93, 154, 163, 170–172
Agricola, 6
Alabi, Taofiz Adedayo, 177
Alberic, 58
Alcidamas, 31
alternate style, 84, 113, 116, 117
Alvarez, Julia, 196
Amare, Nicole, 103
amplification, 7, 34, 42, 60, 69, 167, 206–207
Anaximenes, 23
Annas, Pamela J., 15, 136
Anson, Chris, 156
Antiphon, 23
Antisthenes, 29
Antonius, 36
Anzaldua, Gloria, 135, 196
aoidos, 21
Aphthonius, 206–207
applied linguistics, 169
Aristotle, 28–39, 45–47
ars dictaminis, 57
ars poetria, 57
ars praedicandi, 57
Asiatic, 10, 38, 62, 69, 72, 222
Aspasia, 48, 153, 229
Attic style, 10, 25, 28, 38, 50, 62, 72, 222

Augustine, St., 37, 53–55, 57, 60, 66

Baca, Damien, 48
Bacon, Francis, 70–72
Bacon, Nora, 3, 4, 14, 192–193
Baehr, Craig, 156
Bain, Alexander, 82–83
Bakhtin: dialogism, 94, 101, 116, 230; heteroglossia, 94–96, 100, 116, 125
Bakhtin, Mikhail, 94–100, 141–142, 209
bards, 21
Bartholomae, David, 92, 118, 148
basic writers, 124
basic writing, 17, 85, 125–127
Bateman, Donald, 117
Bawarshi, Anis, 137–139, 141, 143, 175
Bazerman, Charles, 137, 139
Bean, Janet, 93
Beaugrande, Robert, 114
Bell, Alan, 170–171
Berlin, James, 77, 80, 92, 118
Bialostosky, Don, 158
Binkley, Roberta, 48, 52
Birkenstein, Cathy, 186
Bishop, Wendy, 72, 116, 155
Bitchener, J., 133
Bizzell, Patricia, 5, 22, 27, 53, 58–61, 70–75, 118, 127
Black English Vernacular, 129
Bloch, David, 174
blog, 141–142, 149

257

Boethius, 20, 55, 56, 59–60
Bolter, Jay David, 141
Braddock, Richard, 14, 103, 120, 133, 183
Brandt, Deborah, 152, 155
Brereton, John, 77, 81
Brooke, Collin Gifford, 146–147
Brooks, Cleanth, 153
Brueggemann, Brenda, 148
Burke, Kenneth, 103, 165
Butler, Judith, 85–88, 103, 126, 136, 138, 143, 151–153
Butler, Paul, 85–88, 143, 151–153

Campbell, George, 12, 73, 76, 80, 129, 202
Canagarajah, A. Suresh, 119, 124, 128–130, 152, 168, 172–173
Carr, Jean Ferguson, 84
Carr, Stephen, 84
Casanave, Christine, 134
Chatman, Seymour, 111
Chiseri-Strater, Elizabeth, 155
Christensen, Francis, 90, 103, 108–109, 113–119, 149, 184, 189
Cicero, 34–40, 47, 54–55, 58, 60–75, 109
Cisneros, Sandra, 196
Cixous, Helene, 24, 49, 135–136, 150, 153
clarity, 29–33, 36–40, 53–54, 70–80, 121–122, 135, 154, 192
Clark, Donald Lemen, 67
Clark, Gregory, 74
Clark, Matthew, 199–200
classical devices: alliteration, 21, 37, 47, 178, 221; anaphora, 105, 165; *antimetabole*, 159; *antisthecon*, 145; antithesis, 24, 31, 75, 122, 190; assonance, 178, 221; *asyntedon*, 69; *chiasmus*, 36, 189; ellipsis, 49, 106, 217; *energeia*, 29, 31–32; *engargeia*, 31–32, 196; *epistrophe*, 105; *gradatio*, 6; hyperbole, 30–31, 40, 75, 166–167; irony, 35, 65, 70, 86, 140, 160, 167; *metabole*, 38; *metalepsis*, 146; metaphor, 29–37, 46, 65, 69–75, 127, 132, 144, 152, 159, 165, 196; *metaplasm*, 112, 145; metonymy, 35, 40, 52, 65, 70, 146, 196; *ploche*, 159; *poikilian*, 38; *polyptoton*, 159, 200; *polysyntedon*, 69; *sorites*, 6; *symploce*, 105; synechdoche, 146
clause, 45, 79, 106–107, 113–114, 121, 162, 171, 185, 191, 196, 198–199, 204
code-meshing, 100, 128–130, 145, 173
code-mixing, 130, 173, 177
code-switching, 129–130, 173, 222
coherence, 82, 103, 107, 119, 175, 200, 213
cohesion, 75, 105–107, 113, 135, 191
College Composition and Communication, 15, 96, 103
College English, 82–83, 87, 91, 104, 109, 112–113, 121, 129–130, 136, 153, 154
Colomb, Gregory, 121, 193, 195, 218
Conley, Thomas, 36, 53, 56, 60, 64, 68
Connors, Robert, 45, 77–81, 108, 118, 152–153, 201–206, 211
Consigny, Scott, 23
consonance, 178, 221
copia, 42, 68–69, 110, 131, 221
Corbett, Edward, 45, 99, 115, 201–206, 210–211, 224
corpus, 52, 156, 169, 173–177, 181, 186

Index

corpus linguistics, 18, 186
corpus stylistics, 173
correction, 70, 79, 135, 187, 224
correctness, 10–12, 33–34, 77–82, 86–87, 90–93, 100–103, 153, 168
counterpublic, 88, 90, 149
Coupland, Nikolas, 170–171
Crassus, 36
Crowley, Sharon, 77, 103, 152, 166, 205–207
Crystal, David, 142–143, 230
Cumming, Alister, 131
cumulative sentence, 113–115, 119, 199
current–traditional, 80, 103
Cushman, Ellen, 155

Daiker, Donald, 118, 121
Dawkins, Richard, 144
de Pizan, Christine, 59, 61–63
Delpit, Lisa, 126
Demetrius, 19, 45–46, 201
Demosthenes, 28, 38
Devitt, Amy, 137
dialect, 93, 125–128, 170–172; dialect density measure, 171; dialectology, 85, 126, 151, 169–172
diction, 33, 45–46, 69, 73, 75, 95, 100, 141, 146, 168, 173, 191–192
digital genres, 85, 123, 141–144, 146, 148–149, 215, 219
Diotima, 48
discourse analysis, 151, 161–162, 164, 169, 177, 181
dissoi logoi, 27
Donahue, Christiane, 83
Donahue, Patricia, 130
Duncan, Mike, 82, 229, 230

Eagleton, Terry, 85, 88–89

Eastman, Richard, 212–214
eloquence, 9–12, 22–29, 41–53, 64–72, 111, 136, 180
English as a Second Language, 133, 187
Englishes, 123, 126, 130, 151, 154, 168, 172, 177, 181, 187
Enheduanna, 52
Enoch, Jessica, 83, 152
Enos, Richard Leo, 21, 38, 43, 50
Erasmus, 15, 19, 58, 65–69, 109–110, 115, 221
ethos, 47, 86, 130, 165
exercitatio, 202

Fahnestock, Jean, 5–6, 16, 18, 31–35, 42, 85, 103–107, 142, 158, 165–167
Faigley, Lester, 148
Fairclough, Norman, 164
Farmer, Frank, 16, 87–88, 100
Farrell, T.J., 125–126
Faulkner, William, 213
feedback, 9, 66, 133–134, 161, 184, 215–216
feminist rhetorics, 48–49, 61, 123, 135–137, 152, 158–159
Ferreira-Buckley, Linda, 74, 231
Ferris, Dana, 134
figure, 6, 35, 44, 47, 50, 52, 65, 75, 166
figure of expression, 224
figure of thought, 75
Firth, Alan, 179, 180
Fish, Stanley, 86, 88, 112, 157, 160, 167
Flannery, Katherine, 87
Fleming, David, 43, 77, 78
Flesch, Rudolf, 109, 113
Flower, Linda, 90
Fogarty, Daniel, 103
Folk, Moe, 146, 230
Foreceville, Charles, 160

Fowler, Roger, 159
Fox, Helen, 5
Fries, Charles, 108–109
frigidity, 30
Fulkerson, Richard, 156

Gee, James Paul, 162, 164
Geertz, Clifford, 198
gender, 7, 11, 33, 135–137, 157, 171
generative grammar, 8, 113, 157
genre, 45–46, 53, 59, 64–65, 85, 98, 123, 137–151, 158, 167, 175, 206–214
Genung, John, 77, 81–83
Geoffrey of Vinsauf, 58
Giles, Howard, 170–171
Gilyard, Keith, 127, 129
Glenn, Cheryl, 48–49, 62
Gold, David, 83, 152
Gorgias, 10, 22–31, 46
Gorrell, Donna, 197–198
Graff, Gerald, 29, 31, 186
Graff, Richard, 29, 31
grammar, 33–36, 42–46, 64–70, 76–80, 86–95, 99–122, 128–142, 177–187, 191–206
grand style, 10, 20, 37–38, 54–55, 209
Greco–Roman, 42, 49, 52, 97, 99, 201, 211
Greece, 25–30, 35, 41–56, 61, 78, 85, 136, 199
Gregoriou, Christiana, 159
Grusin, Richard, 141
guwen style, 51

Hairston, Maxine, 103
Hake, Rosemary, 121
Halasek, Kay, 16, 99
Halliday, M.A.K., 92, 138, 156–157, 193
Halloran, Michael, 74

Harris, Joseph, 92, 94
Harvard, 76–77, 81–83, 102, 113, 153
Haswell, Richard, 133, 156
Hawhee, Debra, 152, 166, 205–207
Heath, Shirley Brice, 155
Heloise, 48
Hermogenes, 42, 45, 47–48, 55, 63–64
Herzberg, Bruce, 22, 27, 53, 57–62, 70–75
Hesford, Wendy, 148
Hillocks, George, 14, 104, 133
Himley, Margaret, 126
Hodge, John, 78
Holcomb, Chris, 85, 88, 143, 159, 207–211, 218
Homer, 20–22, 27, 205, 211
Horner, Bruce, 80, 124–127, 130–134, 188
Horner, Winifred Bryan, 67, 74
Hortensia, 48
hybridity, 85, 126–127, 135, 137
Hyland, Fiona, 134
hypotaxis, 100, 107

imitation, 42–45, 57–58, 67–69, 96–101, 112–117, 149–150, 199–205; *imitatio*, 43, 202
Indrasuta, 132
invention, 22, 32, 51, 68–70, 98–99, 103, 145, 189, 201–212
Isocrates, 27–28, 36, 47, 50, 201

Jacobson, Roman, 118, 156, 157
Jarratt, Susan, 23–24, 49, 136, 152
Jeffries, Leslie, 160
Johnson, T.R., 25–26, 85, 111, 136, 151–152, 188–190
Jones, Easley S., 78, 83
Journal of Basic Writing, 126–127
Journal of Second Language Writing, 132–133

Journal of Writing Research, 156, 174
Joyce, James, 112, 135, 213

kairos, 205
Karolides, Nicholas M., 184–185
Kerek, Andrew, 118, 121
Killingsworth, Jimmie, 16, 85, 207–211, 218
Kingston, Maxine Hong, 196
Kirkpatrick, Andy, 51
Kirsch, Gesa, 151, 153
Kitzhaber, Alfred, 77
Kolln, Martha, 46, 90, 103, 108, 110, 115, 119–120, 191–199
kosmos, 29
Krashen, Stephen, 133
Kui, Chen, 51

Labov, William, 126, 170–171
Lakoff, Robin, 136, 163–164
Lancaster, Zak, 138, 230, 232
language difference, 123–131, 151, 168–169, 172–178, 187–188, 207
Lanham, Carol, 57–58
Lanham, Richard, 86, 146, 215–217
Lazere, Donald, 126
Leff, Michael, 67
Leki, Ilona, 131
Leonard, Rebecca Lorimore, 154–155
levels of style, 34, 41, 45, 47, 54, 57, 206
Licklider, Patricia, 183
Lillis, Theresa, 168
linguistic, 34, 39–43, 48, 96–113, 122–135, 141–166, 170–183, 191–192
linguistic diversity, 87, 93, 122
Linguistics, 99, 108, 140, 156, 159, 173

Lloyd, David, 109, 165
Locke, John, 70, 72
Lockhart, Tara, 85, 153
logos, 20, 165
Longinus, 19, 45–47, 201
loose sentence, 14, 107, 114
Lu, Min-Zhan, 89, 124–128, 130, 133–134, 152, 188
Lukeman, Noah, 217–218
Lysias, 28

Mac Donald, Heather, 87
Machin, David, 164
Macrorie, Ken, 91
Maier, Paula, 132
Marrou, H.I., 43, 45
Marzluf, Philip, 93
Matsuda, Paul, 13, 80, 93, 127, 132
McCarthey, Guo s., 132
McIntyre, Dan, 160
McNeely, Trevor, 63
McQuade, Christine, 148
McQuade, Donald, 148
Medieval, 57, 59–62
Melanchton, Philip, 6
meme, 144–146
Menand, Louise, 86
Mendoza-Denton, Norma, 158
Menelaus, 20
meter, 21, 31, 46, 138, 201
Meyer, Michael, 164
Meyerhoff, Miriam, 169
Micciche, Laura, 46, 110, 119–120, 167, 183
Middle Ages, 17, 20, 55–59
middle style, 37, 54, 167
Milic, Louise T., 111, 114, 156
Miller, Carolyn, 137, 141, 143, 206
Miller, Thomas, 83, 152
Milton, John, 63, 67–68
Minock, Mary, 97, 98

Modern Language Association, 4, 89, 172
Moon, Gretchen, 83
Morenberg, Max, 118, 121
Moss, Beverly, 155
Mountford, Roxanne, 54
Muckelbauer, John, 99
Mueller, Derek, 148
multilingual, 132–134, 154–155, 180, 204
multilingualism, 130
Murphy, James J., 42–43, 57, 69
Myers, Sharon, 185

Nabokov, Vladimir, 200
Nash, Walter, 159
NeCamp, Samantha, 130
Negro, Francesco, 65
Nelson, Gerald, 178
New Curriculum, 17, 76, 81–82, 90, 102, 113
new media, 146–147, 159, 162
Nichols, Eljenholm, 111
Nikolaus the Sophist, 58
Noguchi, Rei, 182

O'Rourke, Sean Patrick, 23
Obama, Barack, 105, 186–187, 193
Odysseus, 20, 45
Ohmann, Richard, 111–112, 156–157
Olinger, Andrea, 140, 232
Olusunle, Toba, 177
oxymoron, 35, 224

Pace, Tom, 85, 114–115, 136, 151
Pain, Charles, 83
Paine, Charles, 160
Paltridge, Brian, 164
paragraph, 36, 77–78, 82, 84, 114, 190, 194, 200, 204, 213, 217
parataxis, 100, 107, 167

pathos, 165, 166
periodic style, 45, 75, 114
Petrosky, Anthony, 148
plain style, 27, 37–38, 54, 65, 88, 109, 141
Plato, 22, 24–29, 33, 36, 47, 53
pluralingual, 178
Polio, Charlene, 133
Polus, 25, 29
Pratt, Mary Louise, 159
prelection, 203
prescriptive, 77–78, 80, 83, 87, 103, 108, 110
prescriptivism, 73, 84, 108, 110
Priam, 20, 45
process, 94–98, 101, 122, 154, 158, 167, 184, 188, 190; post–process, 118
progymnasmata, 42–44, 58, 69, 86, 149, 205–206, 210
public intellectual, 88, 90, 159, 213

Quintilian, Marcus Fabius, 34–48, 62–64, 68–75, 97–99, 106, 109, 112, 166, 180

Ramsey, Alexis, 153
Ramsey, Shawn, 56, 59
Ramus, Petrus, 69, 70, 76
Ratcliffe, Krista, 136–137
register, 163
Reiff, Mary Jo, 137, 141
remediation, 141, 144
Research in the Teaching of English, 104, 156
rhapsodes, 21, 25
Rhetoric Review, 16, 85, 88, 138, 159
Rhetoric Society Quarterly, 48, 56
rhetorical grammar, 13, 84–85, 110, 113, 120, 122, 138, 167
Rhodian, 72

rhythm, 28–33, 37–47, 57, 65, 68, 138, 191–192, 197, 200–204, 214–218
Rivenburgh, Viola, 109
Romano, Tom, 214–215
Rome, 10, 11, 17, 19, 34–48, 55–56, 67, 109, 118, 156, 158, 166, 202–214
Royal Society, 70, 72
Royster, Jacqueline Jones, 83, 130
Sappho, 48, 153

scheme, 35, 36, 60, 105
Sclafani, Jennifer, 163
Scott, Fred Newton, 23, 45, 62, 77, 81, 205
second language writing, 131–134
Selzer, Jack, 140, 165–167
Semino, Elena, 160, 174–175
Senecan style, 71
sentence-combining, 84, 110, 113, 117–121, 184–186
sermon, 54
Shakespeare, William, 63, 189, 213
Shaughnessy, Mina, 14, 124–128
Shipka, Jody, 148, 215
Short, Mick, 42–43, 58, 67–68, 160, 174–175, 207
Silva, Tony, 131
Simpson, Paul, 160
Singapore English, 176, 178
Smart, Graham, 155
Smitherman, Geneva, 126–127, 154
Sociolinguistics, 163, 168–169
Socrates, 25–26, 106
sophists, 17, 21–33, 38, 49, 72, 136, 152, 205
speech act, 98, 222
Spivak, Gayatri, 85, 88
Spooner, Michael, 5
Sprat, Thomas, 72

Stalker, J.C., 132
Stalker, J.W., 132
Standard English, 3, 17, 34, 41, 102, 110, 122–130, 139–143, 168–172, 177
Sternglass, Marilyn, 152, 154
Stevens, David, 114
Stewart, Martha, 163–164
Stopera, Matt, 147
Stratton, R.E., 126
Strunk, William, 3, 87, 89, 152, 154, 172
Stull, William, 119
style-shifting, 16, 158, 171–172
stylistics, 28, 85–86, 99, 111–118, 136, 139–143, 156–161, 166, 173
stylization, 94, 96
sublime, 47
Sullivan, Patricia A., 20, 31, 151
Sydney, Sir Phillip, 63
Systemic Functional Linguistics, 138

Talon, Omer, 65
Teranishi, Masayuki, 160
Theon, 43, 58
Theophrastus, 34, 39
Thomas, Owen, 20, 28, 36, 72, 83, 108, 110, 125, 196
Tolson, Melvin, 83
Toolan, Michael, 157
Tougaw, Jason, 142–143
Toulmin, Toulmin, 165
Transformational Generative Grammar, 108–119
transformational grammar, 108, 109, 117–118
translingual, 130–131, 196, 231
Traugott, Elizabeth Closs, 159
Trebizond, George of, 48, 63
Trimbur, John, 80, 130, 231
trope, 35, 47, 112, 136

Truscott, John, 133
Truss, Lynn, 87
Twitter, 143–144, 148–149

usage, 57, 73, 75, 102–103, 108, 120, 128, 182, 197, 201–204

Verdonk, Peter, 157–158
vernacular, 66–67, 93, 125, 128, 142–146, 172
Vico, Giambatista, 70
Villanueva, Victor, 48, 127
virtue, 27, 39–40, 44, 63, 68, 109, 205
virtues of style: *decorum* (propriety), 34, 36, 68, 70; *dignitas*, 34, 36; *latinitas*, 34, 36, 39; *ornatus*, 34, 36, 38; propriety (*decorum*), 30, 39, 79, 205
Vitanza, Victor, 23–24
Vognar, Chris, 143
voice, 9–14, 20, 42–45, 67, 79, 82–96, 100–110, 131–144, 167–173, 182, 186–193, 200–208, 212–218

Wagner, Johannes, 179–180
Wales, Katie, 160
Walker, Jeffrey, 46, 205
Warner, Michael, 89
Warren, Robert Penn, 153
Weathers, Winston, 103, 108, 115–116
Weaver, Richard, 182
Webb, Ruth, 43
Weber, Jean Jacques, 157
Wendell, Barrett, 77, 82–83
Whatley, Richard, 75
White English Vernacular, 129, 139
White, E.B., 87, 89, 129, 139, 152, 154, 167, 172, 200
Whitehall, Harold, 109

Williams, James D., 104, 118
Williams, Joseph, 12, 46, 90, 100, 108, 115–121, 149, 193–199
Winterowd, Ross, 117–118
Wodak, Ruth, 164
Wolfram, Walt, 170–172
Women's Language, 163
Woodward, William Harrison, 66–67
Woolley, Edwin C., 78
World Englishes, 18, 129, 169, 176, 181, 187
World Englishes journal, 177
Writing Across the Curriculum, 123, 137–140
Written Communication, 99, 104, 140, 156

Xu, Zhichang, 51

Young, Richard, 15, 103, 117
Young, Vershawn, 128, 154, 173

www.ingramcontent.com/pod-product-compliance
Lightning Source LLC
Chambersburg PA
CBHW030532230426
43665CB00010B/856